D1560090

Sideshow War

TEXAS A&M UNIVERSITY
MILITARY HISTORY SERIES
49

SIDESHOW WAR

THE ITALIAN CAMPAIGN, 1943–1945

George F. Botjer

TEXAS A&M UNIVERSITY PRESS
College Station

Maps provided by Cartographic Service Unit of the Department
of Geography at Texas A&M University

The paper used in this book meets the minimum requirements
of the American National Standard for Permanence
of Paper for Printed Library Materials, Z39.48-1984.
Binding materials have been chosen for durability.

Library of Congress Cataloging-in-Publication Data

Botjer, George F.
    Sideshow war : the Italian campaign, 1943–1945 / by George F. Botjer. —
1st ed.
        p.   cm. — (Texas A&M University military history series ; no. 49)
    Includes bibliographical references and index.
    ISBN 0-89096-718-0
    1. World War, 1939–1945—Campaigns—Italy. 2. World War, 1939–
1945—Social aspects—Italy. 3. Italy—History—German occupation, 1943–
1945. I. Title. II. Series: Texas A&M University military series ; 49.
D763.I8B596   1996
940.54'215—dc20   96-14400
                                                                    CIP

To
Natalina Montefiori
in memoriam.

CONTENTS

ILLUSTRATIONS

PREFACE

The twenty-two month campaign in Italy was in many ways the most exhausting and frustrating Allied operation in the whole of World War II. It commenced with the hope that Italy would fall like a ripe plum. At the bitter end, the Germans were in control of more Italian territory than of territory in their own country. The fact that there was still an identifiable fighting front in Italy when the Battle of Berlin got underway deserved more attention, I thought, than it had heretofore been given. It seemed incongruous, or at least somewhat unique, and deserved an explanation.

This book is the result of an exploration of that seeming incongruity. As the reader will quickly notice, my efforts reached not only into military history but also into political, economic, and social issues. There proved to be, in Italy, a continuous interplay of military and non-military concerns. The latter I lump together under the heading of "social history," and thus call this a social history of the Italian campaign.

Thanks are due, in no small measure, to the National Endowment for the Humanities for summer seminar grants in areas devoted to an understanding of fascism and totalitarianism. These seminars were directed by (in chronological order) Sol Gittleman, Henry Turner, and Andrew Nathan. The advice and insights of colleagues, especially those associated with those seminars, were very helpful. A thank you is also due to Joseph Moriarty, my late uncle and a veteran of the war in Italy, and to my wife, Adriana, who saw the war from the vantage point of a young girl. Their experiences are not detailed here, but their encouragement was most invaluable.

Of course, all the conclusions and opinions expressed herein are strictly my own.

Sideshow War

CHAPTER ONE

SICILY

It was a splendid Mediterranean summer day, a perfect day for spotter planes, which observed even ladies sunning themselves on the beach where an American army would land several hours hence. Toward nightfall, a northeaster sprang up, quite rare for that time of year. The citizens of Gela, on the south coast of Sicily, recognized it as a harbinger of the *scirocco*, the searing dry wind from the Sahara that made life uncomfortable for days, sometimes weeks, on end.

The town's fishing boats, hauled up on the beach, would not go out that night. The northeaster developed into a regular storm, and kicked up a rough sea. Some of the fishermen hauled their boats further up on the sand. The soldier who stood nightly guard on the long pier was soaked by salt spray. His carbine got wet, and he retreated to dry land, fairly confident that no commandos from Malta would venture forth on such a night.

The town, indeed, had never been attacked, though the war was not far away. Allied bombers were attacking airfields in various parts of the island, including Comiso Field, fewer than fifty miles to the north. And it had been quite some time since fishermen ventured out in the daylight hours. The sea lanes to the south were still a British preserve, and every Italian fishing boat was regarded as a potential intelligence-gatherer, subject to attack by any British plane or warship that happened by.

And, of course, most of the town's young men were in the armed forces, if they had not already been killed in the rugged mountains of Yugoslavia or Greece, or in the debacle at Stalingrad during the past winter. Few were in Sicily on this day. Two-thirds of the army were deployed in foreign lands, so it is likely that most were outside the country altogether.

Toward midnight, a sentry outside town noticed dark, silent forms scudding through the dark, moonless sky. He telephoned local headquarters, and the message was relayed to a central command post at Caltanissetta Enna, in the middle of the island. Gen. Alfredo Guzzoni, commander of the island's defenses, immediately ordered the 500-foot pier at Gela blown up. The explosion, in the early minutes of 10 July, notified the Gelans that the war had come to them, that their homes were now a battlefront.

The scudding forms were Waco gliders filled with American paratroopers of the 82nd Division. There were 54 in all, though there should have been 137. Sixty-nine crashed in the water, and the remainder had gotten lost. An estimated two hundred men drowned before the Italians even knew they were being attacked.[1]

Hours earlier, as night had fallen and the wind had begun to blow from the northeast, the invasion force had set out from various ports in Tunisia and Algeria. A companion force made up of British soldiers and sailors embarked simultaneously from ports in Libya and Egypt, their destination being the southeast coast of the island, from Cape Pessaro (the southeast corner of Sicily, east of Gela) to Syracuse, halfway up the west coast.

The North African campaign had ended barely two months earlier, in May, with the surrender of tens of thousands of stranded German and Italian troops in Tunisia. Almost immediately, Axis sources began reporting a major buildup of men and material in the various North African seaports. A guessing game then ensued: Where would the Allies strike next? The Allies played an active role in this game, trying to provide their enemy with disinformation. This included an elaborate scheme called Operation Mincemeat, starring "the man who never was"—a dead British officer who had been set afloat, equipped with a briefcase full of attack plans, near Spain's coast. When the body was found on a remote beach, Spanish dictator Francisco Franco saw to it that Hitler received the packet of material. It indicated that a feint would be made at Sicily, but that the main attack would be made on Sardinia.

Meanwhile, the Italian air attaché in Lisbon was given to understand, through unnamed sources, that the real Allied target was Salonika, the

Italy, 1945

second largest seaport in Greece—but again with a feint toward Sicily to confuse the enemy. The Spanish ambassador in Tangier let on that Sardinia was indeed the main target. The Italian armed forces chief of staff, Gen. Vittorio Ambrosio, was constrained to beef up defenses on Sardinia, issuing orders to that effect in April and May. But he remained wary about the threat to Sicily as well, noting the sharp increase in air raids on both islands.

On 4 June, barely a week before the invasion, a Swiss newspaper predicted an attack on both islands was imminent. Earlier, the Italian consul in Melilla (Spanish Morocco) made a similar prediction, based on confidential sources. The Italian ambassador in Madrid, on the other hand, confidently indicated that Sardinia would be the place.

Closer to the mark was an anonymous typewritten memorandum, prepared at army headquarters in Rome, titled *"Conquista della Sicilia."* Prepared in January, while the North African campaign was still in progress, it set out all the reasons why, if the Allies decided to avoid a hiatus in combat activity once the fighting in North Africa ended, they would most likely jump the narrow stretch of Mediterranean between Tunisia and Sicily, and continue their campaign on that island.

Closest to the mark was a report from a British army training area south of London, sent to Comando Supremo (Armed Forces Command) in February. It indicated that British soldiers were being trained there for an invasion of Sicily. This was the one correct bit of intelligence, but it still had to be treated as a possible effort at disinformation.[2]

The Allies, for their part, had to keep an eye out for any major enemy buildup in Sicily. For this they had the valuable advantage of access to all the German military communications through the ULTRA decoding device, which had been captured during the German invasion of Poland in 1939 and delivered to the British by Polish military survivors. From this and other sources the Allies had learned of a buildup of defense forces in Sicily. One German division and four Italian divisions were introduced to back up the existing coastal defense units, which were also being put on an ambitious training schedule.

But this was a small commitment compared with what the Italians and Germans continued to maintain in the Balkans, and there was no redeployment of forces at all from that area. When the weather turned foul on the night of 9 July, and Allied commanders had to consider postponing the invasion, they felt confident enough in their superior resources to go ahead. They even decided that the storm would abet the surprise, as an amphibious invasion could not be expected to emerge from a stormy sea. It was noted, moreover, that the surging tide would keep landing craft from becoming stuck on offshore sandbars.

The effect that the stiff winds would have on the gliders, however, was not weighed carefully. The British would suffer losses here comparable to those of the Americans, with their airborne commander himself landing in the drink. (His American counterpart, Gen. Matthew Ridgway, was more circumspect and rode in on a destroyer.) And the landing at Gela, scheduled for 3 A.M., was delayed by an hour and a half, although some U.S. Ranger units hit the beach as early as 3:30 A.M. Landing craft wallowed in the heavy sea, making barely two knots an hour. Most of the soldiers staggered ashore rubber-legged and nauseous, many of them with their weapons wet and unserviceable. A division-strength defense on that morning (10 July) would have cast them right back into the sea, but there was only a company-sized coastal defense unit on hand, and immediate reinforcements were not available to bring it up to more than battalion size.

The Americans chose Gela as a landing site because, unlike many other potential debarkation sites, there were no mountains or cliffs nearby. Their Office of Strategic Services (OSS) also estimated that Gela's little harbor could accommodate as many as two thousand tons of supply traffic daily.[3] It was also within striking distance of the Comiso airfield, and fit in with the main Allied plan of conquest. This involved a two-pronged offensive, with the British advancing around the east side of Mount Etna (the massive live volcano to the northeast), and the American force around the west (inland) side. To go that route, the Americans would proceed north from Gela, through Comiso, and on up to the north coast. This would bring them to the ultimate objective of the campaign, the great city of Messina, standing on the Strait of Messina, which separates Sicily from the Italian mainland. They would close in on Messina from the west, along the coast, hugging the slopes of Mount Etna, while the British converged on the city from the south, heading up the east coast, and also hemmed in by the eastern slopes of the volcano.

Given complete freedom of action, General Guzzoni might have defeated the invasion. He had already deployed the German division, and one Italian division, to an area only a day's march from Gela. This was remarkable considering that he had about six divisions (counting the coastal units) with which to defend the whole island, including its two major seaports, Palermo and Messina. There were two divisions near Palermo, on the far northwestern coast, which he decided ought to be moved to the southeast—to be close to the units already deployed a day's march from Gela.

The Comando Supremo in Rome had been dissuaded from this course by the top German commander, Field Marshal Albert Kesselring, who was newly arrived in Italy and headquartered outside Rome. It was the first of many decisions Kesselring would make in Italy (he would be there until 1945), and, as it turned out, the only one that was clearly wrong. Had Guzzoni's recommendations been carried out, the bulk of the Axis defense forces would have been located in the midst of the major Allied attack points, perfectly situated to abort the invasion in its first couple of days.[4]

German generals. Left to right: *Field Marshal Walter Model; Field Marshal Albert Kesselring, German commander in Italy; and Gen. Siegfried Westphal, Kesselring's adjutant.* Courtesy U.S. Army Military History Institute

But the two Axis units near Gela, the Livorno Division and the Hermann Goering Division, were not ready to attack the Americans until the invasion's second day, 11 July. The Germans approached from the east and northeast, the Italians from the northwest. Their progress was impeded by bomb-cratered roads and by shellfire from destroyers and cruisers offshore. On the German front, a hundred U.S. paratroops led by Lt. Col. Arthur "Hardnose" Gorham captured an Italian pillbox that commanded one of the main access roads.[5] This, the only success of the pre-dawn airborne invasion, resulted in several hours of delay for the German panzer attack toward the beach.

The delay gave the Americans time to prepare themselves for the expected onslaught. Another 82nd Airborne unit, commanded by Col. James Gavin, deployed on a ridge line at the eastern edge of Gela. It took the brunt of the German attack. Few of the soldiers on either side had much combat experience. The Hermann Goering Division was a recently reconstituted force that had been decimated in southern Russia early in 1943. It was unusual in that it belonged to the Luftwaffe rather than to the army—which is why it was named after the head of the German Air Force. Starting out before the war as an airfield security unit, it had evolved into a combat infantry force. It was, in a sense, an example of empire-building in the Nazi hierarchy. It also reflected the regime's uneasy relationship with the professional army—the same attitude that helped to give rise to the S. S. divisions so common on the Eastern Front. Officially, it was a product of the close ground-air collaboration that characterized German *blitzkrieg* tactics.

On this occasion, however, there were not many German airplanes to be seen, though most of the American losses on the first day were inflicted by airplanes. (Most notably, the destroyer *Maddox* took a direct hit from a torpedo bomber and sank in a few minutes.) When the Germans attacked, the sky belonged to the Americans. And so did the coastal waters, which stood in clear view. The first attack, which involved thirty of the Germans' fifty-four tanks on hand, was called back when salvoes of naval gunfire cut a swath of destruction directly to the front. It was a unique experience even for the veteran officers who commanded these green troops. They had never attacked before under the guns of nearby destroyers and cruisers.

A second attack showed signs of breaching the ridge line. Units of the 45th Infantry Division were ordered to prepare to reboard landing craft. Italian headquarters in Caltanissetta was apprised that the Allies were in fact reboarding for a possible evacuation. The news were sent on to Mussolini in Rome. But the line held.[6]

The Livorno Division was at this time attacking from the opposite side, against Ranger units deployed on the low hills. The Rangers had dragged some abandoned shore batteries to the hilltops. These were lacking the sights and elevation mechanisms that—the retreating Italian coastal defense squad of 10 July reasoned—would be necessary to make them useful. The Rangers found, however, that the guns were quite useful when fired horizontally into massed ranks of enemy soldiers.

The nemesis of the Livorno fighters, however, was the destroyer *Savannah*. Resting undisturbed a short distance offshore, that vessel fired salvo after salvo in rapid succession—first into the ranks of the attacking soldiers, then into the division's staging area in back of the nearby hills. Five hundred six-inch shells tore into these valiant young men, gouged long trenches into the field of combat, uprooted trees, and leveled hilltops.[7]

It was the last (as well as the first) division-strength assault the Italians would make in the Italian war. Captain Lyle and his Rangers were quite impressed with this display of naval gunfire. On the other side, Colonel Gavin and his paratroops credited the offshore guns with saving the day for the American invasion. There, the Germans lost more than half of their tanks, including ten of the seventeen large Tiger tanks on hand. The Italians, using captured French Renault and their own Fiat 3000 Class tanks, suffered even worse losses.

The Americans had been pushed back to the water's edge, but at the end of the day the beach, and Gela, belonged to them. The enemy forces went their separate ways into the interior, until they reached a rendezvous point at a town fifty miles to the north.

That night, in an effort to impede the Americans' expected move along the coast and into the interior, the Germans and Italians staged a major air raid. Nearly two hundred airplanes strafed and bombed the beach and targets offshore between 10 and 11 P.M. Soon after the last Axis airplane departed, a flight of 145 Allied C-47s came lumbering overhead. To the men on the ground and aboard ship, this was an apparent second stage of the enemy attack. A gun on one of the ships opened up, and then, in an instant, everybody let loose.

The planes continued doggedly through the deadly fire. They were carrying the 504th Regiment of the 82nd Airborne Division. (The 505th—Gavin and Gorham's regiment—had come in the night before.) By the time the firing let up, with the last of the C-47s gone, an hour later, sixty of the planes had been hit. Twenty-three of them crashed, six of these, including the one with the regimental staff, filled with paratroops. Eight of the damaged planes flew back to North Africa. They had a total of ten casualties aboard. All told, 81 men died in this mishap, 132 were wounded, and 16 were missing.[8] The damage was far greater than that caused by the German and Italian raid, but it was the raid that had led to this disaster, so the Axis enjoyed an indirect victory. Part of the 504th's mission was to cut off the roads being used by the two retreating divisions (the Livorno and the Hermann Goering) before they got very far from Gela. Then the American 1st and 45th divisions, the Rangers and the combined forces of the 82nd Airborne, might catch up with them on 12 July and administer the *coup de grace*. That hope was dashed. Allied forces would still be knocking heads with the Hermann Goering Division in 1945.

News of the disaster was carefully censored, and the "official secret" was not leaked until March 1944.[9] In the meantime, Gen. Dwight Eisenhower, in charge of operations, had to defend himself against accusations from the Joint Chiefs of Staff in Washington that too many Allied aircraft were being lost to friendly fire. His report on the matter, which included corrected figures on the number of such losses, indicates that the bulk of them came in this one incident.[10]

Two of the principal targets of the landing at Gela, the Comiso and Ponte Olivo airfields, were taken on 13 July with only slight opposition. The Hermann Goering Division had originally been sent to this part of Sicily to protect those airfields, but now it was well on its way to

Caltagirone, thirty miles to the northeast. The Americans found 125 airplanes on the ground, 20 in flying condition. There were also two hundred thousand gallons of aviation fuel and five hundred bombs.[11] Along the roads leading to the airfields, several abandoned Russian-made field guns were also found. The captured aircraft exceeded by three the total number of German planes in Sicily prior to the invasion. But these were nearly all Italian planes, about a fourth of all the Italian air strength in Sicily.

The British forces that attacked Syracuse and Augusta, halfway up the east coast of the island, were both more numerous and more battle-seasoned than their American counterparts. Their objectives were also more ambitious. Syracuse was one of the important cities of the island. Gela was but a fishing village. Augusta, to the north of Syracuse, was the home of an Italian naval squadron. It was also within striking distance of Messina, the capture of which would mark the conclusion of the campaign.

While soldiers of the U.S. 82nd Airborne were having a bad time in an experimental glider attack carried out in the most unfavorable weather, their counterparts in the British 1st Airborne Division were doing no better. Only 54 of the 115 gliders reached dry land around Syracuse. Of these only twelve, carrying eight officers and sixty-five men, made it to the designated drop zone, near an important bridge.[12] The bridge, Ponte Grande, was supposed to be attacked by an entire battalion. Instead, this platoon-sized group committed itself, unaware that reinforcements were nowhere close by. All but fifteen were killed or wounded, but they managed to hold one end of the bridge for the better part of a day. During this time, units of the Napoli Division were prevented from crossing the bridge and entering the city, as were elements of Group Schmalz, a portion of the Goering Division that had been detailed to the area under the command of Col. Wilhelm Schmalz.

The glider fiasco cost the British 327 dead and 261 wounded or missing. Maj. Gen. G. F. Hopkinson, commander of the glider invasion, was discovered floating in the sea by a passing destroyer. By the time he reached dry land, the Germans and Italians had temporarily recaptured Ponte Grande. (Hopkinson would survive only another month; he was killed on 10 September during the landing at Taranto.)

The main invasion force, carrying the 5th Division from ports in Egypt and Libya, came under a heavy air attack as it approached the shore. The Germans made several attempts to sink the *Reina del Pacifico*, a converted ocean liner and the bulkiest ship on the scene, but their torpedoes all missed the mark. Less fortunate were three transports, including an ammunition carrier whose detonation knocked people down a half-mile away.

The main fighting for Syracuse took place around, rather than inside, the city, most heavily around the Ponte Grande and a couple of lesser bridges. Group Schmalz, approximately a third of the Goering Division, was all the Germans had available. It was, moreover, committed also to the defense of Augusta, and so found itself spread rather thin. The Napoli Division lost some of its effectiveness when its headquarters unit was taken by surprise. The commanding general and most of his staff were captured.

The worst turn of events of all, for the defenders, was the virtually unopposed British seizure of the Augusta harbor. This made a strong defense of Syracuse, to the south, untenable. Lines of retreat toward Messina had now to be made a top priority.

The loss of Augusta caused a stir in Axis circles. It began with an angry protest from Colonel Schmalz to his commanders. The man responsible for the port, Rear Admiral Priamo Leonardi, was accused of abandoning his positions even before the British launched their attack. Mussolini was apprised of the situation. So was King Victor Emmanuel III. So was Hitler. An editorial in the *Regime Fascista*, a North Italian newspaper that had lately criticized military leaders for surrendering in North Africa, suggested darkly that traitors were at work here.

The matter was investigated by Gen. Mario Roatta. Leonardi's contention was that the port had been left with too few defenders, and that several of these were wounded during an air raid the day before the invasion. Colonel Schmalz and others had been apprised of this. After the air raid, Leonardi therefore decided to remove his unit from the port area, and take up a position a short distance inland. Another unit would remain in the city. But, according to Leonardi, when this latter force heard about the redeployment, it decided that it too should head inland—without orders and unknown to the rear admiral. So it was that British commandos were not fired upon when they entered the harbor and found the shore batteries spiked or tipped into the water.[13]

Leonardi was exonerated by his peers, but thereafter the Germans were less willing to trust the Italian officers. Mussolini's already lively distrust of the military was heightened, and more than ever he feared a military coup, which he thought would be led by generals and admirals in need of a scapegoat to cover their incompetence.

The British consolidated their hold on the port area on 11 July, as the battle of Gela raged more than a hundred miles away. During the morning of 12 July, units of the Napoli Division finally made it to the city and launched an attack aimed at dislodging the invaders. A secondary objective was to destroy the harbor facilities—docks and warehousing, which remained intact. But heavy fire from several British warships just outside the harbor had a telling effect, and the harbor facilities were spared. By late afternoon, the city was under the control of the invaders. Augusta became the chief staging area and supply base for the push up the coast toward Messina.

Group Schmalz and the Napoli Division made their way northward to Catania, a short distance up the coast. Here, aided by Mount Etna (which made any landside flanking move by the invaders impossible) and by reinforcements from the mainland, they would engage the British in a three-weeks battle.

Gen. Bernard Montgomery, the hero of El Alamein, was in command of operations on the east coast. Finding himself caught in a sort of bottleneck on the narrow Catania Plain, he began to worry that the Axis divisions (Livorno and Hermann Goering) that had retreated from Gela to Caltagirone, near the southern edge of the great volcano, might launch an attack in his direction. The defenders of Catania might then also attack, catching his Eighth Army in a lethal vise.

Close pursuit of those divisions by the Americans might obviate such a threat, but Monty felt that the Americans were not moving fast enough. The general plan of operations cast them in the role of protecting his western flank, and he felt that they were not doing it quite well enough. They were supposed to interdict any movement by Axis forces around the southern perimeter of Mount Etna, and move on to the northern coast. From there they would threaten Messina from another direction, forcing the Axis to defend that city on two fronts, thus weakening the one facing the British.

Montgomery decided to take matters into his own hands, and sent forces out to secure the Caltagirone-Enna Road (Highway 124), which might be useful for an Axis move against the British rear.[14] The road cut right across the line of advance on the American front. Gen. George Patton's II Corps (the 1st and 45th divisions) was then approaching from the south.

Patton was the kind of commander who would have gladly traded assignments with the Eighth Army, and taken up the challenge of fighting an entrenched and determined enemy in the Catania Plain. He found it particularly galling, therefore, to see the British intruding into his assigned area. The commanding general of Allied ground forces, Gen. Harold Alexander, was himself caught by surprise. His first reaction was to

Allied commanders. Left to right: *Lt. Gen. Sir Oliver Leese, Eighth Army commander; Gen. Sir Harold R. L. G. Alexander, Allied theater commander; and Gen. Mark Clark, U.S. Fifth Army commander.* Courtesy U.S. Army Military History Institute

extend the British zone of operation to fit what Monty had done. This annoyed Patton even more, as it reduced his range of responsibility, which already was basically supporting the main thrust up the east coast, in the British sector. Patton now demanded that a new offensive be mounted for the western part of the island. This was not a part of the original plan. It had been surmised prior to the invasion that once the Allies secured a foothold in the east and southeastern parts of the island and marched toward Messina, any Axis units out in the western areas would themselves converge toward Messina to avoid being cut off.

And in fact this was already happening. General Guzzoni, Alexander's Axis counterpart, had already begun moving the two Italian and the one

German division eastward. The Italian forces (the Aosta and Assietta divisions) were well clear of their original bases near Palermo, and were at least a third of the way to Messina by the time this imbroglio broke out. The German 16th Panzer-Grenadier Division was itself heading toward operational headquarters at Caltanisetta, in the center of the island. (The headquarters itself would soon be relocated to Messina.) Patton nonetheless secured the creation of a Provisional Corps, so that he could command a rapid sweep through western Sicily, culminating in the conquest of Palermo, which would be secured as an important Allied supply base.

And so for a while the two temperamental generals, Patton and Montgomery, were headed in opposite directions, rather than toward one another. The 45th Division moved up through the west-center of the island, toward the north coast. The 3rd Division, also a part of the Provisional Corps, proceeded along the south coast from its original landing site at Licata. By the time the imbroglio broke out, the divison had already captured Agrigento and Porto Empedocle. Patton ordered its commander, Gen. Lucian Truscott, to swing around the west coast and head for Palermo, the ultimate object of the campaign.

This diversion proved to be a considerable waste of time and military resources. The 3rd Division encountered some stubborn resistance in the hills around Agrigento and in the town's narrow, steep streets and alleys.[15] A U.S. destroyer and cruiser also collided offshore, within sight of the Greek temple ruins on the Agrigento shore. But these events proved to be the highlight of operations in western Sicily. Once past Agrigento on 18 July, the campaign took on the aspects of a peacetime maneuver. Few Axis soldiers were to be found. The 45th Division, starting from near Gela, was at Termini on the north coast by 21 July. Its progress was helped along by the fact that Guzzoni's command post was shifted from Caltanitetta to Messina on 19 July, taking with it a German division and an Italian division, both just arrived from the Palermo area.[16]

Another division diverted to this operation was the U.S. 2nd Armored, which occupied Marsala on the west coast on 24 July. That town, home of the eponymous wine, was also in the vicinity of an important air base. The town and the base had been heavily bombed several days before the invasion. The Americans encountered no resistance.

The 82nd Airborne Division rounded out the forces of Patton's Provisional Corps. The division commander, Matthew Ridgway, accepted the sword and binoculars of the commandant at Trapani, Adm. Giuseppe Manfredi, on 23 July. Two days later, the 2nd Armored won the race to Palermo. Gen. Geoffrey Keyes was met outside the city by Italian Gen.

Giuseppe Molinaro, who gave Keyes a ride into the center of town in his staff car.

Patton was greeted by Cardinal Lavitrano and conducted to the medieval royal palace, which became his headquarters.[17] The city had been subjected to an air attack several days before, but its harbor, the main attraction for the U.S. forces, was intact. (Damage from that raid can be seen to this day inside the cathedral, whose massive pillars were gouged by shrapnel when bombs crashed through the roof.) Palermitans were grateful that their city had not become the scene of heavy fighting, considering especially that two divisions had so recently been stationed there for its defense. They seemed happy to see the Americans. The war was over for them, they thought.

From Palermo the U.S. forces headed east, toward Messina. The 45th Division, at Termini (east of Palermo) already, was in the vanguard. The advance covered nearly two-thirds the length of the north coast before meeting resistance. Patton had been crowing about how fast his own *blitzkrieg* had been moving, but from here on out it would be a slugging match, the defense sometimes maniacal in its tenacity. The U.S. forces got a hint of what lay in store for them for the next twenty-one months on the mainland.

By this time control of Axis ground operations had been handed over to the German general, Hans Valentin Hube. The German High Command had decided on a limited commitment of reinforcements to the island on or about 15 July, when Hube arrived at Caltanisseta. There was no matching commitment of new Italian divisions, and in fact both Italy and Germany feared having large numbers of their forces stranded on the island. The loss of tens of thousands of prisoners in Tunisia was still a fresh memory. Yet at the same time they still entertained hopes of a reversal of fortune and a victory over the Allies on Sicily.

These were the stakes when the 45th Division reached San Stefano, the northern end of the Etna Line, which stretched south through Nicosia and then cut east around the southern end of the volcano, ending at Catania, which the British Eighth Army was still trying to capture. The German 29th Division pushed ahead of the Italian Aosta Division along the narrow coastal road as the Americans approached.[18] Machine-gun and mortar positions were set in the cliffs and crags overlooking the road.

To make matters still more difficult for the U.S. forces, the German 15th Panzer Grenadier Division attacked from its base near Nicosia, at the center of the Etna Line. Its objective was the former Axis headquarters, Caltanisetta. The attack was opposed by the 1st Canadian Division and the 1st U.S. Division (the Big Red One). The Allies had by now virtually unchallenged control in the air, and the advancing Germans were bombed and strafed mercilessly. The Allied ground forces gradually pushed them back to Nicosia. Having the initiative now in that sector, and more room to maneuver than was available along the mountain-hedged coast to the north, it was now decided that an effort to breach the Etna Line should be made in that area. Patton in the meantime was plotting an amphibious leapfrog operation around the entrenchments at San Stefano on the coast.

The Canadians battled their way into Nicosia on 4 August after several days of heavy fighting. The American 1st Division meantime pushed around the city and raised a threat to Troina, a crossroads town near the western slope of the volcano. The town overlooks a valley that stretches away to the west—the direction from which the Americans were coming—and through it ran the only good road in the area, close to the shallow bed of the Troina River. The Germans had selected the town as a defensive strongpoint for these reasons. Units of the 15th Division were digging in there even while the battle of Nicosia raged. They were helped by units of the Livorno Division, which at this point was operating at about half its authorized strength.

Advance elements of the 1st Division entered the valley on 1 August. Little progress was made during the first three days of the battle. On 4 August, two air raids by thirty-six A-36 bombers devastated much of the town. By 7 August, the division felt ready for a final assault. The attack was preceded by an artillery barrage that commenced with the simultaneous firing of a hundred guns, all zeroed in on the town's center. Spotter planes then discovered that most of the defenders had already left but were still within the range of the larger guns.

For the soldiers of the 1st Division, the capture of Troina proved somewhat anticlimactic. It was abandoned, except for token resistance, after so many days in which the Americans had sustained heavy casualties under a withering fire from the defensive positions in the town.

Meanwhile, for the retreating Germans and Italians, things were anything but anticlimactic. Eisenhower, touring the area the next day, was amazed by the hundreds of German and Italian casualties still on the ground along the line of retreat. The town itself was totally devastated. The *New York Times* called it the "most savage" encounter for the Americans so far.[19] Ike, in his memoirs, called it "one of the most fiercely fought smaller actions of the war," and noted that the Germans had made two dozen counterattacks into the valley and on the outskirts of town during the battle.[20]

The 1st Division was relieved by the 9th Division, recently arrived by ship via Palermo. The Canadians then joined with the 9th and pushed along Highway 120 toward Randazzo, where the Axis forces had their main supply depot for the western half of the Etna Line.

On 9 August, the Americans resorted to landing craft to leapfrog San Stefano, landing near Sant' Agata. Four days later they repeated the maneuver, rounding Cape Orlando and raising an immediate threat to Messina. Here they were attacked, but held out with the aid of naval gunfire and divebomber raids.

Meanwhile, Catania had finally fallen to the British on 5 August. The battle of Catania had commenced on 11 July with an air raid that wrecked the city's railroad yards and damaged the Gerbini Airfield nearby. On 13 July, the British advance from Syracuse and Augusta was to be aided by a glider drop of airborne troops. Out of 130 aircraft used, 113 were hit by friendly fire from the British ground units, and two gliders collided trying to escape the fire from their comrades on the ground, who believed that these were elements of the German 1st Parachute Division, which was known to be moving into the area. Eighty-seven of the gliders actually made it to the drop zone, where four were shot down by the Germans.[21]

The German paratroops had in fact arrived at Catania the previous day. General Kesselring was also there for a brief visit, arriving just in time to see his troopers float groundward in their parachutes. The Hermann Goering Division's Schmalz Group was already deployed in front of the British 50th Division, along with the Napoli Division. The defending forces at that time had food supplies for only three days, and the civilian population was beginning its acquaintance with a near-starvation diet, amounting to twenty-five grams of bread a day until the end of the siege.[22]

The British captured the important Primasole Bridge across the Sineto River on 14 July. A German counterattack carried out with what a *New York Times* correspondent called "fanatical savagery" took it back the next day, but the British were in control again on 16 July. The battle settled down into a series of abortive attacks and counterattacks, punctuated by frequent air raids and naval bombardments. Colonel Schmalz, in charge of defensive operations, finally ordered a fighting retreat toward Messina on 3 August. The British were in full control of the city, with its harbor "capable of accommodating the largest ships," by 5 August.[23]

To the west of Etna, Nicosia had just fallen, and Troina was about to be surrendered by the Axis forces. The first significant numbers of German prisoners were taken in these latter actions. The San Stefano defense line on the north coast was broken on 9 August, by which time the U.S. 9th Division, from its starting point at Troina (where it entered the line, in place of the 1st Division) had pushed up Highway 120 against only rear-guard action by the retreating Germans.

On 12 August, the Americans reached Randazzo and were ready to round the northern slopes of Etna and converge with the advance units of the U.S. 45th Division. The 45th was just then gaining control of Cape Orlando, after some hard fighting that followed a new eight-mile amphibious leapfrog operation. On the other side of Etna, the British continued their push, against strong opposition, toward Messina.

With most of Sicily now under the control of the invading armies, and with the Axis in control of a mere foothold in the northeast corner of the island, the focus of attention for both sides now was the Strait of Messina. The Axis had to keep it open to save the three German and four Italian divisions still in Sicily—all, at this point, crowded into and around Messina. For the Allies, the task was to block off the evacuation of these divisions. Success here would greatly enhance their impending victory. It was known that the Germans were as yet undecided about the extent of their future commitment to Italy. Gen. Erwin Rommel, for instance, wanted to pull back to an Alpine redoubt. He was at this time in command of the few German forces in northern Italy. Loss of all the German forces in Sicily would probably have strengthened his argument. Kesselring, his counterpart in the south, would accordingly have had to rethink his rosy estimates about the chances for a containment action in the southerly areas of the mainland.

So the fate of Italy—at least its military fate—stood in the balance. Efforts to destroy the port facilities at Messina had begun early in the campaign. On 14 July, the ammunition ship *Patria* was blown up in the strait, and an Italian freighter was heavily damaged.[24] Damage to the harbor facilities was not serious, though, thanks to the very heavy concentration of antiaircraft defenses. Most of the bombing raids were carried out at night, to reduce losses to these batteries, but nighttime bombing in a city under blackout was far from accurate, especially as the airplanes maintained a high altitude to further reduce their losses. The result was that whole bombloads landed in the water, or, much worse, on the densely packed tenement blocks near the port. Traffic in and out of the harbor, under the watchful eye of Capt. Baron Gustav von Liebenstein, was largely unaffected.

At the beginning of August, bombing raids became an almost daily occurrence. The Italian reports regularly cited *"violenti prolongati bombardamenti."* On 10 August there were intense and repeated *("intensi ripetuti")* raids.[25] During those days, also, the British naval forces edged close to the straits, but rarely came within gun range of the traffic lanes. The aircraft carrier *Indomitable* was damaged by a torpedo, and the cruisers *Cleopatra* and *Newfoundland* were also damaged during German and Italian air attacks.[26] Such attacks, coming from air fields on the mainland, were virtually guaranteed whenever Allied ships came anywhere near the strait.

Italian submarines were also in the area. Three *(Dandolo, Alagi, and Nicheliu)* already had hits against British supply ships to their credit.[27] Penetration of the strait was achieved only sporadically by British torpedo boats launched from Augusta and, after 5 August, Catania. They caused some damage, but paid a heavy price.

Efforts to choke off the evacuation, therefore, relied on air power to the very end. On 2 August, a United Press correspondent reported that "an unusually large number of Axis ships gathered in the Strait of Messina were attacked by relays of Allied fighter bombers."[28] On the ground at that point were an estimated five hundred antiaircraft guns, possibly the largest concentration of such weaponry outside the Ruhr Valley.[29] Defending against any breakthrough attempt by Allied armies were the German 29th and Italian Aosta and Assietta divisions on the north coast (in front of the Americans), and the Hermann Goering Division, along with the German 15th Division and (beginning 14 August) the Napoli Division and the Livorno Division.

On the night of 11–12 August, Allied bombs caused some damage to the port and several ships while loading of troops and vehicles was in full progress. Because the air raids always came at night, it was decided to take a chance and resume the interrupted loading operation after dawn the morning of 12 August.[30] Allied spotter planes apparently kept their distance, and there must have been no observers on the higher slopes of Mount Etna equipped with binoculars and radios, for the ships were able to pull away laden with soldiers, trucks, and artillery, and steam across the strait in broad daylight, unimpeded by any Allied aircraft or torpedo boats. That night, shipping hove to in deep water, well clear of the harbor, while the expected bombing raid cut across numerous searchlight beams and braved the effects of thousands of exploding shrapnel shells. Wellington bombers emptied their loads on the hapless city, or were shot down in flames. The port sustained only minor damage.

This day-and-night routine was repeated daily for the next four days. The Italian situation report for 17 August indicated that seventy-five thousand Italian soldiers, along with a hundred pieces of artillery and five hundred trucks, had successfully been relocated to the mainland.[31]

The Germans left nobody behind, removing their three divisions in good order, and taking with them all their antiaircraft guns, tanks, artillery, and motor vehicles. This was a victory of sorts for the Axis forces.

At dawn on 17 August, units of the U.S. 3rd Division rolled into Messina under a full moon. When the sun rose above the horizon, German and Italian guns opened up from the mainland. An officer riding with 3rd Division commander General Truscott was wounded, as were several soldiers. General Moracci of the Italian army had, under orders, detonated explosive charges, already in place, on the day before. Therefore the Allies discovered the harbor area in complete ruin. The battle of Sicily was over.

℃

Why did the Allies invade Sicily, and what did they achieve by its conquest? The campaign was primarily a British initiative. The Americans essentially were dragooned into the operation, and this helps to explain why General Montgomery attacked the more ambitious targets on D-Day, and why his Eighth Army was solely responsible for what was known well in advance would be the most active front (the Catania Plain). This also explains why an American, General Eisenhower, was placed in charge of operations. The appointment helped to break down U.S. objections by giving the Americans a measure of control over the operation.

The British had an attitude toward the Italians uniquely their own. Prior to the invasion, they had fought off an effort to seize the Suez Canal that had been initiated by the Italian army, based in the Italian colony of Libya. Montgomery's great victory at El Alamein in the autumn of 1942 was over not only Rommel, but also over an Italian army.

It was a measure of revenge for the British, but they were still contending with Italian submarines, surface ships, and airplanes in the Mediterranean. Since 1940, ships carrying vital supplies to Britain, travelling via Suez and toward Gibraltar, had been regularly attacked by the Italians on, over, and under the water. And the British naval base at Malta was frequently bombed by planes flying the short distance from Sicily. Malta, being a small island, was not an especially good base for retaliatory raids. Until the invention of radar, which enabled the Royal Navy to carry out destructive night raids from Malta against Italian ships, there was even a chance that Britain would be driven out of the Mediterranean altogether, and lose the Suez Canal and Gibraltar in the bargain.

Sonar, introduced in 1941, gave the British an edge over the Italian submarines, but did not by any means remove that threat. These advances in technology were very timely, for the advent of the Pacific war in December 1941 would take its toll on British shipping. More than a few naval warships set out from Malta for the land of the Rising Sun, never to return.

The Americans, by contrast, had no special grudge against the Italians. To them, Mussolini was a comic-opera buffoon, and Italy's army and navy didn't seem worth much attention. Nobody in Washington was obsessed with the Italians, as were (allegedly) many in Whitehall. Foreign Secretary Anthony Eden, Winston Churchill's right-hand man and heir apparent, nourished a hatred of the Italians that has been characterized as "violent . . . irrational, even psychopathic." Harold Macmillan, in 1943 Britain's chief political officer in liberated Italy (and years later prime minister of England), decried the "childish animosity" of the diplomats in London.[32]

Prime Minister Churchill himself never gave vent to such feelings, and never had such imputed to him. Indeed, prior to the signing of the Pact of Steel between Italy and Germany in 1938, Churchill entertained some fond feelings toward Mussolini—in sharp contrast to his distaste for Hitler. He thought *il Duce* stood for something fundamentally modern, though he could never quite define what that was. Hitler struck him as a dangerous sham. But now Hitler dominated Mussolini, and Churchill no longer had any respect for *il Duce*.

The British leader also had shown an affinity for attacks against what he called "the soft underbelly of Europe." In 1915, as First Sea Lord, he engineered an attack against the Dardanelles. It proved to be a disaster, with a Turkish army first containing an Australian army on the rocky shore of the Gallipoli Peninsula, then unceremoniously kicking the survivors out. Churchill's career was nearly ruined by this episode, but here he was again talking about the "soft underbelly" to President Roosevelt at the Casablanca Conference in January 1943, and having General Alexander work up a plan to invade Italy even while the North African campaign was still in full swing.

Churchill may have sought in Italy a vindication for the costly failure in Gallipoli. But he, of course, instead talked about Italy as "a perfect prelude and accompaniment" to the projected invasion across the English Channel."[33] More to the point, he noted to Roosevelt, "We can't merely sit and watch the Russians."[34] There was in fact the prospect of a hiatus between the end of the North African campaign (in May 1943) and the cross-Channel invasion, during which time the Russian front would continue to be active. The Anglo-American forces had to be doing something more than occasional commando raids and bomber attacks. In a meeting at the White House in May 1943, as the operations in Tunisia were coming to an end, Churchill said again that Allied forces "could not possibly stand idle" while the Eastern front flared and flamed in daily bloodlettings.[35]

There was even a viewpoint, in the British camp, that Italy should be considered a possible substitute for the putative cross-Channel invasion. The principal proponent of this idea was Field Marshal Jan Christian Smuts of South Africa, one of the most prestigious military men in the British Empire and Commonwealth. Smuts apparently sold King George V on this idea, if not the prime minister.

Roosevelt's main objection to the Italian plan was that it would drain resources away from the cross-Channel project. This attitude was fully shared by (if it did not originate with) U.S. Chief of Staff George C. Marshall, who also noted that the flat geography of northern France, the Low Countries, and northern Germany would provide a much better environment for the Allies' abundant supply of military hardware than the craggy mountains of the Italian peninsula.

The decision to invade Italy was made over the relatively weak objections of the Americans, on the premise that Churchill's idea of needing something to do was irrefutable. It was made without consulting the other member of the Big Three, Joseph Stalin, who proved in the aftermath to have very strong opinions about it.

The Russian leader's first response was to recall that the British ambassador to the Soviet Union had made a firm promise that a cross-Channel attack, that would take some of the pressure off the Russians, could be expected sometime in 1943, with a million British and American soldiers taking part. He also recalled an assurance given by Churchill himself, in a letter dated 12 February 1943, that an effort to move across the English Channel could be expected as early as August 1943.[36]

Stalin called that Italian invasion an indication of "disregard of the vital interests" of the Soviet Union. The operation caused "severe stress" in his confidence in the Allies.[37] This observation created some alarm in Washington and London. The Soviets, after all, had made an alliance of convenience with the Nazis in 1939 for the purpose of carving up Poland between themselves. A separate peace between the Soviet Union and Germany might cause mouths to drop open, but it was not out of the question.

The Soviet leader's specific complaint was the same as Roosevelt's: The invasion across the English Channel would inevitably be delayed. The main difference was that Stalin felt much more strongly about it than Roosevelt did. Churchill advised FDR, in the wake of the Soviet leader's blistering complaint, that the "best answer" would be to knock

Italy out of the war, tie down German divisions in Italy, "and let him feel the relief that will come."[38]

The die was cast, but the Allies could have ended their campaign with the capture of Sicily, as the British did during the Napoleonic Wars. Such a move, which might have made possible an acceleration of preparations for the English Channel invasion, even while the Germans were building up their defenses on the French seacoast in preparation for it, would not have been illogical. Possession of Sicily meant greater safety for English shipping in the Mediterranean. Possession of part of the mainland would add to that protection, but arguably there was a diminishing return here.

Even more to the point, the invasion had led directly to Mussolini's removal from power. *Il Duce*, who had ruled Italy since 1922, was ousted about halfway through the campaign, at about the time Axis generals on the scene decided that any chance of driving the invaders back into the sea was past. He was held prisoner, "for his own safety," on the order of Victor Emmanuel, acting through the new caretaker premier, Gen. Pietro Badoglio. Moreover, serious peace talks between Italy and the Allies were now underway. Rome even seemed amenable to the unconditional surrender terms being demanded by the Allied representatives, in accordance with the declaration of Allied war aims made at Casablanca in January.

The conquest of Sicily, in short, produced some major results. As it came to an end, even Stalin might have had trouble claiming that it was not worthwhile.

There is no record, however, that the Anglo-American allies gave even a moment's consideration to ending the campaign in Messina. FDR, for instance, wasn't expressing doubts anymore. Allied commanders and political leaders alike were instead mulling over the question of just how far up the peninsula to go. Churchill now said the Allies should "certainly" invade the mainland and conquer it as far as the Po Valley, "with an option" of also using Italy as a possible springboard into Southern France or even Austria. He was not impressed with the suggestion made by U.S. Secretary of War Henry L. Stimson that now preparations for the English Channel invasion should be accelerated.[39]

These matters were a prime topic of discussion at the Quebec Conference, where Roosevelt and the British prime minister conferred on general policy matters in August 1943. Considering that the invasion force might not reach the Po, Sir Winston settled on a line stretching from Livorno (Leghorn), on the west coast of Italy, to Ancona on the east coast. "If we cannot have the bests," he said, "these are good second bests."[40] The proposed line stood about halfway between Rome and the Po Valley. It assured a buffer zone against any Axis attempt to recapture Rome, which various military leaders, including Eisenhower, had recommended as a worthy terminal point for the Italian campaign.[41]

The most modest proposals, again from assorted generals on the Allied side, favored a line just north of Naples that would also encompass the large airfield complex at Foggia. The latter was considered one of the more valuable specific objectives on the mainland. Located east of Naples, it would be useful as a long-range strategic bomber base. Targets in the southeastern quarter of Germany, now out of reach of aircraft based in England, could be bombed by planes based at Foggia. So, too, could any location in Austria, and even parts of Poland. More than a few of the military commanders felt that a definite law of diminishing returns would set in if operations continued past Naples-Foggia, and virtually nobody took serious issue with this limited objective.

Had the Sicilian campaign been lengthier and bloodier, the Allies would have been less inclined to mull over possible lines of advance on the mainland. But the operation seems to have been regarded, despite its shortcomings, as an unmitigated success. U.S. combat casualties were fewer than 8,000 (including 501 killed and nearly 3,000 missing). British losses were slightly higher, giving a grand total of 17,000 combat casualties.[42] Axis losses (killed, wounded, and missing) were double that, plus a substantial harvest of prisoners, numbering upwards of 130,000. The Hermann Goering Division alone lost 600 men in a single battle, the defense of Gela. The two Italian coastal divisions on the island, the 206th and the 207th, had been "virtually destroyed" after they were abandoned by the retreating Axis forces. These provided a substantial part of the POW numbers, mainly in western Sicily.[43]

About one out of every eight Americans on the island became a combat casualty. This was an extraordinarily high ratio. The British sustained only a thousand more casualties, but they outnumbered the Americans by nearly two to one (115,000 to 66,000). This is all the more extraordinary in that most of the soldiers in Montgomery's command were concentrated on the very active east coast front. Half of the Americans, on the other hand, were diverted during two of the four weeks of the campaign to General Patton's *blitzkrieg* across western Sicily, where no fighting took place once the 3rd Division got past Agrigento and Porto Empedocle, at the outset of the junket. The BBC even felt free to remark during this maneuver that the Americans were "eating grapes in western Sicily" while Monty's boys were slugging it out with Jerry on the Catania Plain. (This elicited an official complaint from

Eisenhower, who pointed out that many of the troops had access to radios powerful enough to pick up BBC broadcasts.)

But the Americans were, both before and after the diversion, in bloody battles. The U.S. landing area at Gela was more hotly contested than the British front at Syracuse and Augusta, and at the secondary British landing site on the southeast corner of the island, at Cape Pessaro. Then, following the occupation of Palermo, the 45th Division's push along the north coast and the 1st Division's attack against Troina involved some intense fighting.

The high U.S. casualty rate can also be explained in terms of a lack of experience on the part of both soldiers and commanders. Americans would also experience needless losses on the mainland as their senior commanders learned what their Allied counterparts had already learned. And casualties would again be increased by accidents of friendly fire, such as occurred to the airborne troops over Gela, although never on quite so large a scale.

The British were more experienced, and their commander, Montgomery, was noted for his cautiousness—an attribute that would drive some of his American colleagues to near distraction in the coming months. These circumstances limited their casualties to a relatively modest level. They also heightened the British leadership's ardor for a continuation of the Italian campaign onto the mainland. The American experience on Sicily, by contrast, offered less in the way of encouragement, though U.S. armed forces came of age on Sicily in a way that they had not in Tunisia. They fought well, displaying their awesome firepower to great effect and earning the respect of Axis military leaders.

As the Allies considered their next move, the German High Command was also weighing its options in Italy. It was inclined to downgrade the role of the Italian forces even more than the Allies were, and so discounted the high Italian casualty count. The latter, at any rate, was inflated by a large number of "missing" personnel who actually had been caught in Patton's sweep through western Sicily. Few of these were regular combat troops.

Field Marshal Kesselring, head of Army Command-South, impressed upon his colleagues in Berlin and upon Adolf Hitler (currently at his forward command post in Poland) that the German loss rate was close to (actually a bit in excess of) that of the Allies—nearly one to one. Kesselring felt that this ratio would improve in fighting on the mainland, where the need to protect a line of retreat would not be so overweening as it was on Sicily. On Sicily, he pointed out, the fear of being cut off from the mainland constricted operations and made them inflexible.

In addition, he noted, defense of the mainland would benefit greatly by the rugged peaks and valleys of the Apennine Mountains, a topography much more daunting than Sicily's to an invader.

OKW, the German High Command, was also busy assessing the effectiveness of combined Anglo-American operations. In the absence of an American diversion to western Sicily, it was pretty clear that a concerted drive around both sides of Mount Etna (the Americans around the west, the British on the east), would have placed Messina, the only viable evacuation point, under inexorable pressure. OKW was fully aware that this was the original plan of attack. It was evident in the deployment of forces prior to Montgomery's maladroit cutoff maneuver in front of the advancing Americans; besides, that deployment impressed the Germans as being the most logical one in the first place. The subsequent split-up of Allied forces was rightly perceived as a sign of dissension. It prolonged the campaign and made possible the eventual evacuation of the German divisions.

Much less clear-cut was the Germans' position relative to their ally. Here political concerns far outweighed the military ones, but let us first dispose of the military ones. Admiral Leonardi's surrender of Augusta nearly destroyed the entire defense strategy. Though the admiral's colleagues in the Italian armed forces accepted his excuses, the Germans did not. Not content to ascribe the surrender to cowardice, the Germans suspected political motives. They believed that many Italian military leaders (including General Ambrosio, appointed chief-of-staff in February) felt ill at ease as German allies. Many did not approve of the alliance and the extensive commitments and risks that it involved.

Just prior to Ambrosio's appointment, the great battle of Stalingrad had come to an end on the Russian front. An entire German army had been wiped out and two dozen German generals captured. The Red Army had broken through in a sector held by Italian and Romanian troops. Many Germans blamed these, quite unreasonably, for causing the disaster. The Italians, for their part, claimed that they were mistreated by their ally in Russia. Food and ammunition supplies were erratic, and they were sometimes insulted.

In addition to the surrender of Augusta, the Sicilian campaign produced a rich harvest of mutual recriminations. Comando Supremo wanted more German reinforcements, asserting them to be "indispensable" and wondering often why more were not sent to Sicily. Those already on the scene, however, were regularly placed in front of the Italian divisions to take the brunt of Allied attacks. Position maps prepared for Commando Supremo show this happening on the north coast and elsewhere. The redeployment on the north coast, near San Stefano, involved soldiers of the two armies passing one another on the narrow coast road. One wonders what they must have thought and said as this happened.[44]

On 13 July, the fourth day of the invasion, Hitler complained to Mussolini that 320 Italian aircraft had been destroyed on the ground in Sicily.[45] *Il Duce* himself wondered if this were not merely incompetence but a case of duplicity in high places. And when the Americans reached Palermo, greeted by an Italian general waiting on the main highway alone in his staff car, the Germans were not amused. The general rode back into the city with an American divisional commander seated next to him. Yet the city had been subjected to Allied bombing raids just before the invasion, as part of the effort to divert defending Axis forces away from the real landing sites. The harbor had not been damaged in those raids, and the Italian commanders did not see fit, either, to sink ships in the channel, destroy the docks and warehouses, or seed the approaches with mines. The place fell to the Americans undamaged, ready for use as an Allied supply depot.[46]

All this fit a pattern begun when the British navy blasted the small island fortress of Pantelleria, out in the Mediterranean, into submission just prior to the invasion of Sicily. This place had been characterized as impregnable, an unsinkable battleship and aircraft carrier combined. It was also a refueling base for submarines and surface ships. Between 1 and 10 June, Allied bombers made 3,500 sorties against the place, dropping 5,000 tons of bombs. An aerial photo taken halfway through these attacks shows the entire island engulfed in black smoke so thick that probably nobody outdoors could breathe. The smoke emanated from fuel tanks at one end of the island, and the breezes did the rest, blowing it in exactly the wrong direction for the defenders. Visibility, and the ability to fight back, must have been reduced to zero while these smoky fires continued to burn.[47]

On 11 June the British 1st Infantry Division landed, and on 13 June the five Italian battalions on the island surrendered. Casualties among the defenders (who included more than a hundred Germans) were two hundred dead and two hundred wounded. Some 4,600 prisoners were taken.[48]

Looking over the weaponry left behind by the defenders, the Allied officers were impressed that this "impregnable fortress" was only modestly equipped with antiaircraft guns, and the shore batteries did not have guns that could match cruisers and battleships of the Royal Navy in range. (In other words, the British could have blasted away without fear of damage from the shore defenses.) All the place had in good supply was infantry. They had been bombed, burned, and smoked into a demoralized state by the time British soldiers landed, although fighting did continue for a day and a half after the landing. By 26 June, a new airstrip was ready for use there as a base for American P-40s.

Still, when the Sicilian campaign was over, Eisenhower could write: "It should be realized also that certain Italian units in the last days of the Sicilian campaign fought determinedly and well." This was in a report to the Combined Chiefs of Staff, dated 19 August. And the OSS concluded that the bad reputation the Italian military had acquired during the North African campaign was undeserved.[49]

General Ambrosio found three causes for the failure of the defense of Sicily. In a final report titled *"Operazioni in Sicilia,"* he concluded that, first of all, the outcome was greatly influenced by the recent loss of North Africa. Specifically, the Allies had the momentum of victory, with large forces mobilized and ready for action against targets of their own choosing. The Axis, in contrast, was still coping with the loss of thousands of troops left stranded in Tunisia.

Secondly, Ambrosio cited the unpredictability of the point of attack. The range of possibilities stretched from southern France, through Italy and Yugoslavia, all the way to Greece. Axis leaders did not appreciate the Allies' sensitivity to the element of air cover, which the Americans in particular had learned in their recent Pacific operations at Guadalcanal. That is why they selected Sicily, the nearest target at hand, and therefore the closest to Allied air bases in North Africa.

These were circumstances that Ambrosio believed were beyond control. Problems that could have been managed better, he wrote, included transport and communication. He did not suspect, of course, that the Allies had access to all German military communications, including those between the German and Italian generals, via their mastery of the German code machines.[50]

Ambrosio also addressed a memo to *il Duce*, noting that the defense of the *patria* was hindered by the deployment of Italian forces in so many foreign lands, from France to Russia, and including a heavy commitment in the Balkans. It was up to *il Duce* to decide whether or not to bring some divisions home, but he couldn't leave his ally in the lurch. Consultation with the Führer was a precondition, as it had been when Mussolini decided to scale down his commitment in Russia following the Stalingrad debacle. A couple of divisions were already back in Italy because of this, but most had been sent to the Balkans, where they replaced some German units that were then sent off to the Russian steppes.

This was a considerable commitment for a nation that could not by any stretch of the imagination be counted among the Great Powers. Moreover, the active combat areas, where partisans and regular army remnants challenged the occupiers day and night, were a military strategist's nightmare: rugged, trackless mountains; semi-arid valleys; and crumbling roads. Lacking the speedy communications and air support of today's armies, many squads and companies were cut to pieces by guerrillas waiting in ambush. It took huge numbers of men to control such geography.

The Italians had tried to fight in the desert without enough tanks. They had also fought in the mountain vastnesses of the Balkans without the resources for victory. But now, was it not time to go home and defend the *patria?*

CHAPTER TWO

A NEW GAME WITH NEW RULES

The bald, portly man bent over, picked up a stone, and threw it as far as he could down the slope. Soldiers and *Carabinieri* (members of the Italian national police) also rummaged about for stones. So did German paratroopers. The bald man seemed nonetheless to be the center of attention. A German captain—a gigantic man named Otto Skorzeny— hovered over him and fixed his gaze first in one direction, then another, over the Apennine peaks, watching, apparently, for airplanes. One was parked nearby. It was a twin-engined Stork plane of German manufacture, noted for its ability to land and take off on short runways and on rugged terrain. Today, 12 September 1943, the plane was to be put to the test. It would trundle over the lumpy terrain toward a precipice, building up enough speed as it went over the side (it was hoped) to hold its own and then soar into the blue. Inside would be the gigantic captain, the bald man, and the pilot. To improve the chances for success, loose stones and large stony outcroppings were being removed from the putative runway.[1]

Finally, the plane started off with its bulky human cargo, bounced along the gentle slope, disappeared momentarily as it dropped off the precipice, then soared into the sky, leaving the cheering, waving soldiers and *Carabinieri* (totalling some three hundred men) on the side of Mt. Cornu, the highest peak in the mountain chain, and the site of the Hotel

Campo Imperatore, the bald man's last abode as a prisoner of the state of Italy.

The man was Benito Mussolini. He was being rescued, under orders from Adolf Hitler, by a German parachute unit that specialized in unusual and highly dangerous missions. Mussolini's Italian guards numbered 250, but they did nothing to prevent the rescue. One reason was that the first German glider to crash-land on the mountain slope contained a kidnapped Italian general. With Captain Skorzeny's Lueger pointed at him, he emerged from the glider and strode toward some Italian soldiers, who appeared ready to open fire. He ordered them to go back to the hotel and secure a general stand-down of arms. They dutifully ran back toward the looming structure, waving their arms.[2] Mussolini, *il Duce*, had watched all this from his window.

He had ruled Italy with absolute power since 1922. Yet no sooner had Sicily been invaded and the Allied beachheads made secure than voices were raised in favor of his overthrow. He was out of office and under arrest by the time the campaign was half over, at just about the point when Axis generals conceded that they would not be able to drive the Anglo-Americans back into the sea.

Yet, when the invasion began, newspapers across Italy had downplayed the importance of the island.[3] It would fall to British and American sea power because it was an island. Meanwhile, the mainland would remain safe. It had been occupied by the British throughout the long years of Napoleon's imperium in Italy, demonstrating that the defense of Sicily and the defense of Italy were two different things.

Some of the newspapers played upon anti-Sicilian prejudices, especially in the northern provinces, where Fascism had first taken root. And there was the very recent memory of Gen. Mario Roatta's remarks in an interview, just before the invasion began, that Sicily could not be counted on to defend itself. Roatta was then in charge of the island's defenses. He was replaced by General Guzzoni. (Subsequently, and paradoxically, Roatta prepared the whitewash report exonerating Rear Admiral Leonardi for the surrender of Augusta without a fight.) Sicilians felt insulted. But in the latter stages of the campaign—after Mussolini's departure from the Palazzo Venezia—the daily reports prepared by operations commanders on the island for headquarters in Rome carried frequent notation of "Sicilians" in the ranks of the Assietta and Aosta divisions deserting their units, sometimes in large groups, and making their way toward Allied-controlled areas, presumably in hopes of making it back to their homes rather than being evacuated to the mainland and an uncertain fate.[4]

There was even a minor separatist movement on the island that received unwonted publicity. It may have been minor, but it was the only such movement in all Italy, except for some of the German-speaking areas and Slovenian enclaves in the far northeast. There were fears that the Allies would cultivate the separatists. Some British officials indeed saw some promise there, but the American OSS resolutely downgraded the movement, saying that it did not reflect the patriotic feelings of most of the Sicilians.[5]

One Fascist leader, Roberto Farinacci, sought to deflect criticism from *il Duce* by suggesting, in his Cremona-based newspaper, that the generals were more interested in getting rid of Mussolini than they were in defending the island, and were willing to surrender the latter in the interests of the former. Mussolini, in his subsequent writings, also entertained this viewpoint. His conclusion was that the military chiefs (or most of them) were traitors.

Had the majority of the Fascist leadership shared Farinacci's view, *il Duce* might have lasted a while longer. He might have even outlasted the war, especially if the Allies decided not to invade the mainland. But the die was cast. The war was very unpopular, and many Fascist leaders now agreed that Italy had to get out as soon as possible.

Such rumblings of discontent had reached Mussolini's ears even during the North African campaign. He was confronted for the first time, however, only when the invasion of Sicily appeared headed for success. Dino Grandi, a senior Fascist official (indeed, a founder of the movement), put matters in stark terms during a personal interview on 22 July. Either Mussolini would have to lead Italy out of the war, he said, or somebody else would have to be found to do it. *Il Duce* raised the issue of unconditional surrender, which became the Allies' declared war aim at the Casablanca Conference in January. And only five days earlier, an Allied declaration had called for Mussolini's ouster as a prior condition for peace. (He was also to be turned over to the Allies as a prisoner.) Grandi then said that *il Duce* should resign, let somebody else make peace for Italy, and hope for the best in terms of his personal well-being.

Mussolini's next visitor—kept waiting in the anteroom during this interview—was Marshal Kesselring, the senior German officer in southern Italy. Kesselring had a quite different message to convey—one of hope and promise, in keeping with his "eternal optimism" (as the Führer himself would later describe the Marshal's disposition).

A meeting of the Grand Council was held three days later, on 25 July. This was the government's board of directors. Mussolini dominated it by virtue of his position as chairman (he presided over meetings from a raised dais, replete with red brocade, which faced out over two long conference tables at which the councilors sat), and his control over the agenda. He also had ultimate authority over appointments to this august body, and most of the membership consisted of Fascists who had helped put Mussolini in power.

Great deference was always shown to *il Duce* at meetings. He would not enter, for instance, until the entire membership was present. Then all would rise and remain standing until he had settled in his ornate chair and bade them be seated. He would then make some opening remarks (sometimes amounting to a speech) which would set the tone for the entire meeting, as others responded to these remarks in respectful terms.[6]

Actual debate was not unknown in these meetings, however. This reflected the fact that each of the Ras' (as these founding Fascists were sometimes called, after an Ethiopian term meaning *prince*) had a power base of his own, which had coalesced in the early days of the movement without *il Duce*'s direct intervention. Grandi, for instance, was the bigshot in Ferrara and its environs—almost a *condottiere* of the old school of swashbuckling adventurers who had once ruled Italy. Farinacci's base was in Cremona, an important town in the Po Valley, the breadbasket of Italy.

And these two, for example, represented different schools of thought on many issues. Farinacci was an outright Germanophile, or at least an enthusiastic Hitlerite. Grandi, who had served once as ambassador to Britain (and before that, as foreign minister), was alleged to be Anglophile. At least, he had always recommended that war with Britain should be avoided at all costs. Similar cleavages existed in the realm of domestic policy. So lively debate was not unknown at Grand Council meetings, even if *il Duce* always had the last word.

At this meeting, however, *il Duce* would not have the last word. He knew something was afoot even before the group convened at 5 P.M., that Grandi was going around sounding out fellow Ras' about a motion calling for the dictator's resignation. Farinacci and other diehards were not approached, but word inevitably got out anyway. Grandi knew this had been likely, and so came to the meeting with a hand-grenade in his pocket, just in case.[7]

Mussolini, for his part, notified the police chief to have a contingent on hand at the Palazzo Venezia in case arrests were in order. Even Victor Emmanuel called upon General Sorice to discreetly place a machine-gun unit and other troops around the Palazzo Venezia once the gathering was underway.

When *il Duce* walked into the conference room, the majority of Grand Council members kept their seats. "I sense the spirit of the Fronde," he remarked, alluding to a band of rebellious aristocrats in the France of Louis XIII. Mussolini nonetheless made his customary opening remarks, devoted this time to the military situation in Sicily. He questioned the military leadership, noting that the commander of the Napoli Division and his staff had been taken prisoner even before most of that division had been engaged by the British forces, and that the port of Augusta had been surrendered through apparent treachery.

General DeBono, one of the so-called Triumvirate that had helped organize the March on Rome in 1922 which catapulted Mussolini into power (and which earned the general a seat close to *il Duce* at these meetings), spoke out in defense of the armed forces chiefs. He and his colleague DeVecchi recalled the advice of the late Fascist Ras' Italo Balbo, founder of the Italian air force: Going to war as an ally of Adolf Hitler, Balbo had said in 1935, would end in a "catastrophe" for Italy. At the time this was said, Italy had no commitments to Germany.

Count Ciano, the former foreign minister who was now ambassador to the Vatican, gave vent to the feelings that had helped bring about his demotion in the diplomatic ranks. Germany was a treacherous ally, he said. The Reich had violated the Pact of Steel by starting a war prior to 1942—catching Italy unprepared for the effort to create the New Order for Europe.

Grandi took issue with the party chairman, saying that he and his predecessors (Carlo Scorza and Achille Starace, respectively) had failed to keep the party in touch with the people, and so had failed to win popular support for the various military adventures that the country had embarked upon. Grandi then made a motion calling on *il Duce* to "return" to the king the powers that had been conferred upon him. This meant specifically the duties of Marshal of the Empire which Victor Emmanuel had conferred on Mussolini in 1940, and which normally adhered to the king himself as commander-in-chief of the armed forces. The motion was general enough, though, to take in Mussolini's official title as *Capo del' Governo* (Head of Government), conferred by constitutional amendment, passed by the legislature in 1926.

The motion passed by a vote of 19-7, with two abstentions. (One "yes" vote—that of Senate president Suardo—was changed to "no" the next day, making the final vote 18-8.) Rather than adjourn, the meeting now

Mussolini posing with wounded soldiers at a military hospital. Courtesy U.S. Army Military History Institute

became very acrimonious (Grandi and Scorza exchanging accusations and insults, for instance). It broke up at 2 A.M., having lasted for nine hours, with a brief recess at midnight.

Mussolini visited the Tiburtino district next day. It had been the scene of the first Allied bombing raid on Rome, the main target being a large railroad freight yard. He also met the new Japanese ambassador, Shinrokuro Hikada. At 5 P.M., he met with Victor Emmanuel at the Villa Ada, one of the king's residences.

The meeting lasted twenty minutes. The king asked Mussolini if he was familiar with the words of a new song, "Alpine Regiment." The king recited some of them, including a reference to "Mussolini's war." It was an anti-war song. The king then opined that *il Duce* was "the most hated man in Italy," and then went on to the proceedings of the night before. Mussolini protested that the Grand Council had only consultative powers. Victor Emmanuel fixed a steely look upon him, noting that this "consultative body" consisted of the inner circle of *il Duce*'s own leadership. Where else might *il Duce*'s friends be found?

So, the king continued, the time had come for him to fulfill his constitutional duty and prerogative, and remove Mussolini from office. The two men shook hands, and *il Duce* left.[8] Outside, he was approached by a captain of the *Carabinieri*, who announced that, on orders from the king, it was necessary that he place the former *Capo del' Governo* in protective custody. "It is for your own safety," he assured. "Nobody will harm you."

Mussolini's fall was announced on the radio by Victor Emmanuel himself, six hours later, at 11:30 P.M. (The airwaves had been blacked out for half an hour before.) In the interim, orders had gone out to the Fascist militia to occupy the city of Rome, orders rescinded when the Militia chief, Monterosi, was arrested.

After the radio announcement, crowds gathered in the streets. By 2 A.M., a huge throng was gathered in St. Peter's Square, where people shouted *"Evviva Il Papa!"* A mob invaded the Casa del Fascio, the national headquarters of the Fascist Party. The offices of the Fascist newspaper *Il Tevere* were sacked.[9] Old scores were settled by the relatives of fascism's many victims: those who had died in jail, those stabbed and shot, those crippled by Fascist beatings—many of them came from families with long memories and even longer patience.

The fire department received an order to remove all Fascist symbols and insignia from public places. It was to be carried out at once, overnight. Off-duty firemen were called to work. Off-duty policemen were called to work, even though no effort was made to stop the surging mobs. Pictures of *il Duce* were sent flying out of many windows. Sicily had killed fascism.

Mussolini was taken to Ponza, a little island not far from Rome. It had a distinctive past as the abode of various political prisoners. Most recently it had housed Ras' Imeru of Ethiopia, the nation conquered by Italy in 1935. *Il Duce* was given the Ras' former cottage. The place had also housed some Socialists, including Pietro Nenni. In the distant past, it had been home to Pope Sylvester Martyr (I); Nero's mother, Agrippina; and Augustus' dissolute daughter, Julia. Mussolini occupied himself with translating, from memory, the odes of the Italian poet Carducci into German. He also read a life of Christ.[10]

On 6 August, he was transferred to another island, La Maddalena, off the coast of Sardinia. His sixtieth birthday had been on 29 July, but presents from family and admirers did not catch up with him until the move to La Maddalena. These included a bust of Frederick the Great (from Hermann Goering), and a deluxe edition of the complete works of Friedrich Nietzsche, sent by Adolf Hitler. *Il Duce* delved at once into the first volume, which containing some early poetry and essays in Greek and Latin philology by the philosopher of the *Übermensch*. The battle of Sicily was entering its last days.

A German reconnaissance plane was spotted near the island on 18 August. The next day, *il Duce* was spirited away in a Red Cross plane.

He was finally sent overland to Gran Sasso, a mountaintop retreat located some distance to the east-southeast of Rome.

It was from there that he was rescued on 12 September. Italy had just surrendered. The Allies had just landed at Salerno.

e/s

Like many revolutionary leaders, Mussolini had come to power acrest a wave of popular discontent. He had not created the wave, nor had he controlled it, but, like any successful revolutionary, he had convinced others that the contrary was true. And so the Fascist revolution of 1922 had seemed as inexorable as a Mediterranean storm. In July 1943, upon hearing that *il Duce* had been unceremoniously fired by the king, and quietly taken into custody, one might have expected the wave to break yet again. But the head of the Fascist militia was easily cowed into ordering the rank-and-file to stand down. And the head of the party, Carlo Scorza, ordered every branch, every precinct, to obey the king and his new premier (who adopted the Mussolinian title of Head of State).

Scorza and other Fascists, fearful of people with old scores to settle, and hearing that some Roman Fascists had been stabbed or shot by unknown assailants or set upon by angry citizens, went into hiding. Thus the revolution, which had arrived with such ferocity, expired in a wave of timidity. Only Carlo Muti behaved like a Fascist in this moment of disaster, heaving a grenade at the *Carabinieri* sent to arrest him, then being gunned down as he tried to run away.

With Fascism apparently evaporated, like a bad dream that one awakes from, Victor Emmanuel now set out to take Italy out of the war. He functioned here as a virtual absolute monarch, but it is obvious that his desires reflected those of the people. For when the armistice was announced, in September, there was celebrating in the streets. The possibility of a military coup, to forestall such an outcome, seemed remote. The new head of state, Marshal Pietro Badoglio, was himself the top man in the armed forces in point of seniority in rank and the various honors he had achieved before his career went into eclipse in 1940 (at the behest of Mussolini). One officer, Gen. Ugo Cavallero, was placed under arrest as a potential threat. He was released in a few days after intensive questioning.[11] General Ambrosio, the chief of staff, advised the king that he need not fear a military revolt even if he acceded to the Allies' standing requirement of unconditional surrender.

Guariglia, the new foreign minister, initiated contacts with the British legate in the Vatican on 30 July.[12] Peace feelers were also sent out, early in August (as the battle of Messina unfolded), to British officials in

Lisbon and Tangier. Roosevelt and Churchill got wind of this as they prepared for their second wartime meeting, in Quebec. Thus they made the matter of peace with this Axis foe a part of their agenda.

Substantive discussions began finally on 19 August, while the Quebec Conference was still in session. These came in the form of discussions between General Castellano and Gen. Walter Bedell Smith (Eisenhower's right-hand man) in Lisbon. Two weeks later, on 3 September, the two men signed an armistice at Cassibile, in Sicily.

The agreement was kept secret for a week as efforts were made (or thought over and discussed) to neutralize any violent reaction on the part of the Germans. Castellano was given to understand, for instance, that the U.S. 82nd Airborne Division would jump into Rome and help the Italian army to keep the Germans away from the Eternal City. As it happened, the Allied chiefs then decided that such a daring maneuver would require assurances of effective support from their Italian counterparts. The second-in-command of the 82nd, Gen. Maxwell Taylor, was sent to confer with the new head of state, Badoglio, and Gen. Giacomo Carboni, currently in command of the Rome military district. They painted a rather grim picture during their late-night conference at the Palazzo Caprara. Taylor and his aide, Colonel Gardiner, sneaking out of the Eternal City in a Red Cross ambulance (en route to a rendezvous with a motor launch and then a submarine), brought back a negative recommendation.[13]

There was no air drop on Rome. And aside from prisoners of war, no Allied soldiers would follow Taylor and his aide into Rome for a full nine months—nine months of brutal, bitter, desperate fighting that would give the armistice the aspect of an oddity of history. It was a peace agreement that ushered in a wave of destruction surpassing the wildest dreams of Hannibal.

∓

The final stage in the political collapse of Italy, following the removal of *il Duce* and the unconditional surrender, was the king's panicked flight from Rome. Victor Emmanuel and his new *Capo*, Badoglio, felt uncomfortable with the five days' grace period between the secret signing of the Armistice and its scheduled public announcement. They exerted great efforts to have that one item changed, on the premise that more time was needed to prepare for any German takeover attempt. And until the very moment when the news came into millions of Italian households over BBC radio, they continued to entertain some hopes on this regard.

Even the matter of an 82nd Airborne drop into Rome was still discussed until the last moment, as Ridgway's men were actually prepared for takeoff from Palermo. Badoglio, who had already expressed strong doubts about the plan while not quashing it altogether, now advised Eisenhower that German divisions were poised for a move into Rome. The impression he conveyed, in a coded radiogram, was that the paratroopers would almost literally land on German bayonets. The message reached Palermo almost immediately after Ike's broadcast announcement of the Armistice was read over BBC radio.

The King and *Capo* thereupon gathered some of their personal belongings, behooved their families to do likewise, and rode out of Rome in motorcars in the dead of night. A motorcade formed itself as various generals with their families, and some royal relatives, got wind of what was happening. The procession stopped at the Pescati Air Field, south of the city. To the amazement and discomfiture of His Royal Highness and his retinue, the pilots indicated an unwillingness to fly him to Sicily. They asserted vehemently that such an endeavor would place the royal person in some danger.[14]

The royal party then proceeded to the small port of Ortona al Mare. Alighting from their vehicles, they crowded onto the lone dock that jutted into the dark Adriatic seascape. Unknown to them at the time, a huge Allied invasion fleet was closing in on the port of Salerno, just south of Naples. Badoglio disappeared for a while, then returned with two motor launches. Only seventy of the three hundred or so refugees on hand could fit aboard. The royal relatives took precedence, and several of the generals, with their now very frightened families, faced the prospect of riding back to Rome.

The royal party ended its trip at Brindisi, on the south coast. The city had just been occupied by Montgomery's Eighth Army, and there was some danger that the royal party, now transferred to the new corvette, *Baionetta*, might be attacked. Challenged by a British patrol boat several miles from the harbor, they were able to convey their peaceful intentions with the aid of a white handkerchief. The Allied chiefs were taken quite by surprise.

Victor Emmanuel's success in avoiding contact with the German air squadrons deployed at various points between Rome and the south coast belied the drastic long-term effects of his surrender and flight on 9–10 September. It is indeed a paradox that a regime that since its origins in 1860 had functioned as a constitutional monarchy, with the monarch essentially a passive figure in the government—a virtual figurehead—now stood suddenly transformed into an absolute monarchy at the hour of its greatest crisis. The decision to surrender was the most important ever made by a modern Italian government. Italians greeted it with jubilation, as they did the king's bold decision to fire Mussolini— also a very popular act. But the euphoria did not last long. People quickly began to wonder about the unconditional nature of the surrender: With most of his country still outside the grasp of the Allies, couldn't the king have negotiated terms?

And when the Germans moved into Rome on the heels of the king's departure, the Italian divisions based nearby were obviously left to respond as they saw fit. This immediately raised questions about the major part of the Italian army, deployed on foreign soil. To assure the secrecy of his planned flight from Rome, Victor Emmanuel (and Badoglio, who simply followed the king's instructions) gave no telltale signs in terms of army directives that might be deemed extraordinary. The entire Italian army was abandoned to its fate.

On 12 September, the newly formed Committee of National Liberation (Comitato di Liberazione Nazionale) condemned Victor Emmanuel and Badoglio for "deserting their posts."[15] The committee, popularly known as the CLN, had a political agenda: replacing the monarchy with a republic, and gaining Allied support for this goal. The CLN consisted of Socialist, Communist and Liberal elements now suddenly resuscitated by the overthrow of fascism. Their long-suppressed newspapers (along with some new ones, on the Liberal side) suddenly re-appeared, often using presses "liberated" from Fascist printing plants and hurriedly squirreled away in cellars and in the Roman catacombs, behind bricked-up walls and secret entrances.

And suddenly German soldiers, German tanks, German trucks, German airplanes were to be seen everywhere. Had Victor Emmanuel really surrendered to the Allies? It seemed instead that he had surrendered the country to the Germans.

乀ᔐ

The political disintegration of Italy had commenced with the removal of Mussolini. The total bankruptcy of the government was revealed with the unconditional surrender to the Allies. The debacle was made complete when the German divisions came pouring in through the Brenner Pass.

The German takeover commenced, not with the Italian surrender proclamation, but rather with the removal of *il Duce* a month and a half prior to the surrender (25 July). Orders went out to the 44th Panzer-Grenadier Division to closely follow the 26th Panzer Division on the main line from Munich through the Brenner Pass. The 26th was scheduled for deployment in Sicily, or, if the fighting there ended quickly, in Calabria, on the adjacent mainland. It was being sent in response to the urgent requests for aid coming from the Comando Supremo in Rome.

The 44th, on the other hand, was an uninvited guest. Comando Supremo was unaware of its approach, for the German High Command (OKW) failed to inform Rome that any additional reinforcements were set to follow the 26th Panzers into Italy. A long train carrying 44th personnel and equipment, including flatcars jammed with trucks and artillery, showed up at Brenner on 31 July, several hours after the last trainload of 26th tanks and troopers steamed off southward down the steep right-of-way.[16]

Gen. Alessandro Gloria, commander of the XXXV Corps, stopped the train at Bolzano, on the Italian side of the pass. The German commander, Gen. Valentin Feurstein, was told that the train could not proceed without authorization from Rome. Both generals then sought guidance from their chiefs via telegraph. Comando Supreme was obviously unsettled by this breach of protocol. There was a strong suspicion that it had something to do with Mussolini's overthrow, but on the other hand, there was no indication that the unexpected Germans were about to do anything but go down and fight for Sicily. Gloria was told to hold the Germans until matters were cleared up.

Feurstein, on the other hand, was told to wait a day; and then, when more elements of his division were on hand (trains began to accumulate along the main line north of Bolzano during the night) he was to continue whether the Italians said it was all right or not. He informed OKW that Italian soldiers had been deployed with machine guns and artillery directly south of the town, and that explosives had been set under the tracks in several places.

OKW then said to wait another day. On 2 August, Rome made the fateful decision to allow this division to pass unmolested, following OKW assurances that there had merely been a foul-up in communications, and that such would not happen again.[17]

But then the 44th Division sprang another surprise. Rather than disappear into the Po Valley, en route to the fighting front, it began to deploy along the right-of-way below Bolzano and in adjacent towns, literally under the guns of the Italian forces. Units also crowded into Bolzano itself. General Gloria questioned the need to build up the defenses around his headquarters. Feurstein complained that the vital rail link between Germany and Italy—the line that ran through Bolzano—was inadequately protected against Allied air attacks. Now that the Allies were established in Sicily (they were then converging on Messina, the last Axis stronghold on the island) they could bomb anywhere in Italy.

General von Rintelen, the military attaché in Rome, responded the same way when General Ambrosio, head of Comando Supremo, put the matter to him. Ambrosio asked him who had given permission for the Germans to "control" ("*presidiare*") the rail lines.[18] Rintelen had no answer for this, except to note that the 44th Division had indeed set up numerous antiaircraft guns, spaced out at regular intervals, for some distance south of Bolzano. It wasn't just to help Germany, he added. It was important for Italy's own self-defense.

Victor Emmanuel and his premier, Badoglio, were not prepared to confront their ally over the matter. They did, however, allow Ambrosio to send two divisions from the French border area to the Bolzano region, ostensibly to relieve the Germans of the responsibility of protecting Italian rail lines.[19]

General Rintelen, taking his cue from Berlin (specifically, from General Keitel at OKW) stormed into Ambrosio's office in Rome to protest this new deployment. He argued that the effect of these units passing Germans on the roads and encountering them in the towns was "intolerable."[20] It was devastating to the morale of German soldiers. Trains, he said, were still carrying Germans southward to the fighting front. Trains were also carrying German wounded back home. What could be the effect of seeing their allies, on whose land they were prepared to spill their blood (or, in the case of the wounded, had already done so), marching in the "*direzzione opposta*"—northward, away from the fighting?[21]

Ambrosio was not persuaded to remove the two divisions, but the dispute had reached a level of shrillness that would surely lead to an armed clash if some *modus vivendi* were not arrived at quickly. Indeed, the foreign ministers of the two countries were now embroiled in the situation (Ribbentrop and his newly appointed Italian counterpart, Sorice), but it was finally agreed, in a kind of summit meeting held at the border town of Tarvisio on 8 August, that the two armies would be deployed in "*equal forze*" along the railroad lines south of the Brenner Pass, and at various other sensitive locations in the far north.[22]

The very next day, Gloria and Feurstein were at it again, this time over unannounced movements of 44th Division troops into the Alto Adige valley towns. Rintelen was called in for an "*urgentissima*" meeting on this.[23] The Comando Supremo then made mention of the basic issue that underlay the whole crisis, in a telegram to OKW. Germany, it said, "distrusts its ally."[24]

Thus did Germany force open the door to Italy a month before the surrender.

Most Italians knew nothing about what was going on up in the Brenner region during those first days of August. The dramatic event of the moment was being played out on the Strait of Messina, as the evacuation of Sicily went into high gear. And for the remainder of August, the Germans maintained a low profile throughout most of the country. They were most conspicuous, of course, in the southerly provinces. Two divisions, the Goering (just in from Sicily) and the 15th Panzers, were based outside Naples. This was the heaviest concentration in the south, and numerous Wehrmacht personnel could be seen every day within the city itself.

In the north, Verona was practically taken over—overrun, one might say—by Germans, as Rommel selected that city as the temporary headquarters for his Army Group B. (Group A, under Kesselring, was south of Rome.) Also, the vicinity of Trieste, in the far north-eastern corner of the country, witnessed a considerable buildup of Wehrmacht units. Indeed, the Germans commandeered the roads into and out of the city, on the premise that Yugoslav partisans were infiltrating the area in order to develop rest and recuperation bases. The roadblocks and inspection points set up here constituted a more direct challenge to Italian sovereignty than even the trespasses at the Brenner Pass. But in contrast to the imbroglio that developed around Bolzano, there was no recorded demur from the Italian authorities over what went on outside Trieste. Yet by the time the Armistice was signed between Italy and the Allies, the Germans were preventing Italians from entering or leaving the city. This policy would continue, with exceptions for people who obtained special passes from the occupiers, until the end of the war.[25]

Except for Trieste, Verona and Naples, however, Germans in uniform were a rare sight in the larger cities. That included even Rome. The situation would change swiftly and drastically after 9 September, when the armistice was broadcast over the radio. The speed and breadth of that change reflects the fact that the Wehrmacht was well established in the countryside, outside the big cities. Rome was seized on 10 September, and most other cities were under the firm grip of the Wehrmacht within a few days.

During the month-long lull between the end of the Sicilian campaign and the Allied landing at Salerno (fifty miles south of Naples) the Reich leadership exercised itself over what to do if Italy dropped out of the war. The main issue was how much of the country should come under German control. Rommel favored an Alpine redoubt, leaving all Italy to the Allies. His argument was that Germany could not spare the man-power for a strong defense of Italian territory. He also doubted that the Allies would accept the heavy casualties that would necessarily attend a breach of the Brenner Pass (the most direct route to Germany) or a move via Trieste toward the Ljubljana Gap (another rare opening in the mountains). He also thought an Allied thrust from Italy into southeastern France could be made equally prohibitive in terms of casualties on the Allied side. There were fortified redoubts left over from World War I in the Brenner and Alto Adige regions, as well as in the Austrian Alps that offered a major headstart in building an unbreachable defense line here, Rommel argued.

His counterpart, Field Marshal Kesselring, who commanded forces south of Rome in Army Group A, took an opposite stand. His main argument was that with a dozen divisions—the number that might be deployed in Rommel's redoubts—the Wehrmacht could bottle up as many as twenty Allied divisions in the rugged mountains of peninsular Italy, where in most places the mountains reach nearly to the seacoasts. The Allies might hammer away at one defensive line there, and finally break through it. But, Kesselring said, they would then encounter yet another line a short distance to the north. A dozen Wehrmacht divisions could hold up a complete Allied conquest of Italy for two years. It could take them two years to obtain what Rommel was willing to concede in a day.[26]

Advantages of such a choice would be threefold: keeping Allied air bases further away from the Reich; a chance to resuscitate Mussolini and give him a territory to preside over; and a chance to rectify the northern boundaries. The second and third points were actually added to Kesselring's proposal by various supporters among the Reich's civilian hierarchy. It was well known, for instance, that the Führer was committed to rescuing *il Duce* from his imprisonment (a move accomplished forthwith). Hitler had indeed long been an admirer of Mussolini. The "Führer Principle" (One Leader) was modelled after a Mussolinian dictum, and the German Brown Shirts had always regarded themselves as the counterpart of Italy's Black Shirts. There were various other sentimental associations. In sum, Hitler found it unacceptable that *il Duce* should possibly fall into Allied hands. On the contrary, Mussolini needed to be re-established as a leader.

Civilian advisers were very quick to point out to the Führer, also, that a German occupation of Italy could gain a mantle of legality if presided over by *il Duce*. The issue of the latter's popularity was not raised. The jubilation that had met his overthrow was certainly not encouraging. On the other hand, there seemed to be a lack of leadership in Italy at this time. The Germans sensed a process of disintegration in the government there. Finding no alternative to Mussolini, Italians might give him a second chance, the Germans hoped.

On the matter of border adjustments, Berlin was thinking of the region from Bolzano (Brenner Pass) eastward to Trieste. Josef Goebbels, Reich Minister of Propaganda, noted in his diary at this time that the Führer was interested in reclaiming some territory lost by his native Austria after World War I. His current thoughts were that it would be constituted, in consideration of its mixed Italian-German-Austrian population, as an Autonomous State of the Reich.[27]

In the Rommel scheme of things, much of this territory would be abandoned to the Allies, although the Wehrmacht would control some of it. In the Kesselring *schema*, there would be plenty of time to set up an autonomous region.

Matters were still hanging fire when the Allies landed at Salerno on 9 September. The fact that they were nearly routed off the beach by a single defending German division lent credence to Kesselring's proposal. By the time the battle of Salerno was over, Hitler had come down firmly on the side of Kesselring, who assumed control of all the Wehrmacht forces in Italy. Rommel was reassigned to France.

That the prospect of border adjustments was no small matter is reflected in the fact that, by the end of September, there was a German mayor in Bolzano. And in Trieste, Italian prefect Bruno Coceani was answering to *Gauleiter* Friedrich Rainer, whose bailiwick included Venizia Giulia and a newly named province called Adriatische Kuesterland (Adriatic Coast), which reached from east of Trieste to the vicinity of Venice. The birthday of Rome, an important holiday, passed without public celebration, by *diktat* of the German authorities.

On 17 September, Kesselring announced the military occupation of all Italy. A few days earlier, Hitler authorized his armaments minister, Albert Speer, to secure all strategic industries in northern Italy. Italian workers in those industries (such as the Fiat Motor Company in Torino, and the Montecatini chemical plants in Milano and elsewhere) suddenly found themselves under direct military supervision. Speer sent an "industry co-ordinator" to Milan (Colonel Aschoff), and for good measure appointed a Baron von Elk as "agriculture co-ordinator."[28] In October the Todt Organization arrived to set up a Commissariat of Labor. The kind of labor this outfit specialized in was civilian levies for the construction of bunkers, pillboxes, tank traps, trenches, ditches, tunnels, caves, blockhouses and, not least, prison camps. Italian workers were often simply grabbed off the streets and trucked off to Todt work sites.

Where was the Italian army in the midst of all of this? It was mentioned earlier that, in the interests of securing his escape from Rome, Victor Emmanuel and his head of state, Badoglio, had not seen fit to leave any advance telltale signs in the form of orders to the generals. Upon arrival in Brindisi, Badoglio found that his principal means of communication was his personal fountain pen and borrowed stationery. He apparently had nothing momentous to communicate anyway, for the armed forces commanders waited in vain for any specific orders as to what they should do now that Italy had surrendered to the Allies.

The army was no longer at war with anybody, apparently. The Germans came forward to offer repatriation back to Italy for the units that were far from their country's frontier. All they had to do was surrender their weapons. But every Italian soldier knew of Germany's insatiable appetite for forced labor. Who was to decide what to do? What could be done? Where was the leadership?

All this can be passed off as a monumental example of defeatism and cowardice. In fact, the king had few options. A constitutional figurehead, he acquired leadership by default. Events, meanwhile, moved too swiftly to allow for the resuscitation of the parties of the pre-Fascist era, or the shaping of new ones, with an eye to establishing an effective popular leadership. The only man who might have exercised real choices was Mussolini, prior to his downfall.

The key to survival as an independent country was the deployment of the armed forces. If most of them were back in Italy as of, say, July 1943, then the country's fate over the next twenty-two months might have been somewhat less gruesome. For one thing, of course, the Allies might then have thought twice about selecting Sicily as their next target after Tunisia. They might indeed have been impelled toward some of those other parts of the "soft underbelly" of Europe that the Italians, homeward bound, left to the manpower-hungry Germans.

In July there were nearly six hundred thousand Italian soldiers deployed throughout the Balkans—mainly in Yugoslavia (current home of the V, VI, XI and XVIII Corps), Albania (IV and XXV Corps), Montenegro (XIV Corps), and Greece (III, VIII and XXVI Corps). There was one division each on Rhodes (still an Italian colony), Samos, and Crete. These forces, combined, nearly equalled the number stationed in Italy; but in fact they comprised a preponderance of the country's trained combat troops.[29]

There was an additional two hundred thousand in France and a slightly greater number in Russia. Through the efforts of General Ambrosio, newly appointed chief of staff in February 1943, this latter force was much reduced from the levels prevailing prior to the Stalingrad debacle. A majority of the soldiers reassigned from Russia, numbering about seventy thousand, were sent straight back to Italy.[30]

This move reflected a desire on Ambrosio's part to begin a gradual disengagement from the German alliance. Mussolini—and the Germans— were aware of his attitude in this regard, and aware also that he had numerous supporters among the army's nearly five hundred generals.

That Mussolini appointed Ambrosio immediately after the end of the battle of Stalingrad, then, was significant with possibilities for the future. It also signalled the tension developing in the Rome-Berlin Axis. Mutual recriminations over that battle have already been mentioned. Some German leaders, and especially von Ribbentrop, the foreign minister, felt that a military coup against *il Duce* was a real possibility. Von Ribbentrop even thought that discontent in the Italian officer corps dated from the events of 1941 in North Africa, when the British repulsed the first Italian thrust toward Suez and overran much of the Italian colony of Libya. Von Ribbentrop believed that since then a virtual *camarilla* of traitors and saboteurs had formed itself within the officer corps.[31]

The fact is that the ranks of the army command became sharply divided at that point. Badoglio, Mussolini's successor in 1943, had been forced into retirement as a result of the poor showing in the Libyan desert in 1941. The field commander, Rodolfo Graziani, blamed Badoglio for the lack of tanks. A Mussolini loyalist, Graziani would later head up the fledgling army of the Italian Social Republic from late 1943 until 1945, and would send Italians to fight alongside the Germans against the Allies.

Berlin perceived the appointment of Ambrosio, in 1943, as an attempt by *il Duce* to mollify the anti-Germans in the army command. Had Mussolini fully taken their side, he would have done more than repatriate some forces from Russia. He would also have scaled down operations in the Balkans and brought hundreds of thousands back to Italy.

Given that such a further shifting of forces was not blocked off by the Germans, it would have given Italy much greater leverage in dealing with both the Germans and the Allies, even as it might (as suggested already) have deflected the invasion from North Africa away from an Italian target.

But what about the pro-Germans in the armed forces? Mussolini was mindful of them also, and so he found himself in a sort of balancing act. It really led nowhere. Some sign of disengagement was given, in terms of the scaling down of forces in Russia, but there things remained.

When the Germans set out to disarm the Italians, they met with a mixed reception. On Corsica, the Friuli and Cremona divisions fought hard against the German 90th Infantry. The unit on Maddalena, the island near Sardinia where Mussolini had spent part of his captivity, also resisted a call to disarm. The division on Rhodes was actually beseeched by Allied radio to attack the German division it shared the island with, the day of the surrender. Two days later, heavily reinforced, the Germans then challenged the Italians and a battle was fought. In Cefalonia, the Acqui Division actually voted on the matter of handing weapons over to the Germans in return for a train ride home. The soldiers chose to keep their weapons, and engaged the Germans in combat. The Firenze Division, in Albania, also decided to resist. A unit on the island of Corfu decided likewise.[32]

The Wehrmacht encountered no troubles on Sardinia, nor in any of the large northern cities. The commander in Turin, General Adami-Rossi, claimed after the war that he feared a leftist uprising if he did not allow the Germans to take over.

The situation at Rome best exemplifies the sharp divisions within the army leadership. It has already been mentioned that the possibility of an Allied air drop into the city was not scrubbed until the day of the surrender—although it was at no time considered a likelihood. It has also been mentioned that the king's secret departure the night the surrender was announced was joined by several generals and their families. Some of these generals were commanders of divisions in the city's garrison. Their departure was no less secretive than the king's. So when the time came next morning to decide what to do about the German ultimatum, whether to fight or give up, division staff often searched in vain for their commanders.

The Germans invaded the city by way of the Magliana suburb, near the pyramid of Caius Cestus. An order was sent out by Gen. Giacomo Carboni, who commanded the city's defenses, for the Ariete Division to close in on the rear of the advancing German unit. This order was never received at the division headquarters. In its place came an order to stand fast—remain in barracks at the *Carabiniere* complex. Carboni himself had tried to join the royal evacuation the night before but couldn't find it. Those generals who had were, most of them, wondering what to do next after they had been left behind on the dock at Ortona.

More than half a million Italian soldiers ended up in Germany. The highest estimate is 615,000.[33] Survivors of fighting against the Germans who came for their weapons went to the worst labor camps. Officers who surrendered peacefully were not obliged to work, but their daily diet of a few potatoes, two pieces of bread, and a cup of tea (this was the regimen in the main internment camp) suggests that the living conditions of the rank-and-file must have been horrendous.[34] Thirty thousand of them never made it home. An additional ten thousand died at the time of the surrender, half of them soldiers of the Acqui Division in Cefalonia—the one that had voted on the question of surrender to the Germans.[35]

Nothing has been said about the Italian navy so far, in connection with the surrender. There were six battleships (two, the *Italia* and the *Vittorio Veneto*, very new), nine heavy cruisers, thirty-two destroyers, forty-eight submarines and numerous smaller craft, such as the new corvette that carried Victor Emmanuel to safety.[36] Adm. Sir Andrew Cunningham of the British Royal Navy ordered all of these to turn themselves in at Malta, whence they might be distributed to various other locations under Allied control. Most of the submarines showed up over the coming weeks, although it is known that the Germans captured or sank no less than eighteen of the total. A majority of the surface vessels also managed to elude capture. The notable exception here was the battleship *Roma*, commanded by Capt. Carlo Bergamini, and steaming southward from the La Spezia naval base (vicinity of Genoa). After shooting down one German airplane, the ship was struck by two glider bombs (forerunners of the modern Exocet missile). One detonated the ship's ammunition magazine in a tremendous, fiery explosion. The *Roma* broke in two and sank, with the loss of more than 1,300 seamen.[37] Had the king been aboard that ship, rather than the corvette *Baionetta*, the monarchy itself might possibly have survived.

Allied preparations for an invasion of the mainland did not go unnoticed by the Germans. So, the consolidation of control over mainland Italy was accompanied by efforts to prepare defense at likely landing sites for the expected invasion fleet. The important harbor of Livorno (Leghorn), situated far up the west coast, north of Rome, was given top priority, with a brigade-sized force of Wehrmacht troops.[38] The south coast, on the other hand, was written off as apparently too close to Allied strongholds. Thus, when the British arrived at Taranto, the site of a major Italian naval base, there was no fighting.[39]

Kesselring looked for hints of a landing near Rome or Naples in the pattern of Allied bombing raids. He did notice that Salerno was never hit, although the roads leading to it received an unusual amount of attention from the raiding aircraft. But then his own headquarters, near Rome, was the target one day of a precision bombing raid which nearly succeeded in killing him. (He emerged from the rubble unhurt.)[40]

There was some concern as to whether the enemy would be caught off guard, as a large American invasion fleet steamed toward Salerno, a short distance down the coast from Naples. The level of anxiety was greatly reduced—possibly dispelled altogether—by a radio message from General Eisenhower. The *Stars and Stripes* described the scene aboard one troop ship:

> At 2032 hours the news of Italy's surrender came over the ship's speaker. Some men dashed around the deck and holds of the ship slapping one another on the back as though they were lifelong friends. Others just yelled as they finally found release from all the emotion that had been mounting for the past few days. . . . As darkness fell over the ship, preparations were made to disembark. Ghostlike forms of troops assembling were visible all over the deck and the stillness of the night was punctuated only by the sharp orders and conversation of the boat crews.[41]

At 0330 the first assault boat left the ship. Most of the Americans belonged to the 36th Infantry Division, a National Guard unit from Texas. They wondered what kind of reception was in store for them, now that the country they were invading had surrendered. The Germans had done much of the fighting in Sicily, these men had heard, but what could the Krauts do now? Maybe the war in Italy was over.

Later, the future First Sea Lord, Sir Andrew Cunningham, who commanded naval operations at Salerno, would criticize the timing of the surrender broadcast. He perceived a lessening of discipline, a loss of the special alertness that characterizes men going into battle.[42]

The sea was calm, like a duck pond, and the stars shone brightly. The seven hundred ships and assault boats, which had rendezvoused from their several points of embarkation off the island of Stromboli, slid past the fabled Isle of Capri. To the north, the Sorrento Peninsula became barely visible in the moonless night. One of the most famous men in Italy, philosopher Benedetto Croce, had a summer home there. The American OSS had actually been assigned to look after his safety. Because he was one of the few Italians who had been allowed to criticize the Fascist regime publicly, it was thought that any mishap to his person would be a mark against the Allies in the minds of many of his fellow citizens.

An American submarine surfaced inside the harbor of Salerno. It was the beacon ship on which the invasion force would home in, relying on its powerful spotlight, pointed seaward.

When the surrender was announced over Italian radio, the German 16th Panzer Division, which was stationed at Salerno, received an order to disarm the Italian 222nd Coastal Division and send its personnel away (on foot) immediately. The Italians, responsible for the defense of Salerno Bay, were quite happy to say goodbye to the war and did not grouse at the alacrity with which they were expelled from their barracks by their former allies. Even so, their commander, Gen. Don Ferrante Gonzaga (a member of one of Italy's oldest and most famous aristocratic families) was shot at the very outset, for failing to hand over his pistol, but nobody else gave the Germans any trouble.[43]

None of the invaders had any combat experience, and neither did the 16th Panzers, except for some of their officers and noncoms, who were veterans of Stalingrad. The unit itself had fought at Stalingrad, but was newly reconstituted after having been virtually wiped out there the previous January. For the veterans who formed the core of the division leadership, Salerno was a happy contrast, with its olive groves and friendly people, to the city of stone and fire where the Reich received its fatal wounds.

Eisenhower was aware that there was "one German division" in the area.[44] He would not have been at all surprised to find Salerno undefended (as Taranto proved to be, for the British Eighth Army), and the timing of the surrender announcement was certainly influenced by the hope that such might be the case. In fact the 16th Panzers, after a holiday the Sunday before, conducted a day of maneuvers right on the shore and in the hills overlooking it. This occasioned the deployment of artillery that was still in place when the attack came. Placed on high alert the day before D-Day, and despite the diversion to expel the 222nd Coastal Division from its barracks and secure its weapons and ammunition, the Germans were in position, looking down into the bay from their hillside deployments. They slept next to their weapons. Awakened by a general alarm shortly after 3 A.M., they did not have to travel anywhere to find the battle.[45]

The 36th (Texas) Division went in along the southern bayshore, its range marked off by the outlet of the Sele River to the north and the Temple of Neptune (Paestum) to the south. On the other side of the river, the British 56th (London) and 46th (Oak Tree) attacked the north shore. U.S. Rangers and British commandos landed on the Sorrento Peninsula, at the far northern end of the attack front. These latter forces came in first, in the hope that any German defenders would be drawn off in that direction while the main attack centered on both sides of the river mouth. The Americans, on the southernmost front, were the last to go in. By that time the guns were booming north of the Sele, and Gen. Mark Clark, commander of the brand-new U.S. Fifth Army, determined that his Texans might slip ashore unnoticed if a preliminary naval bombardment was called off. Vice-Admiral H. Kent Hewitt objected, to no avail.[46]

Clark, it should be said, was one of those rare people who had the advantage of training for this type of enterprise. In 1940, he was in charge of a combat exercise that involved landings at Monterey Bay in California. Observing the action on the Sorrento Peninsula, after dawn on D-Day, he must have been reminded of the no less picturesque Monterey Peninsula. And looking at the deadly hills that loomed over the town of Salerno, he certainly had a sense of *deja vu*, for the terrain in back of Monterey is so very similar. Stuck in the rank of captain for more than a decade, his career was on an upward swing when that maneuver took place. He received top marks for his management of the mock invasion (which had San Francisco as its ultimate target, just as Naples was the main prize here), gained a reputation as an excellent manager and planner, and won another promotion.

Clark was still a colonel, though, when he roomed briefly with Eisenhower in London. Ike sent him on a dangerous mission, by submarine, to contact the French Admiral Darlan in North Africa, in hopes of winning the neutral French forces (neutral on a *de facto* basis since the fall of France in 1940) over to the Allies.

For this exploit he was promoted to general. When the Fifth Army was created, Ike decided that he was the right man for the job. The Fifth Army would be the British Eighth Army's counterpart in the coming campaign on the Italian mainland. The U.S. Seventh Army, which had fought in Sicily, would remove itself to England, whence it would take part in preparations for the cross-Channel invasion.

When the U.S. soldiers set out in their landing ships for the Salerno shore, then, they did not hear six-inch shells whizzing over their heads en route to targets in the enemy's strongholds. Almost until they beached, in fact, it seemed that the battle was confined to the British sector north of the Sele. Then all hell broke loose.

The second wave was delayed by the diversion of some landing craft to the hospital ships or to designated troop ships that served as collecting points for the wounded. Several landing ships had also been disabled, or lost navy crew members. Soldiers on both the British and American sides discovered the smell of blood and sometimes couldn't tell if they had been wounded as they noticed blood on their uniforms, as the landing craft took on the aura of butcheries, replete with red smears and even an occasional body part, left behind by the first wave.

Each of the three invading divisions was expected to clear the beach area by mid-morning and proceed to certain towns located several miles inland. Control of these towns would give the invaders control over the local roads, and the main north-south highway that would bring them to Naples within a week or two. With this hinterland secured, they would then build up for the attack around the Sorrento Peninsula (on the landward side) and head up the road to Naples. This second thrust would be underway, it was hoped, within a few days.

The commander of the 16th Panzers, Gen. Rudolf Sieckenius, was prepared to abandon the bay area after only a few hours defense during the landings. His initial aim was to inflict maximum casualties while the Allies were in the exposed position of carrying out their landings, in the hope that heavy losses of men and equipment would slow their progress toward Naples. That in fact was his basic mission—what one might call a minimum objective.

It did not seem likely that his one division could accomplish more than this, considering that the invasion was three divisions strong, with another (the U.S. 45th—combat veterans from Sicily) in reserve, and supported by close-in naval gunfire. Sieckenius also had to be careful to extricate his forces intact, so they could defend the highway to Naples.

He had a hundred tanks at his disposal, however, and from the outset hoped to stage a counterattack, possibly late on D-Day or the next day at the latest, before the invaders could marshal large quantities of equipment and ammunition. The Germans themselves could expect to be reinforced by the next day, from units deployed just north of Naples. And now that the die was cast, Marshal Kesselring could be expected to send several divisions to the Naples area. The 1st Parachute Division was already heading that way from its base outside Taranto, and two other divisions in the far south, fearful of being cut off from lines of retreat, were also heading that way. So, if the 16th Panzers and local reinforcements could hold for a few days, a rear-guard action might well mushroom into a full-scale battle.

And that is precisely what happened. Sieckanius and his commanders, Gen. Heinrich von Vietinghoff of the Tenth Army and Marshal Kesselring at his bomb-damaged headquarters in Frascati, saw encouraging signs in the early daylight hours. First of all, there had been heavy losses for the attackers. Second, there was evidence of disorganization. On the British side, this was the result of the 46th Division's landing in the wrong place. It was supposed to follow a rocket barrage that concentrated on a stretch of beach, mainly for the purpose of detonating mines.

But the barrage struck the wrong area, and the landing craft obediently took their cue from the explosions there—leaving a gap between themselves and the 56th Division that required some makeshift redeployments to close.[47]

On the American side, the 36th Division seemed sharply divided between units that rushed forward, apparently intent on reaching the town of Altavilla (its official first day objective) and ones that seemed easy to pin down on the beach. Some landing ships carrying men to this sector had also turned around and headed back out to sea when they came under heavy fire close in. The overall picture on this front was of a division that was somewhat strung out and therefore open to various kinds of maneuvers that could result in a portion of it being cut off and forced to surrender.

Third, the defenders saw a weak spot in the overall plan of attack. They noticed that the British and Americans were using the little Sele River as a demarcation line for their separate spheres of operation. They were accustomed to concentrating attacks where allied armies converged, and had done so often in World War I. The spring offensive in 1940 that resulted in the collapse of France had even involved such a maneuver. That the convergence of allied armies—always a weak spot, especially in the communications area—should also be marked by a natural obstacle— the Sele River—was seen as an obvious advantage.

Some Allied leaders had made the same criticism during the planning stages of the invasion. Most emphatic was General Patton's observation that the entire invasion should instead take place north of the river.[48]

D-Day took a heavy toll on Sieckenius's tanks, thanks almost entirely to gunfire from the ships. The first armored formation moved out at 11:20 A.M. Sixteen Mark IVs, some equipped with flamethrowers, headed straight for the beach. They encountered little resistance from the Texans and penetrated deep into the American sector. Within twenty minutes, however, their juggernaut was stopped by a barrage of six-inchers from the American cruisers *Philadelphia* and *Boise*, aided by a spotter plane. Six of the tanks were disabled; the remainder were ordered to break off the attack.[49]

The Germans then resorted to smaller armored formations, on the premise that a smaller target would be harder to hit, and might even escape early detection by ground or air spotters. Attacks were launched all along the front, with infantry units concentrated behind each spearhead. This proved to be no major deterrent to the naval gunners offshore. Moreover, the ground forces were less intimidated by such attacks, and not only the Texans but their British comrades (who were, by and large, as green as the Americans) were able to stop some of these attacks by themselves.[50]

By the end of the day, however, Marshal Kesselring found the invaders still effectively bottled up on the beach, excepting units of the 36th Division, which were in a very exposed position on the edge of Altavilla. The Hermann Goering Division, based just north of Naples, was ready to close in on the Sorrento Peninsula, which was still thinly occupied by the Rangers and Commandos. Units of the 26th Panzer Division and the 29th Panzer Grenadier Division, racing along the roads in long convoys from their Calabrian bases, were also expected overnight. These latter divisions could be on the scene in full strength in another two days, provided Allied airplanes continued to ignore the inland roads.

A counterattack of substantial proportions could be mounted the next day, and it could be expected to gather strength over the next two days at least. Kesselring radioed OKW for permission to commit at least an additional division. The question was forwarded to Hitler at his headquarters in Poland. The Führer clearly did not believe that the Allied invasion could be defeated. His reply was that four divisions were all that should be put at risk in this operation and that their job was to inflict maximum losses on the invaders.[51]

The Germans divided the front into two sectors, just as the Allies had, with the Sele River as the demarcation point. The Goering Division, coming in at the north end of the front, would inevitably draw off British units—away from the Americans. An attack around Battipaglia by the 16th Panzers would further preoccupy their two divisions. Meanwhile, the main thrust could move down the Sele corridor, involving elements of the 26th Panzers and the 29th Panzer Grenadiers. British defenses on their side of the river would be thin and no threat to the Germans' flank, which would use the river as a natural defense. The main attack would move down on the American side—the northern flank of the 36th Division. A secondary attack against Altavilla would hinder an effective response by the Texans, so the Germans might then debouch onto the waterfront and wreak havoc among the landing ships, ammo dumps, loaded trucks, wounded troops awaiting evacuation, command posts, field hospitals, and artillery awaiting deployment.

Such a debacle on the American front would cause the British to take pause, and a general evacuation might even be considered. If the attack did not succeed that first day, 11 September, it could be renewed with equal or even greater force the next day and even the day after that, as the reinforcements continued to roll in.

The German guns boomed on Mt. Soprano from shortly before dawn. Out of the night sky came Dornier and Heinkel fighter bombers to challenge the battle fleet. The Texans were routed from Altavilla. The Mark IV tanks came within two miles of the beach.

The German counterattack continued for five full days. The beleaguered Allied divisions would not have survived without a substantial influx of reserves and reinforcements. The British even brought in five hundred stragglers from the 50th Northumbrian and 51st Highland Divisions, who had missed the embarkation of their units from North Africa back to England. These troopers felt somewhat put upon when they were dumped ashore at Salerno, and their noncoms instigated a sitdown strike—an unprecedented mutiny in the British armed forces. It was defused only when the top British commander on the scene, Gen. Sir Richard L. McCreery, made an impassioned speech on behalf of their desperate comrades only a few miles away. Most of the men got up and marched off toward the sound of the cannons, burp-guns, machine guns, mortars, rifles, and the exploding shells of naval guns. The 192 who persisted in their defiance were returned to North Africa, where they were all court-martialed. The three sergeant ring-leaders were sentenced to be shot, but all accepted an offer of commutation if they would volunteer for combat duty back in Italy. Most of these men saw action at Cassino or Anzio in 1944.[52]

The Americans called upon their ready reserves, the 45th Division (Oklahoma National Guard, and veterans of combat on the north shore of Sicily) and also upon the 82nd Airborne. General Clark requested an immediate air-drop around Avellino, to take pressure off the beach defenders. General Ridgway replied, "Can do." Due to navigational errors and harassing gunfire, however, the drop was no less chaotic than the ones over Sicily.[53]

When Clark sent an air courier to Ridgway's headquarters near Palermo, he was seriously considering an evacuation of the Salerno beachhead. His commander of ground operations, Gen. Ernest J. Dawley, had even responded, to a question about prospects of holding the beach, "All I've got is a prayer."[54]

The German attacks, however, finally came to an end. Kesselring ordered a disengagement to commence on 16 September. That same day, Clark appointed Ridgway to serve as General Dawley's deputy. This was preparatory to relieving the latter of his duties, since it was determined that Dawley was responsible for the near-failure of the invasion.

Eisenhower visited Dawley on 17 December at the "tobacco factory," a battlefield landmark near the Sele River that had been used as a command post by Sieckenius in the first days. Ike took issue with what he saw as confused unit deployments. A question was raised about Dawley's decision to go ashore the first day. He was supposed to have been coordinating the entire landing operation, but instead disappeared among the combat squads and companies for several critical hours.

It should be added that Clark—Dawley's immediate superior—also experienced communication problems when Admiral Hewitt, who was in unquestioned control of all maritime aspects of the invasion, ordered Clark's command ship, the *Ancon,* out to sea when it became the obvious target of German dive bombers. For most of D-Day, the *Ancon,* which was festooned with all kinds of antennae that gave it away as the invasion command post, was out of the battle. Radio transmissions from the shore could not reach it, and second-hand messages from other ships were sporadic and sometimes garbled.

At least one of the many historians of the Salerno campaign has blamed Dawley's troubles on this situation. Dawley "got lost" ashore trying to find out what was going on. The invasion was mindless as long as the *Ancon* was out of range. Then there was the issue of the Sele dividing line between the British and American forces.

The experts on the scene, though, were in full agreement about Dawley. Eisenhower, Alexander, and Clark believed that he had simply gone to pieces under the strain of combat. Ike recommended to his boss in Washington, Gen. George C. Marshall, that Dawley be demoted to colonel. And so one of the casualties of the campaign was the career of the man who commanded it. History has been kinder to Dawley. The consensus of historians seems to be that Clark was the blameworthy party, and his decision to withhold the preparatory bombardment in front of the Texas Division is sometimes cited as a factor in the troubles that beset the invasion. This view is also shared by some military memorists, including Truscott, who succeeded Clark as Fifth Army commander sometime later, when Clark was promoted.[55]

The day that Kesselring called off the attacks also saw the arrival of the vanguard of Montgomery's forces. They had been plodding northeastward from Taranto, and were actually preceded by a group of newsmen who entered the Fifth Army's zone on 15 September. The Eighth Army might have arrived at Salerno two days sooner, but the lack of bridging material caused a hiatus. There had been little fighting on its front, although one notable loss was Gen. "Hoppy" Hopkinson, who was cut down by machine-gun fire at Foggia.

That township was also the site of the largest airfields in southern Italy. They were soon to become the principal base for Allied air operations not only in Italy but against southern Germany and Austria as well. Almost a year later, planes from there would even go to the support of the Warsaw Uprising. Foggia was also the base for air attacks against the Germans in Yugoslavia. It was one of the most valuable conquests of the entire Italian campaign.

Fighting in the Salerno area continued until 20 September. The Germans fought a stubborn rear-guard action as their divisions withdrew. Gen. Fred L. Walker of the Texas Division noted in his diary that the town of Altavilla, which his men had to capture twice, had been reduced to rubble. Despite the great difficulty which his men experienced in and around that place, he was repelled by the apparent indiscriminate nature of the bombardments that had caused most of the damage. The town of Battipaglia was also a ruin, as was Avellino. An officer passing through the latter place found a cheering populace lining the main street, amid the stench of decaying bodies and the rubble of blasted buildings.[56]

The roads leading toward Naples were heavily mined and cratered. They were also blocked by felled trees, burned-out vehicles, and the remains of every mule the Germans had encountered. Allied columns trying to move along these roads came under shellfire from the nearby hills. Spotter planes would hover over some of these emplacements, directing naval gunfire on them or sometimes dropping smoke markers to aid air attacks.

The Germans sustained 3,472 casualties in the battle of Salerno, and lost 630 prisoners. Allied losses were 8,659, plus nearly 3,000 prisoners.[57] The Allied naval forces, who played such a huge part in this battle, also paid a heavy price. The destroyer *Savannah*, which had helped to break the Livorno Division's attack at Gela in Sicily, was disabled by German bombs aimed at Clark's command ship. (Or so it was thought, since German planes pursued the antenna-festooned *Ancon* single-mindedly, and it had actually heeled toward the *Savannah* for protection when guided bombs struck the latter.) The *Savannah* was towed to Malta for extensive repairs.

The HMS *Warspite*, a veteran of Jutland in World War I that had arrived on the scene only in the last days of the battle, was also heavily damaged. It was the *Warspite* that did much of the damage to Altavilla

Cathedral Duomo at Benevento, near Naples. An aftermath of the Salerno campaign, September 1943. Courtesy U.S. Army Military History Institute

that was decried in General Walker's diary. This battleship would survive, nonetheless, to take part in the Normandy invasion.

Also lost were four cargo ships and seven landing ships, plus the battle cruiser *Erebus,* which hit a mine; the HMS *Uganda,* a cruiser that was bombed midway through the battle; and the hospital ship *Newfoundland,* which had to be scuttled after being blasted during a night raid. Another hospital ship, the *Leinster,* was also heavily damaged during the same raid.[58]

The Allied commanders were obviously dissatisfied with the way events unfolded on the Salerno front. It took them more than a week to fight their way off the beach. According to their plans, they were supposed to be in Naples, or very close to it, by then. Yet it was the Germans who made the biggest mistake of the battle—not committing at least one more division.

The combat had a momentous outcome. It resolved Berlin to come down on the side of fighting for every inch of Italian soil. Kesselring's proposal, discussed earlier, now seemed to have been proven out as the preferable course of action. Had the Allies crashed their way through the 16th Panzer Division and rushed onward to Naples, the Rommel proposal—to abandon Italy to the Allies, except for the Alpine areas— would have been accepted. Italy then would have been spared much destruction. Yet one cannot be sure that such a development would have shortened the war. It has been estimated that the combat in Italy may have delayed the cross-Channel invasion by as much as four months, but this is not definitive.

During the entire military campaign in Italy, up to the war's end in May 1945, no large city was the scene of even a minor battle, with the sole exception of Naples. Even there, it was not a contest between the Germans and the Allies. The battle was fought between the Germans and the Neapolitans. It began on 26 September, four days before the first units of the U.S. 82nd Airborne entered the city, and lasted until just hours before those units arrived.

The Wehrmacht had occupied the city on 12 September, and immediately began rounding up young men between the ages of eighteen and thirty for labor service.[59] This involved loading and unloading trucks and railroad cars, helping to repair bombed roadway and railroad track, and assisting in the destruction of the harbor. The latter, of course, was

Capua Cathedral, near Naples, after Salerno campaign. Courtesy U.S. Army Military History Institute

the city's pride and joy. The Germans got only limited use out of it, due to frequent bombing and strafing runs by Allied aircraft. Once it became apparent, by 15 or 16 September, that the attacking forces were not going to be driven out of Salerno, the trashing of the harbor began in earnest.

The conscript labor proved to be very unmanageable. This was partly due to the fact that the Wehrmacht had not been around long enough to gain a firm grip on the city. Men sometimes broke out of their makeshift dormitories in downtown offices and hotels *en masse*. There were also instances of defiance and mass escapes at the work sites. Some were shot down as they ran. Others felt safe against recapture once they reached the crowded tenement neighborhoods.

On 26 September a German soldier was shot off his motorcycle by a sniper. The latter was not a member of any underground group. More likely he had a personal grudge against the Germans. The street where the shooting occurred was quickly closed off, and every building was searched from top to bottom. The soldiers had orders to arrest any "suspicious" individuals. What they found were four citizens with firearms in their apartments. All four were taken out into the street and immediately shot, in accordance with the occupation decree issued on 12 September that made possession of firearms by a civilian a capital offense. A fifth person was shot while resisting arrest.

News of these events swept across Naples in a matter of hours. Hundreds, perhaps thousands, of civilians had not turned in their personal firearms as required by the decree. Now many, encouraged by the approach of the Allied armies and stirred by their hatred of the Germans (who in any case were beginning an evacuation of the city), suddenly assumed the guise of urban guerrillas. Some roamed the city pursuing a lonely vendetta. Others banded together into hit squads.[60]

The conscript labor, meanwhile, virtually evaporated into thin air. So, on the eve of their departure, the Germans found this great city beyond their control. They reacted to the snipers, saboteurs, and grenade-throwers by setting off explosives in the sewers and the water lines. Electric power lines and substations were the special targets on the last night of the German presence.

When the first Allied forces arrived on 1 October, then, they found not only a harbor filled with sunken ships and barges, but also a city without electric light, without water, and with collapsed avenues over main sewer lines that had been blown up.[61] More than three hundred citizens had been killed in the last three days of the German presence. Part of the city's archives was also destroyed in a deliberate act of van-

*Infantryman stands before altar in damaged Catholic church in Acerno, Italy,
23 September 1943.* Courtesy Bettman Archive

dalism. The Palazzo Reale was also heavily damaged. The rumor that
some runaway workers, and even saboteurs, had found refuge in churches
may also explain the heavy damage visited on certain houses of worship,
including San Giovanni's and San Paolo Maggior. The departing soldiers even planted time bombs. One blew up at the main post office on

7 October (a week after the Germans had gone), injuring seventy people, including some Allied soldiers.[62]

General Clark heard that an official welcome was being prepared for him by the city government. When he arrived at the Piazza Garibaldi with several jeeploads of aides and military police, however, there was not a soul to be seen. He discovered that the greeting site had been changed to the Piazza Plebiscito. There a huge and excited crowd awaited its liberator, and British, American, and Italian flags flapped in the breeze. When he finally made it to this new location for the official greeting, Clark felt a bit uneasy about the three flags being thus intermingled. He was also impressed with the attitude of the crowd, but the total effect was a bit confusing for him, the man responsible for governing this metropolis of the lately surrendered enemy. These cheering people were the exact opposite of an enemy, even one that had just surrendered.

The three flags flew over the city hall for the next few days, but then the Italian one was removed. This occurrence was accompanied by the appearance of some public proclamations, tacked up conspicuously all over the city, that one historian characterizes as "belligerent."[63] They dealt with penalties for the possession of private weapons (an issue that helped spark the anti-German uprising), for black-marketeering, and assorted other offenses. Clearly, the Allied leaders were not ready for the spirit of camaraderie that imbued the local populace in those first days of October.

Water was restored to parts of the city on 10 October, and by the end of the month most of Naples had water. The restoration of electric power was completed for the downtown area by the end of October, but downed power lines in the outlying neighborhoods were not replaced for many weeks thereafter. U.S. Navy Seabees connected sunken hulks with makeshift causeways that could even accommodate trucks, while sunken vessels in more obtrusive locations were removed with remarkable speed. Eisenhower cabled his boss, General Marshall, that by 22 October ships were unloading nearly seven thousand tons of supplies in a single day. By the end of the month, port tonnage was approaching pre-war norms.[64]

Such an extraordinary feat of reconstruction indicates the importance that the Allies attached to the port of Naples. It would in fact serve as the principal supply base for the Italian campaign up to is conclusion in 1945. For some major upcoming military operations, such as the battle of Monte Cassino and Anzio, and in fact for all military activities leading up to the capture of Rome in June 1944, Naples can fairly be described as the main staging area for supplies and reinforcements. This helps to explain the fact that the Allies established their permanent headquarters not far away at the town of Caserta, where the old Bourbon kings maintained a country estate. The generals were careful not to set themselves up in the royal palace. Clark himself would inhabit a trailer on the palace grounds; even so, some visitors criticized the sumptuousity of the trailer itself.

CHAPTER THREE

VIA APPIA

The liberation of Naples was punctuated in a spectacular way by the eruption of Mt. Vesuvius. The ancient Romans would have taken this as a bad omen. Perhaps the Allies should have. True, they would win victory after victory, but at great cost—cost enough to leave the Germans satisfied all the way to the bitter end.

Highway 6 passes through a narrow mountain defile where the town of San Pietro then stood. (It is not there now.) The Germans decided that this place would be good for a more ambitious delaying action. Especially useful was the town itself, whose stone buildings could mask a buildup by units of the 29th Panzer Grenadier Division. Moreover, San Pietro stood on a promontory jutting out from the steep mountain in back of it. This promontory also had steep sides, thus giving the effect of a stage upon which the town stood like a set. Entrance to San Pietro was afforded solely by a narrow, winding road coming in from the front of this stage.

Alternatives to the high road were hard to come by in this sector, so it was expected at Kesselring's headquarters that the Americans would just have to bull their way through, at some cost—not only in men and matériel, but in time also.

Expecting the usual short but sharp engagement, ending with the liberation of some more Italian territory, General Marshall in Washington sent a Hollywood film unit to make a pictorial record of the liberation of San Pietro from start to finish. It would be used as a training film back in the States, to show the recruits what combat was all about: some battle heroics, then a happy greeting by the townspeople, including perhaps some photogenic young ladies.

On 12 December, a line of American tanks made its way along the narrow road into town. The road, like every other feature of the local geography, had precipitous sides. As the lead tank approached the first buildings, the Germans opened up on the whole column. Antitank projectiles struck from hidden positions on both sides of the road. Mortar shells fired from within San Pietro and the heights overlooking the town rained down from above with deadly accuracy. Soldiers who tried to exit disabled tanks faced a hail of rifle and machine-gun fire.

Three days later the Americans tried to storm the town again, this time helped by a flanking maneuver by infantry along the ridge line in back of the town. Tanks of the 1st Armored Division ran a gauntlet that proved to be no less destructive than the one of three days before. But a few of them made it into the town, as did some of the soldiers descending from the lower slopes of Mt. Lungo. The tanks and many of the soldiers were captured when the attack was broken off. By now, twelve of the original sixteen tanks that had been committed to the capture of San Pietro had been either captured, destroyed, or heavily damaged.

Strong reinforcements began to arrive the next day, however, and the Germans now had to worry about their line of retreat along Highway 6. The Americans had not been dislodged from the ridge line, and on that day, 16 December, they even gained the top of Mt. Lungo, the highest point in the area.

The third attack on San Pietro was launched on 17 December. Most of the troops of the 29th Panzer-Grenadier Division were now clear of the ridges and heading north. A heavy artillery barrage prepared the way, and tanks and troops rolled in without much opposition. San Pietro was now a heap of rubble over which hung a sickening stench. A third of the 900 townspeople who had not chosen to flee were dead, and most of the others were injured. One hundred and fifty of the soldiers of the 36th (Texas) Division were dead. Another 250 were missing, and there were 800 wounded. The 82nd Airborne Division (mostly its 504th Regiment) sustained a loss of 50 killed, 225 wounded or missing. Other units—the Third Ranger Battalion, the 753rd Tank Battalion, the 111th Engineer Combat Battalion (which had to make the road into town passable after the first two attacks)—also sustained casualties.[1]

The documentary record of the battle proved to be one of the most realistic combat films ever made. Cameramen frequently came under fire, and accompanied lead units of infantry through some very dangerous maneuvers. But in place of a welcoming committee and soldiers throwing candy bars to children, all the film had to show was a scene of total devastation. A shot of a tank turret lying in the road was bound to make trainees at Fort Knox wonder what it must feel like to be hit with something that could cause that turret to fly off. The sight of a young man no older than twenty, his eyes still wide open, being lowered into a body bag would not give trainees at home a taste for combat. The film was canned and shelved for the duration.[2]

After this unexpectedly difficult operation, the Texas (36th) Division was sent back to Naples for two weeks of rest and recuperation. The ravages of illness and injury, on top of the heavy casualties sustained at Salerno and San Pietro, had removed from the scene nearly half the men who rode into the Salerno beachhead on 9 September. The ranks were refilled mostly with draftees, a great many of them from the Northeast, shipped over from Fort Dix to Naples and then assigned to this National Guard unit.

Its place in the line was taken by the new French Expeditionary Corps, or more specifically by the Moroccan and Algerian brigades of that force, which was commanded by Gen. Alphonse Juin. The Allied advance during those two weeks—the last two weeks of the year—was fairly rapid. Concern that the Germans would turn Mt. Trocchio, a high peak standing in the midst of a rare open plain close to Highway 6, into a bastion, proved unfounded. Kesselring decided that such an isolated promontory might be cut off and its defenders forced to surrender.

Instead, he decided on a forward front line which, it was hoped, would blunt and slow down the advance on his main Highway 6 strongpoint—the one located at Cassino. This forward line was located on the north shore of the little Rapido River, a westward flowing stream, and along the Garigliano River into which it flowed and which in turn emptied into the sea, about halfway between Naples and Rome.

The flatlands that surrounded Mt. Trocchio end on the south shore of the Rapido. On the other side of that river, which is only thirty to sixty feet across, the terrain turns into steep hills and narrow defiles. The hills, in fact, quickly give way to low mountains, although it is possible, from certain angles, to see the abbey atop Monte Cassino from the flatlands south of the river. The terrain afforded the Germans an open field of fire from well-hidden positions that could be disturbed only by accurate artillery strikes from the other side. The S-curves on the Rapido also enabled them to set up machine guns so as to catch most crossing places in a crossfire.

LCI burns at Anzio, 22 January 1944. The lightly opposed initial landing of Allied troops would be followed by ferocious German attacks aimed at driving the Allies back into the sea. Courtesy U.S. Army Military History Institute

The approach to the little river was made more difficult by the "thick mine fields" (as the *New York Times* noted)[3] and by the temporary diversion of its waters upstream, so that the lowland came under a couple of feet of water for several days. When the first American engineer units entered the plain to clear a path to the river with their minesweeping equipment, their efforts were greatly hampered by the ooze, into which they sank up to their ankles. The mud had such great suction qualities that if a soldier had to hit the dirt when gunfire came too close, there was some question as to whether he would be able to get up again unaided.

The engineers managed to set up pathways to the river's edge under cover of darkness, and also a thick smokescreen, which was maintained over the field for several days. This smokescreen was supposed to protect the men from accurate gunfire. It also tended to diminish communication among the soldiers who had to walk through it, and sometimes a soldier had no idea where any of his cohorts were. If the tape strung along the "safe" pathways by the engineers broke (which it did in many places during the attack), then the fogbound soldier lost his sense of direction and entered the mined area. The smoke also made breathing difficult.[4] Together, inhaling the smoke and navigating the mire for a mile or more left many men—those who survived the steady gunfire and mortar explosions—exhausted by the time they reached river's edge.

Many, indeed, determined that they were becoming seriously ill as they trudged through the first assault, and turned back to seek medical attention. So those valiant men who managed to reach the river bank were greatly discomfited by the thinning out of the ranks that this exhausting maneuver caused. Rafts, skiffs, and bridging materials that some of them helped to carry toward the river were also lost—jettisoned by sick-call soldiers or dropped when their carriers strayed into mined areas, or just cast aside by exhausted men who nonetheless continued to move forward.

Artillery was deployed in the rear, on Mt. Trocchio, which also served as the command post for the attack. But there was no effective spotting of the kind that saved the day at Salerno, and few specific targets were found. Firing across the river at crossing points was also ineffective, partly because communications broke down at this point. Radios were broken, and lines were cut. The command post sometimes believed that soldiers still struggling to cross the stream were already established on the other side, in places where, instead, enfilading fire was coming from enemy machine-gun positions.

Such were the conditions that weighed down upon the young men who attacked the Germans at the Rapido River. In addition, throughout the engagement, there was "a steady drizzling rain smelling sourly of death," wrote Cyrus Sulzberger of the *New York Times*.[5] "Welcome to sunny Italy" became a popular greeting among the Americans for new arrivals from stateside, who were surprised to find Italy not only wet but cold. The first Italian winter was at hand for the Allies and their German adversaries.

Deployed on the north bank of the Rapido was the German 15th Panzer-Grenadier Division, under the command of Gen. Eberhard Rodt. It stood athwart the American line of advance. Next to it, spread out westward along the Garigliano and nearly to the coast, was the 94th Division.

The first attempt to ford the Rapido was made during the night of 20–21 January 1944. Nearly two hundred soldiers of the 36th Division (recently returned from rest and recuperation in Naples) had made it across when a retreat was ordered shortly after 6:30 A.M. By then the rubber boats and rafts and the little footbridge that had been strung across were shot to ribbons, and these men had no functioning radio. They were abandoned to their fate.

General Walker, the division commander, then received an order from Fifth Army headquarters that another try should be made by 2 P.M. The thought of a repeat performance, so soon, struck the Texas Division like a bolt of lightning. The 111th Engineer Battalion was at that moment under heavy fire while trying to set markers and tape along the safe paths through the mine-strewn mud flats. The problem of moving watercraft and bridging material to the water's edge also seemed, in light of the earlier attack, insurmountable.[6]

Walker's 143rd Regiment got underway two hours late, at 4 P.M. Five hours later, with the aid of the engineers, this force once again had a footbridge strung across the river. Then, very quickly but with heavy losses to steady enemy machine gun fire pouring in through the light of flares and searchlights, two companies made their way across. The footbridge was by then shot apart, but another company made the crossing in rubber rafts. The smokescreen obscured much of the action, and Rodt later expressed surprise at his grisly achievement: a thousand Americans killed or missing, five hundred taken prisoner.[7]

This particular operation, which was only one part (albeit an important one) of a general advance across some riverine obstacles south of Cassino, has generated nearly as much controversy as the subsequent bombing of the Abbey of Monte Cassino. Walker made some denigrating comments about it in his diary, at the time, calling it "stupid" and in violation of the basic principles of infantry warfare.[8] He had taught his present commander, Clark, at the Army War College, when Clark was two ranks below him. Hadn't Clark retained anything from his courses there? Walker's diary entries, even before the battle began, were quite fatalistic, and it is apparent that he was not in the least surprised by the outcome.

Nearly all of the generals on both sides in Italy agreed (if not explicitly) with Walker's complaints. Kesselring and Senger wrote in their memoirs that the British move across the Garigliano, which commenced a day earlier, did not need the support of a major attack on the Rapido. It was enough, they wrote, that the presence of the U.S. 36th Division tied down the German 15th Panzer-Grenadiers, and prevented them from coming to the aid of their comrades in the 94th Division. The latter had been given no time to prepare defenses on the Garigliano, and in any event had to be wary of the Allies' naval guns—to the extent that they would not stand and fight for long so near the shore.[9]

Allied memoirists, especially Walker and the 3rd Division commander, Lucian Truscott (Clark's successor a year hence), are similarly disposed. When the war was over in 1946, officers of the 36th Division appealed to the Texas state legislature to pass a motion demanding a congressional investigation. This resulted in some hearings in Washington, but the Senate Armed Services Committee concluded that nobody should be brought to book over the matter.[10]

Throughout the controversy, Clark had been identified as the main villain. The Texans, indeed, hoped that he would be court-martialed. Had they tried to enlist the support of politicians in other states, on the premise that the Texas Division by then was only half Texan—its ranks having been filled out mainly by draftees after the Salerno bloodletting—they might have given Clark more cause of concern. Texans, as it happened, were second to New Yorkers on the casualty list.

The Rapido-Garigliano offensive was part of a one-two punch strategy that was supposed to speed the Allies along to Rome. The second punch consisted of an amphibious invasion force that departed from Naples on 21 January. A fleet of 343 ships first headed southward, then doubled back on open sea and steamed at full speed toward the sleepy little seaside resort of Anzio-Nettuno, thirty miles south of Rome.

The Führer's initial reaction to news of the Anzio landing was that it must be a feint to cover an amphibious invasion of Civitavecchia, Rome's little exurban seaport.[11] The German response to Anzio was swift enough for the Allies, who at first were pleasantly surprised to discover no defenders on the beach when they arrived. But in fact it was held back for nearly a day out of concern for Civitavecchia. To a lesser extent, there was also concern about Livorno (Leghorn), although that place, the most important harbor between Naples and Genoa, was almost fifty miles north of Rome.

These concerns continued even as the battle of Anzio unfolded. They were fed by the curious posture of the Allies on their beachhead. The Allies had failed to exploit an easy opportunity to move twenty miles northward, two-thirds of the distance to Rome from Anzio, to seize the strategic Alban Hills and gain immediate control over Route 6 as it passes by on the inland-side hills (near Mt. Artemisio). On D-Day, an Allied officer could have ridden out there in a jeep and not been fired upon. At the end of this twenty-minute jaunt, he could have selected a command post from among the hilltop villages, and then called up the artillery and infantry to secure the place.

Something else that puzzled Kesselring, and Hitler, was the total absence of good intelligence on their side about the Anzio invasion. The chief of naval intelligence, Adm. Wilhelm Canaris, was visiting Kesselring only the day before the landing, and informed him that Naples was quiet and normal, and no amphibious landings up the west coast were in prospect.[12] The German theater commander, still headquartered at Franscati (not far from the battle site), had to conclude that another amphibious landing could come at any time, without advance warning. As a result, a minimum of one division (sometimes reinforced) was maintained at both Civitavecchia and Livorno throughout this crucial phase of the Italian campaign.

On the other hand, the Germans were in no mood to soft-pedal their defense on the Anzio front. They were convinced that one more division could have gained them a victory at Salerno. Kesselring had asked for that division and been refused. Now his requests would be treated with respect, and it was his intention to call for reinforcements even from outside Italy to throw the Allies back into the sea. Units were sent in from France and Germany, while those which had been based at Rome held the Allies on the beach.

Gen. Eberhard Mackensen, commander of the Fourteenth Army, enjoyed an excellent view of the landing beach from his command post in the Alban Hills. His big guns zeroed in on the narrow swath, which was jammed with landing craft, tents, thousands of vehicles (some five thousand, leading Churchill to wonder if all the soldiers were being employed as chauffeurs and mechanics), and milling crowds of men in uniform. The houses and beachfront hotels of Anzio and Nettuno (to the south but immediately adjacent) were the only obstacle to a perfect view. These diminished in size and numbers as the battle wore on. It was a rare German shell that did not find some victims at the end of its trajectory.

And yet the Allies did enjoy certain advantages. The most important one was sea power—the naval guns that had saved the day at Salerno. They would do it again here.

Another was the unusual evenness of the terrain in this part of Italy. It was a lowland that began with the Pontine Marshes, which formed an anchor for the Allies at the southern end of their line. They were safe from a southerly flanking attack thanks to the marshes. The gray ground, rising gradually toward the Alban Hills that marked off the northern end of the front, was "flat country . . . excellent for maneuver with armor."[13] Both sides had plenty of that, but the Allies had the lion's share. So the terrain was an advantage for them.

Moreover, the open ground made spotting for the ships' guns and for tactical air strikes much easier. This restricted the Germans' movement greatly, except in the vicinity of the hills. All of their counterattacks would by necessity come down the roads from the north, because it was not possible to marshall large forces anywhere except within the cover provided by the hilly terrain.

This does not mean that the lowland was uncontested. Here Mackensen succeeded in maintaining blocking forces. This was helped by the presence of numerous little hamlets all made up of sturdy stone buildings. The area had been the site of Mussolini's most ambitious public project during the 1920s and 1930s. A portion of the Pontine Marshes had been drained and the land made available to farmers. With the buildings came drainage facilities, with the Mussolini Canal serving as the main avenue of excess water runoff to the sea near Nettuno. The drainage system was an obstacle to tanks, but at least it did not have the high embankments that characterized so many of the rivers the Allies had fought their way across. And at this time of year, the canals were not yet brimming with water. The light rain that fell almost every day (though not on D-Day, which was bright and sunny) made for muddy fields, but it did not fill up the canals and ditches.

The Allies came ashore, thirty thousand strong, on 22 January. The soldiers seemed "let down," in the view of a *New York Times* correspondent, by the lack of fighting.[14] Next day, Alexander advised Churchill that things were "proceeding satisfactorily," although he indicated that there were no reports of any significant moves toward inland objectives.[15] For Alexander, a prime target was the town of Cisterna, about fifteen miles distant. Both Highway 7 and the main railroad line to Rome went through the town. Its capture could result in the German divisions down on the Cassino front being deprived of an effective route of retreat.

Some German planes had come over during the landings on the first day, but had caused little damage. The second day a hundred Focke-Wolf 190s came strafing and bombing not only the beach but also some of the ships offshore. The damage was somewhat heavier this time, but the Germans lost fifteen of their planes in the process. Nine Allied planes were shot down as well.[16]

All the while, German infantry and Panzer and artillery units were heading down the roads from the Rome area, thirty miles distant. Six divisions based in France and Germany were in the process of being entrained and transported through the Alpine passes. Hitler, Jodl, and Kesselring were determined that this would be no repeat of Salerno, where stinginess over manpower had deprived the Wehrmacht of a signal victory in a year filled with defeats.

The British 1st Division, commanded by Gen. W. R. C. Penney and containing veterans of Tunisia and the Pantelleria operation, prepared a defensive position along the little Moletta River. This was intended to be a shield against any sudden German moves from Rome. General Truscott's U.S. 3rd Division, which had distinguished itself in the crossing of the Volturno River north of Naples, and before that had spearheaded Patton's *blitz* in western Sicily, was positioned just south of Anzio.

This was the unit that was to attack Cisterna. With it was a part of the 45th (Thunderbird) Division, which had seen some hard fighting on the north coast of Sicily, at Salerno, and also north of Naples. Colonel Darby's three Ranger battalions were in Anzio. They were going to serve as the shock troops for the move inland toward Cisterna. The 82nd Airborne's 504th Regiment, under Colonel Tucker, veterans of nearly all the major operations thus far, were positioned in Nettuno.

General Mackensen was transferred from his headquarters at Verona to take charge of the German forces on the Anzio front. He visited Kesselring at Franscati en route, and was told—this was the day after the landing, 23 January—that the front was already "consolidated" and that "no major reversal" seemed likely in the short term.[17] This avowal, given before any significant contact had been made between the two armies, was more than just an expression of Kesselring's well-known optimistic nature. It put his general on notice that this was not just a delaying action. It was a battle the Germans could win, and Mackensen was angling to be supplied with all the resources required to accomplish that. It was the first and last instance in the Italian campaign where a German general would be called to account, if, instead of just carrying out an effective holding or delaying action, he did not force the enemy to abandon the field of battle and go away. Such was the responsibility that fell upon General Mackensen.

His counterpart on the Allied side, Gen. John Lucas, who had relieved Dawley at Salerno, was less aware of the fateful consequences of success or failure. This was mainly because he did not expect to be held directly accountable for what happened. He wrote in his diary before the landing that the whole operation had "the odor of Gallipoli," the notorious disaster of 1915. Gallipoli, the invasion of a rocky peninsula on the Turkish seacoast, had been the brainchild of Winston Churchill. So, to a certain degree, was Anzio. Lucas also had the impression that Anzio was basically a sideshow of the Cassino campaign, and that even the capture of the Alban Hills was the responsibility of the Allied forces on the Cassino front. He got this impression from his own boss, General Clark, who also told him not to "stick your neck out." Clark cited his own experiences at Salerno on the matter of daring maneuvers.[18] So the two commanders at Anzio had widely divergent impressions of what their commanders expected of them. But both would end up the same way: disgraced and demoted.

The first German forces on the scene were the 4th Parachute Division and parts of the Hermann Goering Division—the force that had met the Americans at Gela on the first day of the Italian campaign. The headquarters unit from the 1st Parachute Division was transferred from Cassino to coordinate the early stages of the buildup. A regiment from another Cassino-front unit, the 3rd Panzer-Grenadiers, was another early arrival. It was sent into Campoleone, opposite the British forces. The Goering Division, in full force by 29 January, occupied Cisterna.

The first serious fighting took place on that date. By then the British had ventured ten miles up the Albano-Anzio Road, toward the Alban Hills. The Americans had gone about two-thirds of the way to Cisterna, and were within four miles of the town. Allied strength had doubled, reaching about sixty thousand men. At this point, as German divisions arrived from Rimini on the east coast, from Livorno up the west coast, and from France and Germany, neither side could claim a manpower advantage. This was not a very promising situation for an amphibious army that had its back to the sea, facing an army that controlled a large hinterland that provided it with room for maneuver, extensive transportation routes, and substantial back-up resources, both in men and matériel, that were ready at hand.

Once fighting was under way in earnest (from 29 January on), the Allies would depend on forty truck-laden LSTs per day, sent a hundred miles up the coast from Naples. Three hundred truckloads of supplies and ammunition would be driven ashore, and a near-equal number of empty trucks from the day before would then drive onto the LSTs for a return trip to Naples. The Germans exerted themselves to disrupt this supply system, which Mackensen could observe daily through his binoculars—at least when the usual smokescreen was blowing thin, an event that happened several times daily. He tried to administer a knockout blow on the very first day of combat, sending two hundred planes in. At least six of the LSTs were damaged, but none were rendered unseaworthy. On the other hand, an American Liberty ship that was anchored offshore was sunk, and the British cruiser *Spartan*, which had maintained a lively antiaircraft fire against the Germans throughout the morning hours, was sunk by torpedo bombs. Such attacks, repeated several times, could have choked off the Allied supply lines. But the Germans lost a number of planes, and they never again attacked from the air on so large a scale.

During the night of 29–30 January, the Rangers attempted to take Cisterna by surprise, proceeding down an irrigation canal that ran right by the place. Two-thirds of their forces, numbering 767 men, took part in this maneuver. Goering Division scouts spotted these men early on, but General Conrath ordered his men to hold their fire as units were sent down past the Rangers on both sides of the ditch. He was assisted in this operation by advance elements of the 715th Infantry Division, just arrived from Avignon, France.

Flares were fired over the ditch, and the Germans opened up with everything they had. Rangers exiting the ditch were promptly captured. Some of the captives were then led up toward defended positions—serving as shields to their captors—while a German officer called out for the rest to surrender, threatening to shoot the captives if they did not. The Germans took nearly five hundred prisoners. Only six of the Americans made it back to Anzio. In this manner did two of Colonel Darby's three battalions disappear in the dark of night.

The Germans gained the advantage in manpower on the ground. When their all-out attack on the beachhead was ready to go, it was 90,000 against 62,000 Allied soldiers.[19] The latter, if ever they looked over their shoulders for a route of retreat, would see only the blue waters of the Tyrrhenean Sea.

Kesselring, for the only time in the whole Italian campaign, also tried to gain the upper hand in the air. On 16 February, as the German offensive reached its peak of intensity, waves of dive bombers came in at three-hour intervals. The largest attack occurred at 11 A.M., when forty-five planes strafed and bombed the beach and the ships offshore. An ammunition dump was detonated, producing numerous casualties, but only a single landing craft was sunk.[20] The next day, while the 29th Panzer-Grenadier Division was striking down the Albano Road in an effort to breach the 45th Division's line, more waves of bombers swooped down on the beach area.

On those two days, the peak days of the German offensive, the Allies were forced to yield one mile of territory along an attack front that was two and one-half miles wide. During the next three days the Germans made further, but smaller, gains. By then it was clear that they would fail—the Allies would not be overrun. Advance units struck to within a few miles of the beach, but no division-size unit got closer than fourteen miles.[21]

Winston Churchill confided to a friend, at the height of the German offensive, that this was his most anxious moment of the whole war.[22] It was a remarkable statement coming from a man who had been directly involved in the desperate evacuation of Dunkirk in 1940, a man who lived daily under the wings of German bombers. Several days later, General Lucas, commander of the operation, was replaced by U.S. 3rd Division commander Lucian Truscott. There has been considerable debate among memoirists and the authors of various books on Anzio as to Lucas's relative responsibility for the hardships suffered on that front. Not much

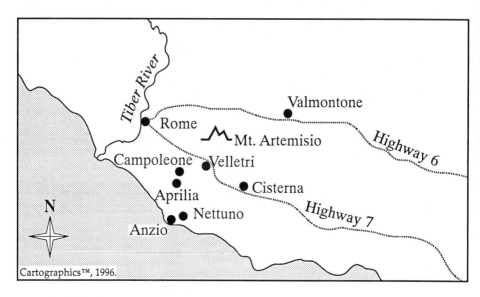

Anzio Region

attention is paid to the fact that Lucas guided the Allied defense through the crisis of the German onslaught. His replacement was indeed ill-timed, for that onslaught was not yet quite over. It was only in a brief pause, preparatory to a final, nearly hopeless effort. The choice of a successor was a good one, however. The leather-jacketed warrior in high boots did not require time to orient himself. Truscott's promotion showed a rare moment of lucidity at Fifth Army Command at this critical juncture, which in more ways than one was the crisis period of the whole campaign.

The crux of this crisis was the Cassino front. Anzio was launched in support of the Cassino offensive. But with the danger that the armed forces would be driven out of the Anzio beachhead, Clark had to turn things around and consider applying more pressure on the Germans at Cassino. So it happened that as the Germans made their main attack on the beachhead in mid-February, the Allies launched their own all-out offensive against the bastion of Monte Cassino.

The significance of the Abbey of Monte Cassino lay in its position overlooking the Via Casilina, Route 6, the main highway between Naples and Rome. The Allies had experienced huge difficulties in coming within hailing distance of this place. It now presented them with a singular challenge, for it was one of the most impregnable defensive positions anywhere on the continent. St. Benedict had founded the first Western monastery there in the sixth century. Saracen invaders overran the place early on, but only because it was virtually undefended. The remaining parts of the original construction were reduced by earthquakes in the thirteenth and eighteenth centuries. Most of what the soldiers could observe, standing out brazenly atop the western end of a long mountain line, dated from the latter century.

The highway cut through a gap in the mountains—the Liri Valley—directly below the building, the mountain slope on that side being as steep as a mesa. The Abbey also overlooked, quite literally on its south side, the town of Cassino, which before the battle had a population of twenty-five thousand. Inside the building lived fifty-five monks and their abbot, Gregorio Diamare, who at seventy-nine was about to see more excitement than he ever imagined to exist outside the precincts of Hell. Was there no alternative to Cassino—say, a flanking move up the east coast?

British forces had only lately occupied the port of Bari (where the king found refuge) down in the heel of the peninsula, and there was talk among the German planners at Frascati of losing the campaign on the neglected Eastern (Adriatic) front.

A flight of a hundred JU-88 bombers was sent against Bari in mid-December to disrupt the supply line in this sector. (Nothing so ambitious would ever be attempted against the port of Naples on the opposite coast, where the air defenses were much more of a challenge.) This proved to be the largest and most successful German air operation of the whole Italian campaign. Seventeen Allied ships were destroyed. One was loaded with mustard gas, on reserve in case the Wehrmacht resorted to gas attacks. The burning hulk exuded clouds of this gas, which wafted over the city and caused more than a thousand civilian deaths.[23] The incident was held in strictest secrecy by the Allies and went unreported in the press.

Eighth Army, undaunted by the temporary disruption of their supplies, captured Ortona on 28 December. The defending 90th Panzer-Grenadier Division (formerly based in Sardinia, which the Germans abandoned to the Allies) and the 334th Infantry (a melange of eighteen-year-olds and men over forty, all seeing their first combat) fought a stubborn delaying action through the city streets. The city, already a ruin, was then shelled by the departing Germans.

The prospect of a breakthrough along this "quiet" front disappeared with the new year, as the Allies—daunted by daily blasts of snow, icy winds, and sleet; and facing a succession of fast mountain streams, often just a few miles apart, that fed the Adriatic Sea—faced the need to rebuild the port, to repair heavily damaged roads, and to conserve perilously low resources of men and matériel. The Allies now gave their undivided attention to the Cassino front, and so did Marshal Kesselring.

The Anzio invasion of 22 January was supposed to pry the Germans loose from their Gustav Line defenses, as they were known. After sizing up the situation at Anzio and determining that it was more an opportunity than a threat, Hitler issued this order: "The Gustav Line must be held at all costs."[24]

So the stage was set for the Allied February offensive, the timing of which was at least in part determined by the need to provide some relief to the beleaguered forces at Anzio during the height of the German attacks there. This Allied effort would have benefitted greatly from lengthier preparations, considering the great hardships experienced merely to arrive within striking distance of Cassino. It was intended from the first not as a sideshow to the Anzio situation or as a limited operation. The intent at Fifth Army headquarters was to overrun the town, capture the monastery mount, and send the Germans into headlong retreat back toward Rome: in short, to break the Gustav Line.

Selected to spearhead the attack was the recently arrived New Zealand Corps, which included a division of Sikhs and Gurkhas from India. The British commander of that division, Gen. Francis Tuker, proposed that an effort be made to occupy the Abbey itself, even though it had been informally agreed by both sides that the four-story structure should be off-limits for combat operations. Tuker had heard rumors (mainly alleged sightings by soldiers in forward positions) that the Germans had entered the building and were using it as an observation post, possibly even as an ammunition dump. After a flyover, British Air Marshal Ira Eaker claimed to have seen German uniforms hanging out to dry on a line, and thought he had seen somebody looking out an upper window with binoculars.[25]

He pored over a book about the Abbey with his commander, General Freyberg. They were impressed with its fortress-like dimensions, and especially the ten-foot thick walls. Tuker proposed that if his Indians could fight their way to within a thousand yards of the structure, fighter bombers could then attempt some close air support by blasting an opening in the wall facing the attackers. The Allied soldiers would then rush in and gain control of this dominating feature of the battle zone.

The plan was presented to General Clark for his approval. It was well-understood on all sides that bombing such an important historical site (one of great religious significance as well for Catholics, though not for the non-Catholics who dominated the Allied command structure) would be most controversial. Clark ordered another flyover to determine if the Germans were in fact using the place. The report from the aerial observers was inconclusive. The situation was confused by the Germans' failure to observe their own off-limits policy for the ground immediately adjacent to the building. This policy had been set forth in a memo to every German unit by the chief of operations on this front, Gen. Fridolin von Senger (a practicing Catholic); but the soldiers ignored it with impunity, and could be seen at the very foot of the building walls.[26]

Questions persisted about the assumptions of Freyberg and Tuker. At this point the issue of morale was raised. Freyberg put it most eloquently: If his two divisions, the Indians and the New Zealanders, launched an all-out attack on the ridge where the Abbey stood, and if, after desperate fighting and heavy casualties, they were forced to give up their attack—what would the surviving soldiers think when they looked up at that intact building looming over the fields of slaughter? How, Freyberg asked, could he then justify to his men, leaving this veritable fortress—the dominant feature of the battle scene, and entirely at the enemy's disposal—off-limits?

In a meeting on this issue at Caserta, General Keyes raised the issue of a German unit filling any gap in the wall blasted by the tactical bombers. The first bomb would remove the figurative "off-limits" sign, and the Germans would then have the free run of the place before the Indians could make their way up the steep slopes.

This argument did not sway the generals from the New Zealand Corps, but it moved Clark to propose that if the Abbey had to be bombed, it should be obliterated in a saturation raid by heavy bombers. Freyberg and Tuker did not argue with this. Now that they had the ball rolling, they were content to let matters take their course at Fifth Army headquarters. Tuker went a step further. His arthritic pains had become unbearable from the rigors of the campaign, especially the incessant icy drizzle that sometimes gave way to snowfall or, more often, to wind-driven mountain squalls. Tuker asked to be relieved, and command of the Indian Division was assumed by Brig. H. N. Dimoline. The latter supported the bombing of the Abbey as one of the unfortunate necessities of warfare.

Had an American division been designated to lead the new offensive, and such a request come from an American commander, Clark might have denied it. In his memoir he states that the deciding factor was the need to maintain Allied harmony.[27] The fact that his own chief, British Field Marshal Harold Alexander, seemed partial to bombing the Abbey probably sealed the decision. Alexander himself later expressed the view that the Abbey was bound to sustain significant damage before the campaign was over, and indeed it had already been peppered by shrapnel and flying debris on numerous occasions.[28]

Alexander was also concerned about morale. Since the landing at

Salerno, the fighting front had been an unmitigated hell. He was impressed by a report from General Truscott, forwarded initially to Clark, regarding the condition of 3rd Division troops after the Volturno River crossing, north of Naples. Men cycled out for rest in Naples after only ten or twelve days of living in ditches and tramping through brambles and thorn bushes on the mountainsides, much of the time soaked through from the chilly rain, were a sight to behold as they waited for trucks that would bring them back to civilization. Their uniforms were tattered and filthy; often even their boots were torn. Behind several days' growth of beard were yellow-green complexions, decidedly unhealthy even by the standards of Patton. Bloodshot, bleary eyes showed their lack of sleep. Many shivered incessantly, for the damp cold had penetrated to their inner depths. Few could sit or stand still, unless they were very sick with heavy colds or pneumonia. These were men who had been pushed to the limit.

Alexander, though he didn't say it, remembered the mutiny of British soldiers on the beach at Salerno. About this time he also questioned Clark about the close-spaced and lengthy bouts of combat duty being endured by the American 34th Division. That National Guard unit from Minnesota and Iowa seemed on the verge of a breakdown of discipline, yet it fought on.

Tuker's initial request was made on 11 or 12 February. The bombs began falling on Monte Cassino at 9:30 A.M. on the fifteenth. The first wave of aircraft scored few hits on the assigned target. This was mainly because they were flying at more than fifteen thousand feet, and were aiming at a single building. Their bombs plastered the adjacent area, where the Germans actually were, and in light of subsequent developments it can be said that this was the most effective part of the raid. Mitchell and Marauder bombers coming in at a low altitude proved more accurate, and columns of dark smoke spurted up from the Abbey, resembling the plumes of some monstrous bird. Newspapermen circulated among soldiers at a safe distance, and could not find any who disapproved of the raid. The consensus was that if it saved lives—and all assumed that it would—it was worth it.

Altogether, 137 B-17s and 43 Mitchells and Marauders took part in this effort to demolish a single building.[29] Most of the monks and up to two thousand refugees were still inside at the time. Later investigation shows that there were no Germans killed or wounded inside the building. Clark was aware that the place was being used as a refuge by the local people, and the day before had managed to have warning messages dropped on the place. But to evacuate meant running a gauntlet of shell and gunfire, so practically everybody stayed put.

The ground trembled under the Sikhs and Gurkhas waiting to invade this Catholic shrine. Then, with the last bombers droning off into the distance, came the order to attack. Above them, the German 1st Parachute Division quickly opened fire with machine guns and rifles. The Germans moved into the rubble and behind the broken walls and found there among the bodies of the dead and wounded monks and townspeople a stony bastion. They would remain there until May.

On 18 May, soldiers of the Podolski Lancers planted the Polish flag atop the Abbey rubble, indicating that at long last the battle of Cassino was over. The Germans disengaged when setbacks at Anzio exposed Via Casilina and Via Appia—the two viable routes of retreat—to capture if the Allies became unusually daring. It was also influenced by a breakthrough on the inland flank, where Moroccan soldiers of the French Expeditionary Corps were in a position to cut in behind the Germans at Cassino.

The German disengagement was quiet and orderly, carried out on the night of 17–18 May. A rearguard unit gave the Poles a hot time as they stormed the heights. Germans had not seen much of Polish fighting men since 1939, when nearly a quarter-million Polish soldiers were killed or wounded during the first campaign of the war. These men, under the command of Gen. Wladislaw Anders, had been taken prisoner by the Russians, who were then Germany's partners in the dismemberment of Poland.

When Russia joined the Allies in 1941, following the German invasion of Russia, these prisoners were returned to duty as Allied soldiers. But instead of using them on the Eastern Front, Stalin had sent them down into the Middle East, where they linked up with the British, including Freyberg's New Zealanders. After an interval of garrison duty on that quiet front, the Poles were sent to Cassino and their moment of glory, vindication, and revenge.

The German withdrawal may have been orderly, but it was hurried. Kesselring now felt his line of retreat in great jeopardy. He was especially concerned about the Via Casilina, more westerly of his two highways but the one more exposed to action coming out of the Anzio front. It was also by far the better highway, for Via Appia cut through undrained portions of the Pontine Marshes at one point, and around some steep mountainsides at another. These two constricting points would prohibit any effective evasive action if a well-timed Allied air attack took place.

Monte Cassino, 6 February 1944. A reconnaissance photo that may have influenced the Allied decision to bomb the historic monastery. Courtesy U.S. Army Military History Institute

Bombing of the road ahead, with a pursuing enemy in the rear, would have presented grave problems.

Allied commanders were well aware of these matters, and Field Marshal Alexander hoped that the Germans might be forced onto Via Appia if Clerk's Fifth Army could break out of Anzio in a timely fashion and occupy Valmontone, a town astride Via Casilina barely thirty miles to the southeast of Rome and not at all far from the main fighting front at Anzio.

Alexander envisioned nothing less than an envelopment of Senger's Cassino army, in which units breaking out of Anzio would move across to Via Appia or, if the Germans insisted on staying on Via Casilina, would dig in to meet them. In either case, the pursuing troops from Cassino would soon catch up, and a whole German army, or at least a substantial part of one, might then be forced to surrender. The only units capable of escaping would be those which had fought at Anzio and then redeployed directly toward Rome.

Such a victory could be compared with Stalingrad. It would be a Little Stalingrad, and a vindication of the entire campaign.

CHAPTER FOUR

WAR COMES TO ROME

The priest walked briskly up the street holding his Bible in one hand, a holy water dispenser in the other. He was in the middle of the street, but waved the dispenser first toward one side, then the other. You could see drops of holy water flicking out of the thing if you were up close. He heard a moan from under a collapsed tenement as he reached the corner, and gingerly approached the building, stepping over chunks of stone and shattered furniture and glass. He flicked some holy water at it, and then looked closely into a few fissures in the piled-up debris.

Some onlookers started toward the wreckage, but then the papal limousine came into view, and everybody's attention naturally was turned toward His Holiness, Pope Pius XII. The black vehicle caught the edge of a bomb crater and nearly went out of control as the driver revved the engine to avoid getting caught in the hole. Then it bumped to a stop in a street filled with bits of stone, wood, metal, and the ubiquitous glass, in front of the Basilica of San Lorenzo.

The Pontiff got out and was immediately surrounded by a large crowd. Some in the crowd were covered with white dust and looked almost like ghosts. Others had blood in their hair, or on their faces or clothing. Some of the women were crying loudly. There were shouts of *"Pace! Pace!"* (Peace! Peace!) and *"Aiuta!"* (Help!), and a general cacophony of plead-

Pope Pius XII (in white) *in prayer outside the Basilica of St. John in Lateran after bombing of Rome, 1944. The Basilica, officially neutral territory of the Vatican State, was damaged in this first Allied bombing raid against Rome. Shortly thereafter, Rome was declared an "open city."* Courtesy UPI/Bettmann

ing as the pontiff attempted to survey the bomb damage to the face of his basilica in the waning sun of that summer evening.

It was 19 July, the tenth day of the Allied invasion of Sicily. Mussolini was away meeting with Hitler in the town of Feltre, in northern Italy. News of the first bombing of Rome was brought to *il Duce* as he talked with the Führer. The timing was quite deliberate; the raid had been perfect in that regard. The raid was only near-perfect in its pinpointing of targets, because of intense antiaircraft fire (which brought down five of the American bombers) and a defensive smokescreen rising from the San Lorenzo Railway Yard, across the street from the basilica. The yard had been the raid's prime target.[1]

This was one of Rome's outlying neighborhood, but its jumble of multistory tenements made it look like anything but suburbia. And it had its share of historical monuments; no part of Rome could be presumed to be free of such things. The basilica was two hundred years old, as were the many statues and murals inside. A short distance away stood a monument, the pyramid of Cestius, from the days of the Emperors. Close to that was an ancient cemetery—ancient, but in use all through the centuries. Some victims of this raid would be buried there. The great expatriate English poet John Keats also lay there. His headstone was damaged by shrapnel.[2]

The *New York Times* report of the raid, two days later, was apologetic: Rome had been invaded and sacked numerous times before, it noted, listing all the capital cities of Europe already subjected to aerial bombardment. More than any other city, though, Rome was a living museum. Its open-air artifacts were vastly more numerous than those of Athens, its sole rival as the birthplace of Western civilization. Every creative era was represented among its monuments. Thoughts of bombing such a place, or fighting a battle in that city that was unlike any other in the world, quickly turned to spiritual reflection. Rome was like a thousand Monte Cassinos.

Victor Emmanuel visited the scene of the damage the next day. A crowd gathered near him, too—kept at bay by dozens of *Carabinieri*. The mood was much less pleading and reverential than it had been for the Pontiff the evening before. People cursed and made obscene gestures. They shouted *"Cornuto!"* and, addressing his daughter, who stayed by his side, *"Putana!"* Not since the days of political turmoil and labor riots following World War I had the king encountered such public anger. Even then, it had not been directed at him personally. These American bombs had brought the war to the royal doorstep in more ways than one. They revealed that he was reviled as a leading author of the country's misfortunes.[3]

Mussolini arrived back from Feltre the same day. Hearing about the king's reception in the streets of the Tiburtino district, he hid at the Palazzo Venezia. A Fascist Militia squad patrolled the square outside, to prevent people from gathering there. *Il Duce*'s downfall was to take place within the week.

A second bombing raid took place on 13 August. This time, an arriving passenger train was hit by three bombs, but no Vatican property (legally neutral and outside the jurisdiction of the Italian government), historical monuments, or great poets' graves were hit. Nonetheless a large crowd gathered in St. Peter's Square. The pope went out to the scene of destruction to assist in administering last rites. In the Piazza di Villa Fiorelli he began a sermon on the futility of war, but had to break off because of the wild shouting and chants of *Pace! Pace!*

By this time the government had unilaterally declared Rome an Open City. This meant that the city would not resist any invaders and therefore they should not inflict any damage on it. Secret peace talks were just beginning with the Allies, and the status of Rome quickly entered the discussions. Eisenhower's desire to keep the Germans out of Rome, once surrender was announced, cast a shadow over the city's fate. Mussolini's successor as head of state, Badoglio, seemed open to Allied proposals that U.S. and British paratroops be brought in at the moment of surrender, to assist the Italian forces in keeping the Wehrmacht at bay. But Badoglio scuttled that plan at the last minute.

Berlin was partial to the "open city" declaration for reasons that had little enough to do with preserving cultural artifacts. In practical terms, "open city" meant open to the Wehrmacht when the rumored Italian surrender to the Allies took place. As soon as the surrender was announced over the radio on the night of 9 September, Marshal Kesselring summoned Gen. Calvi di Bergolo (the king's son-in-law) to Frascati, and told him flatly that if the Italian army resisted a German move to occupy Rome, the city would be bombed mercilessly. The general immediately passed this information to Marshal Caviglia by telephone from Kesselring's office. In the absence of any orders from Badoglio or the king (both fleeing southward at this time), Caviglia was, as the highest-ranking officer on the scene, the *de facto* commander of Rome.[4]

He resolved immediately that Rome's official status as an open city not be tampered with in any way, but the commanders of the four divisions of the Italian army deployed around the city were not ordered to stand down until next morning, 10 September. Already units of the Ariete Division had opened fire on approaching tanks of the 93rd Panzer-Grenadier Division. Kesselring's aide, Gen. Siegfried Westphal (the youngest general in the German Army) set out to negotiate the details of disengagement with Caviglia. Meanwhile, Calvi di Bergolo's Centauro Division stood aside and allowed the first German troops into the city—the first occupying troops, for they were greeted by hundreds of other German military personnel who had materialized in the city during the last days of Mussolini and who were not invited to leave by Marshal Badoglio. "Open city" meant, then, that four Italian divisions stood aside while a single German one came in to introduce the German military occupation of Rome.

The Allies may have been intimidated by the papal visits to the scenes of the bomb damage, for their August raid proved to be the last of any consequence. A pinpoint attack, involving only a few planes, was launched against the German Army's Rome headquarters at a converted hospital (the Policlinica) on the edge of Vatican City on 18 March 1944. On 3 March, an important aqueduct was hit outside the city limits, causing a severe water shortage that lasted a week.

Eugen Dollmann, the Rome Gestapo chief, reports in his memoirs that Pius XII made a "tenacious effort" to secure universal recognition of Rome's status as an open city. A secret meeting with Ambassador to the Vatican Weizsaecker and Italy's SS chief General Wolff, was "decisive," in Dollmann's view. The meeting took place at the Convent of the Savior in late March 1944. Wolff, Weizsaecker, Dollmann and *Gauleiter* Rainer from Trieste were first treated to a guided tour of the Sistine chapel and other historic places in the Vatican.[5]

The Vatican, a neutral country situated in the heart of Rome, could not escape heavy damage or even destruction, Pius said, if the Wehrmacht chose to stand and fight in the city. He pointed out the fate of Monte Cassino, which he had bitterly denounced without pointing a finger at either side. Even the papal summer residence, Castel Gandolfo, located a short distance south of Rome, had already been damaged by Allied bombers.

The Germans were quick to point out that they had not occupied Castel Gandolfo. The only casualties there had been refugees and some escaped British prisoners, including the son of a general. (This was General Freyberg's son, who instead of serving in his father's New Zealand Corps at Cassino had been assigned to the Anzio front.) That suggested the Allies might blast Rome no matter what the Germans did.

But General Wolff and his comrades did not wish to discourage the pope, as they sought to keep their options open. Rome was the major converging point for Italy's railroads south of Milan, and through its four major train yards flowed the manpower and supplies that fueled the combat to the south. Rome was not only a transit point, however. It was a place where weapons, ammunition, and supplies were stockpiled, where wounded soldiers were taken, and where exhausted soldiers went on leave. Just fifty miles from the Anzio front, it was a rear staging area for operations there.

The Allies had made no formal commitment to the "open city" claim. Attacks on Rome were at the discretion of Alexander, the theater commander, and Fifth Army commander Gen. Mark Clark. But actions spoke louder than words. Air raids concentrated on the track north and south of the city, but the big yards within the city limits remained intact. In those yards could be found at any time track after track lined with boxcars, passenger cars and locomotives. They comprised a huge transportation bottleneck, and the most important strategic bombing target in Italy.

So, until the front reached the outskirts of the city, the Germans could consider Pius XII an invaluable *de facto* ally. They certainly were not interested in making him give up his "open city" propaganda, and were heartened when Vatican Radio warned of the "indelible stain" that would attach to any country that became involved in the destruction of the Eternal City.[6]

The deeds of Pius XII have come under close scrutiny since the war ended. He has been excoriated on the stage (in Rolf Hochhuth's play *The Deputy*) and even in painting. Some writers have characterized him as a Germanophile, if not a Fascist sympathizer. He spoke German fluently, and was papal legate in Berlin (as Cardinal Pacelli) during World War I. Certainly the pope's relations with Mussolini were by no means cordial, despite the fact that *il Duce* restored a remnant of the old Papal State in 1929, in the form of Vatican City.

There were many Church properties scattered throughout the city, and all were recognized as outposts of the Vatican's sovereign territory. This made them—not only churches, but also convents, seminaries, and priests' residences—off-limits to the authority of the Italian government.

On taking over the city, the Germans chose to honor this sovereignty, even though they knew that it would be a source of some trouble to them. The film *Open City*, made by Roberto Rossellini shortly after the Germans departed Rome in 1944, well illustrates the problem. One of its heroes is a priest, active in the anti-Fascist partisan movement. The priest exploits the sovereign status of Church property to the hilt—hiding fugitives, storing weapons, and so forth. In real life, not many priests were active in the underground, but there was considerable passive involvement in the way of allowing fugitives to hide on Church property. Such involvement may actually have been non-partisan, in many cases, for even in medieval times the worst criminal could find a refuge from his pursuers in a church. The pursuers could not trespass and assert their secular authority on religious property, and the Church jealously guarded its rights on this matter.

So it happened that Church establishments became the frequent refuges of various kinds of fugitives, including not only partisan fighters but also escaped prisoners of war, Italian officers who had opposed the German occupation of the city, and Roman Jews. Occasional Gestapo demands to search a Church building were met with stony silence. The pope, surely aware of the problem that existed, never once compromised the sovereignty of Vatican territory in favor of the Germans. Many fugitives survived the occupation because of this. There was only one clearcut instance of a German violation of Vatican territory. General Monti of the Italian air force and five officers were on the Gestapo's wanted list for their hostile activities during the takeover on 10 September. They were known to be housed in St. Paul's Basilica. On 9 February—at just about the time the big German push against Anzio was getting underway—soldiers invaded the basilica and arrested Monti and his men. After a speedy trial, all were executed the next day. The Vatican issued a strong protest, and no flagrant incident of this type occurred again.

The Seminary of San Giovanni housed another military fugitive, General Bencivenga, during the latter days of the occupation. Bencivenga had been arrested and then escaped. At San Giovanni he received a message from Marshal Badoglio, the king's head of state, appointing him governor of Rome, the appointment to take effect as soon as the Germans left. This order came down as the Wehrmacht disengaged from the Cassino front, in anticipation that Rome would soon be liberated. Bencivenga welcomed Mark Clark into the city on 5 June, on behalf of the Italian government, in a curious anticlimax to the months of fighting that had preceded the Allies' arrival in the city.

Badoglio's move was at least partially inspired by his knowledge that anti-royal partisans were also hiding in the Eternal City. Foremost among these was Giorgio Amendola, a Communist official who spent much of his time in a convent.

Partisan activity within the city was, with one big exception, low-key, and was probably inhibited by Rome's status as an open city, which both Axis and Allies seemed interested in maintaining. Plans for an uprising as the Germans left—something more coordinated than the outburst of the Neapolitans at the end of the previous September—were squelched by the Allied chiefs, who saw this as an end-run by leftists around the royal claim to authority. As elsewhere, the partisan movement within the city was dominated, but not fully controlled, by the Communists.

Also as elsewhere, fugitive soldiers of the Italian army made up the second largest partisan element. The very night Italy announced its surrender, Col. Enrico Nuti and several of his marines from the San Marco Battalion (based at Civitavecchia) attacked the German embassy with grenades and submachine guns. Other marines at the port of Civitavecchia resisted the approaching Germans. Many of them found their way into the city and took refuge in the ancient catacombs.[7]

The catacombs, home of the early Roman Christians when Christians were fed to the lions at the Coliseum, housed a substantial number of fugitive Jews during the occupation. Early in the occupation, all the Jews in the city were required to register with the police. It was well known that this requirement, which had severe penalties for noncompliance, was the first step toward slave labor, the breakup of families, and, for those who could not work, a cutoff of food rations. Noncompliance in Rome, where half of Italy's Jews lived, was rather high. This was because Mussolini, under the Führer's prodding before the war, had initiated a similar registration of Jews. Administration was much more lax in pre-war Italy, however, and the result was that a number of Jews came up with altered identity papers, including birth certificates. Most importantly, the Jews found that they had the sympathy of those around them. Tattletales and anti-Semites were few, at least compared with some other parts of Europe. So the German effort to control Rome's Jews was not a total success. The tolerant spirit of the city was helpful to the great majority of Jews, who did not have altered identity papers and new names. It encouraged noncompliance with the new Gestapo registration decree, and so the Gestapo did not know where many of the Jews lived.

The newspapers carried stories about Jews who defied the law, the Gentiles who helped them, and how both were suddenly set upon by the police and sent to labor camps. Some of these stories were probably fabricated, but the occupation authorities exerted enough pressure to send many of the Jews into hiding in the catacombs or elsewhere. The chief rabbi was told to collect gold as an alternative to forced-labor requisitions. Fifty kilograms in gold coins, watches, necklaces and bracelets, and even a few pieces of bullion were forthcoming. But then the authorities staged a roundup anyway, which netted slightly more than two thousand people. At least as many evaded the soldiers and policemen, who made their move suddenly in the dead of night. Shouts and screams in the first apartments they entered alerted everybody within earshot, and the Jews among them often clambered down fire escapes or across rooftops to seek an uncertain refuge. The city was willing to hide them.[8]

Besides hunting down renegade soldiers, partisans, and Jews, Occupation authorities also exerted efforts against unreliable elements and "economic criminals." Just a few days before the Americans arrived, a merchant accused of selling food at black-market prices was shot by a firing squad. Prior to that, black marketeers were generally sent off to forced labor or incarcerated in the Regina Coeli prison. Prices shot up by more than four times during the period of German control (September to June—almost nine months), and, according to one estimate, two-thirds of the food sold in the city was on the black market. There were severe shortages in everything but bread, which was rationed out at a meager hundred grams per person daily.[9]

The Occupation also singled out "war profiteers" for special attention. A leading Roman industrialist, Volpi di Misurata, was arrested, as were members of the Cini family. They were accused of price-gouging on supplies sold to the Wehrmacht, mainly in the early days before official prices were set for virtually everything; and for selling shoddy goods and undercounting on deliveries.[10]

In November there was a roundup of supposed monarchists—lead-ing citizens, especially ex-government officials and their relatives—whose loyalty to Mussolini's newly proclaimed Fascist republic was in doubt. The king's son-in-law, Gen. Calvi di Bergolo, was already in custody for objecting to the policy of taking hostages in reprisal for acts of sabotage. Friends and relatives of Count Galleazzo Ciano, the former foreign minister and Mussolini's son-in-law, and including "smart women of the Ciano set," were incarcerated.[11] Ciano himself had been arrested else-where, and turned over to Mussolini at his new base near Lake Garda in the far north. Ciano was regarded as the driving force in the move to oust *il Duce* in July, and in fact he had been one of the main conspira-tors. The other principal conspirator, Dino Grandi, had been prudent enough to exit the country as quickly as possible. He ended up in En-gland, where he had once served as ambassador, and was treated with remarkable respect there. (He would live in England until his death, of old age, in 1989.)

The Germans also disarmed and arrested all of the city's *Carabinieri* (national police) and sent them off to work on the planned final defense line—the last and largest one south of the Alps, stretching from coast to coast in the Northern Apennines, and known as the Gothic Line. This group numbered nearly 1,500 men—not far short of the number of Jews arrested in November, the following month,[12] when the citywide Jewish roundup took place.

For the average Roman, the most onerous aspect of the Occupation was the practice of labor drafts. When the Germans needed workers, they simply grabbed them off the streets. The sight of a truck with a couple of submachine-toting guards riding on the back was enough to send men scurrying for cover. If there were not enough able bodies on the streets, then the search would be brought into the tenements. Men might even be routed out of closets and from under beds. A complicat-ing factor for men of military age was the fact that Mussolini's shadowy republic had issued orders for military draft registration. Men in the armed forces when the king surrendered were likewise ordered to report for duty under the Italian Social Republic. It was a rare soldier who answered that call, but failure to meet the deadline (or deadlines, as there were a few extensions accompanied by well-publicized amnesties) resulted in classification—if captured—as a deserter. The regime warned that violators were subject to the death penalty.

The Germans had their own needs, though, and rarely worried about the status or identity of the people they rounded up. Anybody from about the age of fifteen to about fifty was fair game. Aside from the usual needs for lifting, hauling, and repairing bomb damage on the roads and rail-road tracks, there was also the substantial project run by the Todt Organization in the northern Apennines.[13] For this workers were being "recruited" from all over northern Italy, for it involved the construction of the Gothic Line.

Working conditions there were not vastly different from those that prevailed during construction of the Great Wall of China. Workers starved and suffered from exposure, and the only medical attention was an infusion of bullets for "malingerers" who claimed that they were too sick to work. Romans also had to worry about being shipped off to Germany to work in factories, for the Reich labor chief, Fritz Sauckel, regularly appealed to the military government and sometimes even to Mussolini for workers, skilled or unskilled, male or female.

German soldiers were known to fire upon fleeing conscripts, and the man who did not move quickly enough to the waiting truck might be prodded along with some hard blows from a rifle butt. Wives, sisters, and mothers of labor conscripts who got in the way might be physically abused and possibly even arrested. When not performing such duties, however, soldiers were under orders to behave themselves with the Romans. It was the same all over occupied Italy.

Except for reported incidents of looting during the initial takeover of the city on 10 September, these orders seem to have been obeyed. Pius XII even made some favorable comments to General Wolff along this line, during his penultimate appeal for the continuance of Rome's "open city" status.[14] There was no practical advantage for the Wehrmacht in stirring up popular discontent, especially when it was trying to shore up Mussolini's new Social Republic. German treatment of Italians seems in fact to have been *il Duce*'s major preoccupation, as the latter sought especially to end the labor requisitions and to have Italians in Germany repatriated.

The Wehrmacht was also not above an occasional public-relations stunt. Upon entering the city and seizing the Italian Army bakery, cameras were brought in to record a gratuitous, one-time distribution of bread to a large crowd of neighborhood people. (Off-camera, according to one observer, soldiers took it back.)[15] And upon leaving, they cleaned out the flour supply and distributed a large "surplus" of bread loaves through the bakeries. When the Allies arrived, therefore, most of the Romans had a good supply of bread at home, but no prospect of any bread at all a few days hence. The Germans hoped that they would be going hungry by the third day after the Liberation, and then remember the generous distribution made by the departing forces of the Occupation.[16]

Civilian damage caused by the two bombing raids against the railroad yards also received a lot of publicity, but this was the work more of pro-Fascist newspapers than of the military command. The black-shirted element had been resurrected with the arrival of the Wehrmacht, and even though *il Duce* himself remained clear of the Eternal City (he would never see it again), his followers exerted themselves to create the impression that Rome was, once again, a bastion of Fascism.

Most of the high-ranking Fascists were up north, in the lake country, with the new so-called government. What remained in Rome were the Fascists of the streets—the rank and file of the disbanded Militia. The Wehrmacht made virtually no use of this element, but there seemed no harm in allowing them to erect signs with the word *"Liberazione"* on the ruins near the rail yards, or to engage in vigilante efforts against underground newspapers. Such low-key activities were no problem, but the occupation authorities knew, or remembered, that the Romans rejoiced when *il Duce* was fired by the king. They knew that Fascism was dead in Rome.

Pictures of Mussolini and Fascist insignia, once ubiquitous, were now extremely rare, even under the German occupation. On the other hand, a rendition of the Fascist anthem, *"Giovanezza"* (Youth), preceded every performance at the Rome Opera and at various other theatrical events. It was assumed that Fascist displays would be vandalized, but it was not so easy to interfere with the *"Giovanezza"* in a public place without running the risk of being arrested. Still, one evening, as the opera orchestra cranked into the obligatory playing of the anthem, a blackshirt jumped onto the stage and waved a submachine gun at the crowd, threatening to shoot anybody who did not stand up.

Elsewhere in public, blackshirts sometimes brandished firearms and hand grenades in efforts to extort food and money from merchants. Blackshirts shot up a movie screen when they found the film boring. And at one of Rome's largest movie theaters, several jumped on the stage to sing the *"Giovanezza."* In this instance, they were heartened to hear many members of the audience join in. When they tried this at another theater, located in a workers' neighborhood, they were jeered instead.[17]

The Wehrmacht's biggest publicity stunt involved the rescued art works from Monte Cassino. This effort was not limited to Rome, but was trumpeted all across Europe in an effort to characterize the Teutons as the true conservators of Western culture. Once it had become clear, in December, that the Allies were heading straight for Cassino, Lt. Col. Julius Schlegel of the Hermann Goering Division decided that a mission to rescue the art works of the Abbey should be mounted immediately.

His division was currently bivouacked near Civitavecchia, having been withdrawn from the line for rest and recuperation after the retreat from the Volturno River.

Schlegel was well aware that more was at stake than the gilded chalices of the Abbey. Also deserving of rescue were the establishment's archives and rare books. In addition, thirty crates of artifacts from Pompeii were in temporary storage at the Abbey. These had been removed from the Naples Archaeological Museum by the retreating Germans. And there was more. The Germans—specifically, units of the Hermann Goering Division—had also "rescued" no fewer than 150 crates of art works from the Naples National Art Gallery.

The officer secured several days of leave time and visited Abbot Diamare. The key to success was the availability of trucks, emptied of supplies brought to the front, being diverted to carry these art treasures back to Rome. Up to now Schlegel tried to accomplish these things on his own authority, and through negotiations with regimental commanders of the 1st Parachute Divisions. He was afraid that higher-ups could bring the project to a sudden end with a simple "no." It quickly became clear, however, that the transport resources of his own division would have to be tapped if the project was to succeed. Schlegel appealed to his commander, Gen. Paul Conrath, who at first was reluctant to send his weary truck drivers down to the front. One of his concerns was that a convoy of division trucks, caught up in an Allied offensive, might be shanghaied by a front-line unit. The trucks might be bombed and strafed while travelling on the Via Casilina. He also wondered if they might cause logistical problems for the fighting units.

Schlegel believed that the artworks were worth the risk, and argued that the Allies constantly accused their enemy of looting Italy's art treasures. This argument swayed Conrath, especially after he heard a news broadcast from Naples that accused the Germans of looting Pompeii and the city's museums. In the background was also the division's ultimate commander, the man after whom it was named—the Reich Air Marshal and member of Hitler's inner circle. Hermann Goering was not brought into this discussion, but his personal interest in art was widely known. What would happen if, after the artworks were destroyed at Cassino, Goering were told that Conrath had vetoed an effort to save them?

Conrath decided to go along, agreeing with Schlegel that this could be a major counterblow to the incessant propaganda from the other side about German looting. And if Hermann Goering decided to claim some of the rescued works for his own fast-growing personal collection—well, that might not help in the propaganda department, but it would not be bad for the two men's career prospects. In all, a hundred truckloads of crated paintings, statues, books, archival documents, Pompeiian artifacts, antique furniture, gold and silver churchwares, old coins, and other objects were shipped north. Some were lodged in a church basement in Spoleto, but most went to Rome.

There, a public ceremony was held outside the Palazzo Venezia, in which General Conrath formally presented the rescued art to the "Italian people," here personified by some of Mussolini's Cabinet ministers. Also on hand were art historians from Germany and Italy, plus a large contingent of reporters and photographers.

Most of these rescued artifacts did not remain in Rome when the Fifth Army finally arrived. A substantial number of crated items were to be found in Venice at the end of the war. Some went to Berlin, one painting being presented to Goering as a birthday present from "his" division. (Goering later claimed to have returned the painting to Italy.) Others were found, after the war, stored in salt mines in Austria.

Only days after the last truckload left the Abbey, and Abbot Diamare posed for the photographers shaking hands with Lieutenant Colonel Schlegel, the place was blasted by the American bombers. Pius XII did not publicly congratulate these saviors of Italy's cultural heritage. Neither, for that matter, did he openly condemn the bombing of Monte Cassino. The Vatican newspaper, *Osservatore Romano,* waited three days to mention the bombing and—despite its considerable devotion to cultural matters—had little to say about the art rescue. When the destruction of the Abbey was reported, it was in a very brief, objective despatch on the front page. Behind the scenes, though, U.S. legate Harold Tittmann had his ears pinned back by papal aide Cardinal Miglione, who condemned it as "a colossal blunder . . . gross stupidity."[18]

There was one major exception to the rule that partisan activities inside Rome were quite restrained. That exception inspired the occupiers to commit a great atrocity that totally negated efforts to win the hearts and minds of the people, and instead won for them the undying hatred of most Romans.

A company of the SS *Polizeiregiment* "Bozen" was quartered in a tenement building on Via Rasella, in the heart of the city. It consisted of 156 men, some of whom were old enough to be veterans of World War I, and virtually all of whom were over-age for the military draft. They were volunteers and, as members of the *Schutz-Staffel* (Heinrich Himmler's vast security police apparatus) may have been inspired by a greater sense of devotion to the Hitler regime than was to be found among the rank-and-file of the Wehrmacht. They all came from the Bolzano (in German, Bozen) area of the Italian Alps, which had a mixed German-Austrian-Italian population. This territory had been handed over to Italy at the end of World War I, but it was now being governed by a Nazi *Gauleiter*—to the great annoyance of Mussolini and most Italians. The spirit of volunteerism that gave rise to this unit was certainly fueled by the hope, among the men of the Bozen Regiment, that the place would soon be formally annexed by the Reich.

One day, the men were marching back to their quarters, accompanied by an armored car and a few trucks. It was 23 March, a date that meant nothing to them but which was remembered by many Italians as the birthday of the Fascist Movement in Italy—one year shy, in fact, of the movement's silver anniversary. A streetsweeper dressed in a white uniform and standing next to his wheeled trash barrel lifted his cap respectfully to the formation. He then went into the vestibule of one of the tenement buildings that lined the street, leaving the can and large street broom outside.

The tip of the cap was a signal to a man peeking out a window nearby, who then pushed down on the handle of a contraption with wires sticking out of it. The contraption was a timed detonator. Inside the can down in the street was forty pounds of TNT. Less than a minute later, as the two men ran pellmell out the back of the building, a thunderous roar went up. Limbs and heads went flying, and even the armored car was cracked open. Twenty-eight of the SS men were killed instantly, and four others died later. All of the others were injured, most seriously, including some who would be permanently disabled.

General Maelzer, the military commandant of the city, arrived in short order. His first reaction, on seeing the ambulances and the blood, was to shout, *"Vendetta! Vendetta!"* He ordered all the residents of the street to line up outside, to be trucked off to a detention area as hostages. Many of them emerged from their flats with cuts and bruises. All had their homes ransacked by soldiers and policemen in search of the culprits. Most were women and children, and there were some elderly people among them. Maelzer himself took part in some of the impromptu questioning that all were subjected to. Nobody knew anything, and it was pretty obvious that they were victims, too. Getting over his initial shock and rage, the commandant then changed his mind about placing them all under arrest. But he was sure that a great chastisement would befall the Romans forthwith—all the heavier if the killers were not promptly captured.

The incident was so serious that Berlin was notified immediately, and the highest authorities were asked for instructions on the matter of reprisals. This was in fact one of the worst instances of terrorism to occur thus far in occupied Europe, matched only by the activities of Tito's partisans in Yugoslavia in terms of attacks upon German forces. General Jodl, chief of the military High Command in Berlin, relayed the Führer's sentiments that a substantial number of hostages be seized and shot in retaliation. He also confirmed that General Mackensen, whose Tenth Army command encompassed Rome as well as the Anzio front, was the man responsible for all the details, including setting the number to be killed.

Following brief telephone conversations with his commander, Marshal Kesselring, with General Maelzer and with General Wolff, the SS chief for Italy who came to Rome to offer assistance, Mackensen settled on a ratio of ten to one. Thirty-two Germans had died, so 320 Italians would pay with their lives. Responsibility for actually carrying out the punishment fell to Maelzer and to Col. Herbert Kappler, the police attaché. Kappler was supposed to work with the Rome chief of police, Pietro Caruso. The latter enjoyed a fierce reputation when it came to dealing with suspected partisans—sufficient to earn him a conviction for torture and murder only six months hence in a Rome courtroom. But killing innocent hostages was a little bit beyond his ken, and he refused to play an active role. His job would have been to actually select the hostages, conduct the roundup with his police force, take them to some appropriate location and then to kill them all. Kappler would have been essentially a liaison with the German authorities and perhaps an advisor on the selection of appropriate victims. Instead, Kappler ended up running the whole operation himself.

Mackensen had recommended that condemned criminals be used—men who were slated for execution anyway, and at that point he ceased to actively involve himself in the matter. It turned out that the prisons could only yield three condemned prisoners. Gen. Wilhelm Harster, the SS chief of Vienna who was visiting Rome at this time, urged that Jews should fill out the ranks of victims. This would have made things easy if the deportation of the Roman Jews had not already been carried out. But it was well-known that more than half of them were still at large in the city, and rarely did a week go by when at least a few of the fugitives were not rooted out of the catacombs or some walled-up room. A canvass of the jails plus the immediate arrest of certain Jews who were under surveillance (either "suspected" Jews, with fake identity papers, or persons who might inadvertently lead the police to other Jews) yielded a total of seventy.

It was important for the Germans that the reprisal should be carried out with despatch, to show that punishment was not only sure but swift. Posters were already being pasted up around the city the next morning stating (falsely) that "ten criminals" had already been shot for each victim of the terror bombing—that the reprisals had already been completed. Kappler, in his haste, ended up selecting the requisite number from the jails, most of them coming from the Regina Coeli prison. One was an Italian air force wing commander (General Renulli, who had resisted the occupation in September). Several were awaiting trial and had not been convicted of any crime as yet. Eleven were foreigners. Twelve had no identification papers and there was no certainty even about their real names.

Meanwhile, relatives of the thirty-two men who had been killed in the bombing were flown in at German government expense. This was in preparation for a mammoth funeral procession that would snake through the major boulevards and squares of Rome, with a marching band playing funeral dirges and patriotic anthems. Also, Romans were being urged over the radio to contribute to a fund for the victims' families.

Kappler ended up with 335 hostages—three more than needed. They were taken to the Ardeatine Caves, outside the city, and massacred by machine-gun fire. After each group of prisoners was mowed down, German soldiers would walk among them looking for signs of life. Any who appeared still alive received a bullet in the head. They were then dragged in and explosives were detonated, thereby sealing the cave entrances and effecting instant mass burial.[19]

Lieutenant Colonel Kappler had been a security adviser in Rome since 1939 and had even brought his parents to live there. He had an adopted son from Himmler's *Lebensborn* Program—the SS agency that matched blond couples for the purpose of breeding Teutonic children. In 1948, Kappler was sentenced to life in prison by an Italian court for his role in the Ardeatine Massacre.

Marshal Kesselring was also tried for this massacre, and offered a defense that placed responsibility on the SS—an entirely independent command over which he had no control. Still, he was sentenced to death. The tribunal then received letters from Mark Clark and other Allied chiefs, attesting to Kesselring's adherence to the rules of war. The judges then commuted the sentence to life, noting that the massacre was beyond the scope of his authority. Fourteenth Army chief Mackensen was convicted along with General Maelzer in a British military court in 1946. Both were sentenced to death, but the sentences were then commuted to life. Maelzer died in prison; Mackensen was paroled in 1952. The massacre was included in a long list of charges against the chief of the High Command in Berlin, General Jodl, who was hanged after being convicted by the Nuremberg tribunal. Kesselring was paroled in 1951.

Who carried out the bombing, and why did they do it, and what was their fate? The attack was the work of Communist partisans known as *Gappisti*, in retaliation for the execution on 7 March of Giorgio Labó, one of the group's founders. It had the approval of the top Communist official in Rome, Giorgio Amendola. The man who tipped his hat to the troops was Rosario Bentivegna. He became a hunted man when a confederate, who helped reconnoiter the area, was captured by agents of the "Special Department of Republic Police," a small free-lance collaborationist police intelligence unit headed by Pietro Koch. Anybody captured by the Koch groups was guaranteed to undergo the most heinous tortures at the unit's headquarters in the Pensione Jaccurino. The capture of this confederate led to the capture of other *Gappisti*, but those who actually carried out the attack were still at large when the Americans rolled into Rome, ten weeks after the incident.[20]

In addition to the Communists of the *Gappisti*, there were various other underground groups, ranging politically all the way to Victor Emmanuel loyalists. Only the Communists and the monarchists indulged in acts of sabotage and terrorism within the city. The more politically moderate groups in between these two extremes of left and right limited themselves to propaganda activity and plotting against both the communists and the supporters of the king. Most of the latter were actually military officers rather than civilians, and when the different factions organized themselves into the Committee of National Liberation (CLN), these military people remained aloof. They were influenced by the idea that the military should not get itself mixed up in politics, and they justified their support of the king on the premise that his was the only legal government. The CLN, which maintained a board of directors clandestinely in Rome, was firmly committed to ousting the monarch. It was also dedicated to preventing a Communist takeover, even though Communists were admitted to membership.

With but few exceptions, the royalist officers became quiescent after the first days of the German occupation. Thenceforward the *Gappisti* enjoyed a virtual monopoly on violent anti-German acts, and the bombing on the Via Rasella was only the culmination of a series of deeds. These included hand-grenade attacks on police guard posts, and the tossing of grenades at two train stations on 23 January. On 2 March a couple of members of the Black Brigade (a paramilitary unit serving Mussolini's government) were shot down on the street in broad daylight—this to avenge the execution of Teresa Gullaci, a *Gappisti* courier who went through Pietro Koch's torture chamber without revealing the identity of any of her comrades.[21]

The *Gappisti* also had a running war with Koch's special police, because the latter had political informers in working class neighborhoods where the Communists usually had their hideouts. These contacts seemed more dangerous than anything the regular Rome police or the Gestapo had. The latter two groups found it easier to let Koch have his fanatical way than to try to get any of this privileged information out of his men through coercion. That Koch seemed to be a genuine sadist did not faze them. Stories that his girlfriend used to sit on his lap to watch suspects being mutilated and burned, and that she composed poems about the tortures, were bandied about in police circles in a spirit of black humor.

But even the moderate underground could find things difficult at times. Raids on clandestine presses were common, but even the capture and execution of the editor of *Italia Libera*, Leone Ginzburg, failed to silence that widely distributed paper for even a few days. His group, the Action Party, did not carry out any violent reprisals, even though it was fast becoming a mainstay of the partisan war that was developing in the north. The Action Party, along with the CLN, hoped that the Eternal City could be spared from destruction. In this one thing they agreed with the monarchy and with the pope—and, thus far, the Germans. The Communists were the main disturbing factor. Orders had come down to them from on high, however—from party chairman Palmiro Togliatti, even before he returned to Italy from his long exile in Moscow: They were to cooperate with the Allies and with the CLN. United Front was the order of the day, but within that restraint lay the hope that the seeds of the Revolution might today be planted with hand grenades and with bombs hidden in trash barrels.

The Allied landing at Anzio electrified the city of Rome with confidence that the German occupation would prove short-lived and that the front would sweep past, hopefully around, the city. The imminent arrival of the Americans and the British would mean that, for the Romans, the war was essentially over. The more than two hundred thousand refugees who had found their way into the city from the various fighting fronts to the south would at last go away. Shortages would gradually disappear. There might even be elections for a new government. Forced-labor roundups and Gestapo raids would seem like a bad dream from which they had awakened.

Anzio, after all, was barely fifty miles away. A car could cover the distance in an hour. So if they had to fight, it might take days. And if the

Germans fought hard, it might take a couple of weeks. As days turned into weeks, and weeks turned into months, Romans were apt to imagine that any noise—a commotion in the next apartment, a shout in the street—signalled the approach of the Allies. Some would ask, "*A giunta l'ora?*" (Has the hour come?)[22] This became something of a catch-phrase. It was even scratched on walls, along with humorous sayings such as "Allies—don't worry! We are coming to rescue you!"

Once the invading forces became bogged down at Anzio, their ability to break out was undercut by the approaching deadline for the English Channel crossing. Ships and landing craft had been "loaned" to Fifth Army in January—very grudgingly, and with an understanding that they could not be spared for long. The main German counterattack in February prevented any significant withdrawals until the end of the month, when fear of a new thrust by the Wehrmacht waned considerably.

From then on, Anzio was steadily bled of maritime resources. LSTs, supply ships and warships disappeared one after another. There was no question of making good on naval losses to German aircraft, either. The Royal Navy lost two cruisers and three destroyers along with smaller vessels, and a total of 429 sailors. The Americans lost two minesweepers, two Liberty ships and five landing craft, and a total of 326 sailors.[23] These losses not only could not be replaced; they were criticized as a menace to the success of the cross-Channel invasion, for many of the ships and sailors had been slated to take part in the D-Day Invasion.

In April alone, forty-six LSTs were withdrawn from Italy, many from the Naples-to-Anzio supply shuttle. The cruisers HMS *Dido*, USS *Brooklyn*, and USS *Philadelphia*—all of which had a telling effect on Mackensen's February offensive—were sent to England. Along with them went destroyers and all kinds of other watercraft.[24]

By mid-May, the Germans had six thinned-out divisions strung out from the coast through the Alban foothills and then southward along Via Casilina, through the towns of Belletri and Cisterna. The Channel attack was less than a month away, and Fifth Army had been informed that the bleeding of its resources would actually accelerate once a foothold was gained in Normandy. This raised the prospect (the way things had been going) that the Romans might not be rid of their German masters until the Allies were in Berlin. The Italian campaign would then have to be counted a failure, and the reputations of its commanders would be reduced to ashes.

Mark Clark and his staff set plans for a one-two punch at Cassino and Anzio, with a breakout attempt from the latter place set for 23 May. The immediate objective was Cisterna, which had been the scene of an Allied disaster in the first days of the campaign, when two Ranger battalions were wiped out by the Hermann Goering Division. Now General Truscott, the front commander, sent the Third Division (from which he had so recently graduated) against the town and its current defenders, the German 362nd Infantry Division. Also taking part in the attack was Gen. Ernest Harmon's 1st Armored Division.

With complete control in the air—the front by this time virtually abandoned by the Luftwaffe, due to its heavy losses in the early going—and possible support from the remaining ships outside the harbor, this looked like a sure thing. Cisterna was finally taken after two days of intense fighting (during which Master Sergeant Audie Murphy earned his Congressional Medal of Honor). The cost was very high: 476 Americans dead and 2321 wounded, and Harmon's tank force sustained losses of such magnitude that the division's role would be diminished for the remainder of the Italian campaign. A hundred tanks were either destroyed or damaged.[25]

Gen. Heinz Greiner maneuvered the 362nd Infantry up the highway toward Velletri. During this retreat the last salvoes of the Anzio Express were heard. They were not especially effective, these huge shells from railroad guns that occasionally rolled out of their railroad tunnel sanctuaries inland to loft shells toward the beach, upon which they had over the months established a deadly accuracy. Firing now at a mobile battlefront, they went without aerial spotters and landed shells perilously close to their own people.

Meanwhile, the Hermann Goering Division moved into Valmontone. This was a key position, for the Via Casilina passed right by it, and there was a direct road from there to Anzio across the open country, just south of the Alban Hills. If Fifth Army forces broke through and captured that place, the retreat from Cassino, which was now in progress, might be cut off and a major part of the Fourteenth Army forced to surrender. The only hope for the Germans would be to rely on Route 7, the Appian Way—further inland but marked by various geographical hazards and bottlenecks that could be exploited by Allied aircraft. The Via Appia would be a bloody gauntlet. Via Casilina had to be kept open.

Field Marshal Alexander espied the opportunities here, and issued an order to General Clark to send his Fifth Army troops against Valmontone. The order actually was received by Clark's chief of staff, Gen. Alfred M. Gruenther, and Clark immediately decided to ignore it, acting as if he had been out of Gruenther's reach and didn't receive it in time. Clark also hoped that Alexander would not catch up with him for a day or so, and in fact there was no follow-up from the theater commander's headquarters.

Thus began the next and perhaps greatest controversy in inter-allied relations. General Clark perceived the order as a diversion from the main objective, which was Rome. The breakthrough at Cisterna and the fact that the initiative was clearly with the Allies on both the Anzio and the Cassino fronts assured that Rome was finally about to fall. But Clark worried that British units from either the 1st or 5th Division would be the first to enter the city, due to their present location. They were near the seacoast, facing the German 4th Parachute Division, and therefore at the furthest remove from Valmontone. An attack on that place would be an American operation, and heavy fighting could be expected. Moreover, movement along the Anzio-Valmontone Road would be subject to constant artillery fire from German positions in the Alban Hills, immediately to the north.

Clark was well aware, though, of the possibilities that the capture of Valmontone would raise. Later on, in his defense, he said that these were far from being certainties, and that the Germans heading north from Cassino might well effect their escape anyway. Alexander, in any case, found the Fifth Army's move directly into the Alban Hills and straight toward Rome "inexplicable."[26] Clark later confessed to being "shocked" by the order, which in any case (he added) was not in writing. He would also explain that Eighth Army did not deserve the glory of being first into Rome, because it "lacked aggressiveness . . . [and had] done little fighting."[27]

General Senger, commander of the forces retreating from Cassino up Via Casilina had a decided opinion on the matter. Years later, he wrote that the capture of Valmontone would have "vernichten" the Tenth Army.[28]

A unit of the 36th (Texas) Division expedited matters for Clark and for the entire Allied offensive when it discovered that Mt. Artemisio was entirely free of defenders. Located at the northern end of the east-west strip of rugged, mostly hilly terrain—the Alban Hills—that separated the Anzio Plain from the Roman Plain, this was a major find.

General Mackensen had made a little oversight, or else he gambled that the American would avoid this steep promontory that had no roads on it. The front guarded by his 4th Parachute Division ended on the western side of the mountain, and then units of the seemingly ubiquitous Goering Division were deployed on the other side—with not even a reconnaissance team on the mountain itself.

General Walker, who had guided his Texans (now about half "adopted," or honorary, Texans from New York City) through Salerno and the Rapido bloodbath, immediately dispatched engineer units to find a route for tanks that would not have impossible gradients. The engineers quickly accomplished their task in the darkness during the night of 30 May, and then went to work with a bulldozer to remove obstacles, laying tracks that would grip tank treads in the steeper areas. The division then went over the mountain and debouched into the plain below.

The German units to the west suddenly found themselves faced with entrapment, and the front broke in that direction. Tanks from the battered 1st Armored Division reached the outskirts of Rome on 4 June, but were stopped by heavy gunfire. At 7:15 A.M. the following morning, the 3rd Reconnaissance Platoon of the U.S. 88th Division (noted as the first all-draftee division to go into combat) entered the city and encountered only sporadic rifle fire. General Clark himself was in Rome less than an hour later.

The Romans, who had shown a certain bitterness during the long months of waiting, were jubilant.

CHAPTER FIVE

THE POLITICS OF CHAOS

The fall of Rome, on 5 June 1944, marked the high point of the Italian campaign. It was indeed the putative main objective for the Allies, to the extent that a continuation of the offensive after Rome had always been considered problematical. Adding to the glory of the moment was the fact that the Eternal City had gotten off with only slight damage. This was no thanks to Mussolini, who had wished to avenge the giddy celebration that had greeted his downfall in July 1943. He had desired that Kesselring do to Rome what Czar Alexander had done to Moscow on the approach of Napoleon in 1812: Leave the prize a smoldering ruin—but without any provision for an advance evacuation of its citizens.

And it was no thanks to the partisan groups, who feared that the king would resuscitate his blasted reputation by riding in as a participant in the liberation. The groups affiliated with the Action Party, especially, plotted a preemptive uprising once most of the Germans were gone. They hoped that the citizenry would rally to their side and together they could claim credit for liberating themselves and then dare to proclaim a republic.

Marshal Kesselring, however, had struck an informal bargain with the Allies. The city, including even the Ponte Vecchio and other bridges across the Tiber, would be left intact as long as there were no air strikes or other direct moves against the Germans leaving the metropolitan area. The Allies in turn put pressure on the partisans within the city to restrain themselves, and they did.[1]

The occasion was a political milestone. For one thing, it marked the end of the period of royal absolutism that had commenced with the firing of Mussolini. For another, it set Italy along the road that it has traveled to the present day—toward a multi-party representative government. This remarkable transformation was accomplished without a revolution or even an election. It would not be until 1946 that Italians would have an opportunity to vote, and then they would basically ratify what was accomplished in the June days of 1944.

Victor Emmanuel realized that the liberation of Rome confronted him with a dilemma. To continue as the ruler of Italy he would have to go there. But how could he face the people he had so ignominiously abandoned? In truth, the future of the country had no place for the aging monarch. The Allies were more aware of this than the king was, and they had to tell him to stay away from the city.

The king decided to retire, and made his announcement on 4 June. Marshal Badoglio, head of state since the end of Mussolini, resigned his post on the same day. He had attempted to shore up the king's position in April, by appointing a Cabinet that contained some anti-Fascist politicians. The Communist leader Palmiro Togliatti accepted a post, but many other leading politicians stayed away. Togliatti, for his part, was just obeying the Moscow line, which was predicated on the demarcation of spheres of influence in postwar Europe. Stalin was ready to assign Italy to the West, provided the West assigned such places as Romania and Hungary to him. He had recently ended Russia's official state of war with Italy and recognized the regime of Victor Emmanuel. Togliatti then showed up, ending his long exile in Russia, coming into Naples aboard an American destroyer.

As it happened, though, the West was not altogether sold on the monarchy. But the issue was still very fluid in 1943, and Moscow was ready to acquiesce in anything the British and Americans might come up with. Stalin even agreed that he should not have a vote on the Allied policymaking board, the Allied Control Commission (ACC), and was content only to have a liaison man on the scene. This was a precedent which would then be held up to the Allies as the Red Army rolled into Romania not long thereafter. Russia would control the occupation of that country (which, like Italy, would then change sides) and the Allies could send observers and liaison men. This *quid pro quo* did not end, of course, in Romania. It provided the framework for the later division of Europe into two hostile camps, marked off by the infamous Iron Curtain of the Cold War era.

This unexpected help from the Communist side, with Togliatti suddenly materializing to take his seat in an absolutist government, was not enough to save Victor Emmanuel. Neither was the still more important help given by Winston Churchill, who in February 1944 delivered a speech to the House of Commons in which he referred to the aging monarch as the rock of continuity and stability in Italian politics. He characterized any departure from the monarchy into republicanism as a leap in the dark, and suggested that it would probably result in a left-wing takeover.[2]

Churchill at the time was responding to certain signs that the king was in trouble, and he was eager to stave off a royal abdication. The very day that Victor Emmanuel left Rome, a group of pre-Mussolini era politicians got together and proclaimed the founding of the CLN, which they obviously intended to be taken for a provisional government. When the Germans rolled in during the next two days, this group promptly went underground. It didn't have much effect on events in Rome during the subsequent occupation, but the CLN's directors and their numerous followers mounted a serious challenge to the royal authority in the liberated provinces of the south.

In December, they attempted to hold a convention to lay the groundwork for a new republican constitution. The chosen site was Naples, and the Allies told them that political activity was impermissible in an active operational area. Naples was in fact the prime staging area for combat activity then in progress north of the Volturno River. The politicians then selected the somewhat quieter confines of Bari, and the Allied Military Government (AMG) acquiesced. It was stipulated, though, that there would be no radio and no audience. The meeting place, the Piccinni Theater, was even surrounded by military policemen to keep curious onlookers at bay.[3]

Such restraints might suggest that the Allies disapproved of the CLN. In fact, their major concern was with maintaining order. The CLN was still an unknown quantity, even to its own members. The original executive committee consisted of Ivanoe Bonomi and Alcide De Gasperi, two veteran legislators of the pre-Mussolini era; Meuccio Ruini, of the Democratic Labor Party, Alessandro Casati, of the Liberal Party; Ugo La Malfa, of the Action Party; Pietro Nenni, of the Socialist Party; and Mauro Scoccimaro, of the Communist Party. De Gasperi, a founder of the new Christian Democratic Party, was a restraining influence when the talk among his colleagues turned to the fate of the monarchy. With the return of Togliatti and the enunciation of the new Moscow line, he would have added support against hotheads.

The Action Party was the most militantly anti-monarchist group. This party dated back only to 1941, and, according to the OSS, lacked any clearly defined antecedents in the pre-Fascist era. Its anti-royalist and also anti-Church stance accorded with the traditional attitudes of the left-wing parties, but the Actionists did not espouse socialism in any form. Most of its membership was, in any case, too young to have been involved in the political life of Italy before Mussolini. An exception was Luigi Einaudi, a Turin publisher and probably the group's wealthiest and most influential member. An important element in the party was the veteran chiefs of the pre-Fascist General Confederation of Labor— comprising another important exception to the generally youthful membership. These people organized the April 1943 strikes in Turin and Milan, the first serious instances of labor unrest in the twenty-one-year history of the dictatorship.[4]

In fact, although the party's rank-and-file consisted of college professors and businessmen, the Actionists were much more militant than even the Socialists and Communists, prior to the founding of the CLN. They set the tone for activities on the labor front, and would quickly enjoy the wholehearted cooperation of the other parties of the left when it came to planning and directing strike activity.

A party made up of seemingly contradictory elements, the Actionists were also the most difficult to restrain during the Germans' departure from Rome. They also would become the strongest proponents within the CLN of action independent of the Allies, including the seizure of territories in the North. Yet, these contradictions in the membership would have a telling effect once the war was over. The union organizers would find a home in the Socialist ranks, and the middle-class majority would move toward the Liberals and the Republicans. The party survived the war by only a few months. Curiously, the Republicans found the CLN to be insufficiently adamant in its opposition to the king, and refused to join. Thus they joined the much less important political groups, the Trotskyite party known as the Italian Communist Movement (the "Red Flags"), and the Catholic Communists (whose name annoyed any Catholic or Communist who was not a member).

The CLN parties were each allowed to send one delegate for every province in liberated Italy—at that point (January 1944) extending northward to the vicinity of Monte Cassino on the west side of the country and Ancona on the east coast. Since voting on resolutions and motions was not weighted in any way, most of the parties (the big exception was the Labor Democrats—the smallest and newest group in the coalition) enjoyed a parity in voting. In other words, no single party dominated.

The Bari Conference did not produce factions, either, even though there was much heated debate and many impassioned speeches during the two days (28–29 January 1944) that it met. The sessions were co-chaired by a Socialist (Tito Zambone, who had spent much of the Fascist era in jail) and the Communist Alberto Cianca. A naive and unknowledgable spectator would not have suspected from the demeanor of the co-chairs that their parties had long been bitter enemies whose mutual antagonism had helped to pave the way for Mussolini's rise.

The meeting produced a resolution asking the king to step down.[5] Actionists and Socialists favored a direct repudiation of royal authority, but Christian Democrats and Liberals cautioned that this would undercut the CLN's hope for Allied support. This was good advice, insofar as the mild resolution that was passed greatly annoyed Churchill, although it was respectful enough to keep him from adopting an inflexible position, such as a public denunciation of the CLN. It also had an effect on General Eisenhower, who was still commanding operations in Italy. Eisenhower thought the CLN was showing signs of being a responsible organization. The CLN's other resolution, that it be recognized as a provisional government—either with or without the king at the helm— piqued his interest further, and he became a CLN advocate in U.S. policy circles.

The Americans, indeed, were less well-disposed toward the monarchy than were their allies, the British. Nonetheless, Victor Emmanuel scored a major political victory the following month (February) when the Allied Military Government turned over control of the southern provinces, from Sicily to Salerno, to his government. The following month, the temporary royal headquarters was moved from Brindisi to the somewhat less isolated town of Salerno. There it would remain until the capture of Rome.

The king's decision to retire, the day before Fifth Army entered Rome, was not a surrender to republicanism. It was a personal sacrifice on behalf of the monarchy and the family dynasty—the House of Savoy, Piemonte, and Sardinia, which had led Italy to unification in 1859–60. His son Umberto (namesake of Umberto I, assassinated by an anarchist in 1896) was named regent and sent to Rome. Since the royal retirement also occasioned the resignation of Marshal Badoglio as head of state (this, too, was announced on 4 June), Umberto felt lost when he arrived in Rome. Italy for the moment had no discernible government at all—other than occupation authorities in the war zones and of course Mussolini's

Social Republic, which was a chimera from the perspective of liberated Italy.

By this time the Allies were decided on the matter of the CLN and the monarchy as well. Once the war was over, the voters would decide what form of government they should have. Meanwhile, the CLN could go ahead and form a provisional government. There would be no king now that Victor Emmanuel was retired. His son Umberto would see no coronation ceremony until and unless the voters ratified the monarchy after the war. Meanwhile, he could hold forth as the Lieutenant General for the Realm (a title his father bestowed on him), and establish himself in Rome. Umberto would have no specific duties to perform, but this did not appear very unusual, since the Constitution under which his father had served for so long provided for a figurehead monarch, with actual power being vested in the various organs of government.[6]

Ivanoe Bonomi announced the formation of a new CLN government on 16 June. Bonomi, an independent with no party affiliation, assumed the office of premier. Badoglio was offered a cabinet post but refused. Over the next two months, AMG transferred government powers for the territory extending from the Naples area (but excluding Naples itself, because of its continuing role as the major entry point for supplies and manpower) all the way up to and including Rome. In September, the last important addition to the government's geographical area was made. This new frontier extended from Viterbo on the west coast to Pescara on the east—well north of Rome, but excluding Florence (for Allied operational reasons) until late in the war.

Such authority for a coalition of political parties, some of them boasting large mass following, looked very good on paper. The reality was something else, because there were few resources to govern with. AMG had done some reconstruction work, mainly to serve the immediate needs (such as for passable roads) of the armed forces, and to stave off plague and riot. But much of the southern half of Italy was still severely dislocated. A majority of men, for instance, didn't have jobs. There was a dreadful food shortage, partly the result of the country's principal granary being located in the northern plain, where the Germans held sway. Thousands were homeless—tens of thousands. Conditions had never been worse, except perhaps when Hannibal and his Carthaginians had roamed the countryside, and even that was debatable. The situation was a scandal, because the people here were, after all, liberated. The movie cameras rolled when they stood by the roadsides to greet passing Allied divisions. But the cameras did not stay to show what it was like after the army passed by.

Bonomi, the seventy-three-year-old neutral at the head of his coalition, seems to have been resigned to this situation, because he devoted his limited energies elsewhere. At one point he wrote a letter to U.S. Secretary of State Cordell Hull, complaining that the free-spending ways of the American GIs were fueling inflation. But for the most part, people were left to fend for themselves. The main energies of the CLN government went into efforts to organize the German-occupied area politically, and to root out Fascist remnants in the liberated territory.

This latter task was daunting enough, considering that Italy had spent the last twenty-two years as a one-party state. The Fascist Party was an originator of what has come to be known as totalitarianism—a system in which everything is considered political, and no organization, not even a sports team, could function without some kind of official supervision. The Fascist influence pervaded Italian society, even if the events of July 1943 showed that it had failed to take root.

In August, the government established a blacklist which barred Fascists from holding public office or serving in any police or civil service position. It also published a list of Fascist criminals, and urged citizens to come forward with information that might lead to the arrest of persons on this list. By mid-September, more than two thousand alleged political criminals had been arrested. This campaign taxed the judicial system, which had had its share of Fascist judges. In fact, AMG had set up a blacklist of its own, based on OSS reports, and completed a fairly thorough housecleaning of Fascist judges. Some of their places were being taken by practicing lawyers who did not have a Fascist background— but whose lack of experience on the bench could sometimes prove disruptive of the legal process. A few were criminal lawyers in the pay of the Mafia.

The first of the important Fascists caught in the roundup to go on trial was Pietro Caruso, police chief of Rome under the German occupation. The recent warden of Regina Coeli Prison, Donato Canetta, came to testify. As he emerged from a police car in front of the courthouse, a riotous mob broke through a protective cordon of mounted and unmounted *Carabinieri* and seized him. Canetta was beaten and dragged to the edge of the nearby Tiber River. Then he was thrown off the wall into the water. When he tried to come ashore men beat him on the head with sticks. As a large force of *Carabinieri* struggled with the mob, Canetta died under the blows and was taken to the morgue. Unknown to the crowd, this Fascist official had been in league with the underground since the Germans occupied the city, and had assisted the escape of some partisans from the prison.[7]

Most of the big-name Fascists were out of reach, settled in with Mussolini's Italian Social Republic up north. In November, however, General Mario Roatta was arrested. Army chief of staff from May until November 1943, Roatta was considered a Mussolini loyalist. Since he also had a reputation for being anti-German, he belonged to that group of Fascists who could not feel safe in either the south or the north. Roatta's trial was delayed because of complaints of ill health. At the beginning of March 1945 he was admitted to a hospital in Rome for observation. On 5 March he escaped, not to be heard of again until the war was over. For this, a mob invaded the Viminale Palace and ransacked the government offices there.

The Bonomi government's preoccupation with that half of Italy (the northern half) still under German control was the result of the fast-growing partisan movement there. Most of the partisan bands had a distinct political affiliation. Even the *Autonomi*, mainly Italian soldiers who had managed to evade the Wehrmacht at the time of the surrender, were thought to be led primarily by monarchist-leaning officers. The twin mainstays of the more clearly political partisan groups were the communists, first and foremost, and the Action Party. They outnumbered the *Autonomi* by a considerable margin and therefore raised the possibility that, given a free hand, they could carve out a strong left-wing power base in the north. (The Actionists were considered left-liberal, and the Communists represented the far left.) The Communist Party enjoyed the special pedigree of being the Fascists' worst enemy, and in the liberated territory had an estimated following of a hundred thousand, of whom twenty thousand were in the strategic port of Naples. The party's following in the north was more difficult to estimate, but in pre-Fascist times, the north had been the party's power base.

Allied Military Government was no less concerned about the political prospects in the north than was the Bonomi regime. As it happened, a counterpart of the CLN had come into existence in the north in January 1944. That was the same month that the CLN had coalesced into a real political entity at the previously discussed Bari Conference. The northern group was dubbed the Committee of National Liberation for Upper Italy (CLNAI). Its presiding officer was Alfredo Pizzono. Unlike Bonomi, Pizzono had no political background; but, like his counterpart in the CLN, he was regarded as politically neutral. He was a banker who found it not overly distasteful to hobnob with leftists during his non-working hours in Milan.

In August, Bonomi appointed Gen. Raffaele Cadorna as coordinator of all partisan activity in the north, with the prior consent of the CLNAI.

Cadorna parachuted into a field near Milan and promptly took up his duties, thus establishing the Rome government's authority over the partisan bands of the north. At about this time the CLNAI issued a proclamation declaring its adherence to democratic principles, and its abhorrence of *"reazione"*—apparently a reference to the monarchy. Its political program, in other words, was indistinguishable from that of the Bonomi government in Rome, and the group seemed quite happy to consider itself simply a branch of that government. This status was not formalized until December, in the Rome Protocols, when the CLNAI was recognized as the government's delegate in north Italy.

The Protocols coincided with a commitment on the part of the Allies to assist the CLNAI and the partisan bands in the common struggle against the Germans. That this commitment was long in coming—barely six months before the end of the war, and after the partisans had been fighting the Wehrmacht for more than a year (since partisan warfare actually pre-dated the establishment of the CLNAI)—reflects the intense distrust on the Allies' part of the CLNAI and the partisans.

Churchill had little use for the Bonomi government. He once referred to it as "this extremely untrustworthy band of non-elected comebacks," his main objection, of course, being its decidedly anti-monarchist viewpoint. That the minions of this regime should be roaming the occupied territories with weapons supplied by the Allies—weapons which might later be turned against the adherents of the House of Savoy—was a prospect he did not relish. While the Americans did not share his concern for the monarchy, they did share Churchill's fear that armed Communist partisans might stage a revolution once the war was over. OSS reports of an impending move in that direction by the Greek Communist partisans—who had been generously supplied with Allied weapons—made more of an impression than Togliatti's seeming cooperativeness.

The Caserta Agreement, signed at Fifth Army headquarters outside Naples, committed the Allies to supply the partisan bands, virtually all of which by now were clearly affiliated with the CLNAI and, by extension, with the Bonomi government in Rome. The CLNAI's military arm, the Volunteer Corps for Liberation (CVL), was designated as the executor of the Allies' military orders. In newly liberated areas, CLNAI would have the right to nominate local government officials, but AMG would have the final say on whether those officials would actually be allowed to take office.

The agreement might never have transpired were it not for the growing impact that partisan operations were having in the north. The Allies seem not to have especially welcomed partisan activity. Negotiations at

Caserta were difficult and prolonged, and the agreement was in fact something of a compromise. But it did effectively place the CLNAI and the partisans under the direct control of Allied military commanders. OSS and British intelligence operatives were already keeping a close watch on the bands. A British liaison officer, Colonel Temple, was flown in to maintain an official watch over adherence to the pact signed at Caserta. When he was killed during a German mop-up operation, he was replaced by British colonel John M. Stevens, who was later joined by Maj. Basil Davidson, direct from similar liaison duties with Tito's army in Yugoslavia.

The agreement also stipulated that the partisans would turn in their weapons at Allied checkpoints once the war was over. This included not only weapons supplied by the Allies, but also weapons of the Italian army carried over from the surrender, and captured German weapons—the materials that were in fact the partisans' mainstay of resistance up to this point and, as it happened, beyond. Coupled with the Communists' devotion to the Moscow line on spheres of influence, the Caserta Agreement effectively defanged all radical elements on the wartime political scene.

Meanwhile, as noted earlier, people went hungry whether they lived in the north or the south. AMG and the Allied Control Commission recognized a need to alleviate the hardships of the people, but the large and populous territory of liberated Italy presented a daunting challenge. But Great Britain did not place Italian relief programs high on its list of priorities. At one point British officials complained that Italy was better fed than Greece, a country that had never sunk British ships in the Mediterranean or attacked British soldiers in the Sahara Desert. This was not saying much, since it was the Germans who were responsible for feeding most of the Greeks until very late in the war. Britain also refused to divert any of its merchant ships to the transport of grain from the United States to Italy.

There had been a time, not far past, when Italy had taken part in an effort to starve Britain into submission, and Britons remembered going hungry in 1940–42 while their ships sank to the bottom in incredible numbers. That country was still standing in line for food aid, and American CARE packages would still be going there two years after the war was over. The net effect of all this is that responsibility for feeding the people of liberated Italy (or more exactly, making up the deficit, estimated at a third of total food requirements, left by local farming resource limitations) fell to the Americans. They were already helping Britain—and to a much lesser extent, Russia and China—with food.

The problem in Italy was exacerbated in 1943 by drought conditions that prevailed in the south, and especially in Sicily, during the growing season.

In normal times, there would have been more shipments from the granaries of the Po Valley in the north, which normally produced a surplus. But those areas came under effective German control in late summer. Italians hadn't even seen serious food rationing until 1942 (about the same time that Americans did), but now there was suddenly a real emergency in the southern provinces, and especially in Sicily.

The first response was to ship in six thousand tons of grain from the military reserves stored in North Africa. Additional emergency supplies proved difficult to come by. In Messina, during the long winter of 1943–44, as the Cassino-Anzio campaign unfolded, more than a hundred people died of starvation.[8] The toll was only slightly less in Syracuse. On the mainland, in Apulia, farmers were regularly accosted by hungry townspeople who accused them of hoarding, and violence was not uncommon. At the Circo preserves plant in Naples, it was deemed practical for all concerned that the workers should receive their pay in jars of jam, which they could easily use to pay their rent or purchase other necessities.[9] The only other Neapolitans who had the opportunity to bring food home from the job were the stevedores who unloaded American Liberty ships. The *Camorra* (Naples' version of the Mafia) put together a logistical system that would spare dockworkers the risk of having canned C-rations hidden in their clothing. Some workers were caught anyway with canned goods stashed in hidden pockets, when the MPs occasionally staged shakedown inspections at shift changes. But they had the option of exchanging the little notes they received for being part of the smuggling system (and no dockworker could avoid taking part) at any of the black-market outlets in exchange for food.

When refrigerated ships brought in meat for the soldiers, the contraband included, along with the ever-present cans of C-rations, everything from hot dogs to steaks. The workers never qualified for the best cuts, though. These went to the well-connected—especially to the *Camorra* membership, which appreciated that it was just emerging from a long period of hard times, when its role in Neapolitan society had largely been preempted by the local Fascist organization.

Most Neapolitans were desperately hungry, despite the fact that the port was an inexhaustible cornucopia of all kinds of supplies for the troops. The local farm country, noted for its cash crops—oranges, tomatoes, and so forth—had been severely disrupted by the Salerno campaign, and in any case was not a grain producer. Salerno province itself was among the hungriest areas in all Italy, as the onset of autumn saw the end of local fresh vegetable supplies. The first winter of Allied control saw the bread ration as low as five hundred grams a day.

Worst off were certain Sicilian cities. Catania, Syracuse and Messina, the main cities on the eastern side of the island and also the most heavily damaged, seem also to have been last in line for the scarce American food handouts. The island as a whole suffered desperately, and food riots were particularly rife in Palermo. On one occasion, American soldiers had to fight off a surging mob outside a waterfront warehouse, where grain had just been offloaded from a Liberty Ship. When this happened, the Allied Military Government was still headquartered in Palermo. This unrest was noted in German intelligence reports, including the *"blutig"* attacks involving American soldiers.[10] The Germans also heard that there were instances of people starving to death, and they saw to it that the news of such things was trumpeted forth in the northern press. Such stories do not seem to have made them any less hated there, and it is likely that people discounted such stories as propaganda.

The onset of hunger in liberated Italy came as a shock to all of the citizens. The appearance of American and British soldiers in the communities signalled, for most, that the war was at last over for them. The war had swept past, or through, their cities and towns. The hated Fascist regime was gone, and now it was time to rebuild and shape a new life. For those without sons in the armed forces, the burdens of the great conflict had heretofore been relatively light. Italians ate at least as well as their Axis partners north of the Alps until mid-1943. They were among the best fed—or least poorly fed—people in Europe at the time, and certainly better off than the British.

So this, coming in the wake of liberation, was something of a shock. As month followed month in 1944, and more areas and more people were liberated, the enormity of the problem finally seeped in at the White House in Washington. The American chief of staff, General Marshall, was in receipt of intelligence from Armed Forces Headquarters at Caserta that the food shortage could undermine Allied authority in occupied areas. This was a serious matter, for one singular advantage that the Allies enjoyed over the Germans was that the latter were faced with a fast-growing insurrectionist movement in the north, while in liberated areas deliberate acts of sabotage or attacks on Allied soldiers were extremely rare.

But if it was correct that as much as 50 percent of a shipment of military food supplies passing though Naples was not finding its way into soldiers' stomachs, the overall food crisis had to be construed as a threat to the war effort. (The problem here was not just pilferage, but soldiers' trading food for valuables and services, available to them at a very generous rate of exchange.) There was also the issue of Italy's political stability. Southern provinces were being transferred from military control to civilian Italian control in accordance with a timetable that seemed advantageous to the Italians. But what could people think of the CLN and its mainstream parties—including the parties that expected to govern in the future, when the war was over—when the CLN presided over hunger and starvation?

Politically closer to home, at the White House, was a press conference called by U.S. Representative Claire Booth Luce at the end of a tour of liberated territory. A platoon of newsmen, representing all of the major daily newspapers of the United States, was treated to an account by the outraged congresswoman that was truly embarrassing: emaciated children, young girls driven to prostitution, scenes that might invite comparison with the Warsaw Ghetto. What kind of liberation was this? she asked.[11]

It was 1944, an election year in the United States. President Roosevelt could pass this off as Republican political hyperbole, but would millions of newspaper readers do so? Mayor LaGuardia of New York chimed in with excerpts from letters written home by soldiers in Italy, passed on, apparently, by their families. Italian-American organizations took up the issue. The liberation of Rome had been one of the crowning events of the war, but at the Democratic and Republican party conventions convened during the summer, that moment was being overshadowed by the issue of living conditions in liberated Italy. The Italian-American vote was important in several key states, not the least of which was New York, where Roosevelt's Republican opponent, Thomas Dewey, was governor.

Winston Churchill and his Italophobic foreign minister, Anthony Eden, were far from elated when the news reached them that emergency runs of U.S. grain were to reach Italy by late summer.[12] But they appreciated the political exigencies on the American scene which lay behind the White House's decision. They also appreciated that such increases might be only temporary. This was not only because the American elections would take place on 4 November, but also because the impending liberation of France and the Low countries would place unprecedented strains on the Americans' ability to provide emergency food relief. Then it would become necessary to feed even the Germans.

The situation would in fact remain desperate until the enemy was driven out of the Po Valley. Plans called for a major push against the Germans' Gothic Line shortly before the U.S. elections, and a possible breakthrough into the open country. There, it was widely assumed, Allied air and armored superiority would produce a quick rout of the Germans, who would speed northward to the relative safety of the Alpine Barrier. But spring planting would have to await the spring. And harvest time seemed a long way off, even if the war was over by then.

This desperate situation was made worse by the presence of a horde of refugees in the areas south of the fighting front. AMG's Refugee Field Section estimated that there were two hundred thousand in the Fifth Army section alone, as of March 1944. The capture of Rome, three months later, meant an additional hundred thousand. There were at least half as many in the Adriatic and Eastern Apennines areas that were the responsibility of the British. That meant close to a half-million. Some of these, to be sure, were from southern Italy in any case—people who had fled their homes before the advancing battlefront only to have it catch up. But such were only a small minority, since the average citizen looked forward to the arrival of the Allies, and sought only to lie low, close to home, until the big moment came.[13]

Most of the refugees fell into one of two categories: They were either Italian soldiers who had escaped the German dragnet at the time of the surrender; or they were northerners who for some reason found life under the German occupation especially perilous. Among the soldiers was the greater part of a division that had made its way across the Adriatic from Albania, along with parts of other divisions that were stationed in Greece or Yugoslavia when the surrender was announced in September 1943. Virtually none of these men returned to Italy overland. All had braved the waters of the Adriatic aboard often unseaworthy skiffs and small motorboats, or, if they came across on military transports, the machine guns and bombs of German divebombers. Several of the latter were sunk, with heavy loss of life. The safest crossings were made aboard confiscated Albanian, Greek, and Yugoslav fishing boats, which could cover much of the distance in a single night. Some of these vessels were so overloaded with soldiers, however, that they foundered in deep water.

The ranks of the dislocated were swelled further by teenage runaways, orphans, escaped jail inmates, Fascist party members who feared their neighbors' vengeful wrath, and survivors of the villages and towns (such as San Pietro, Cisterna, Anzio, and Cassino) destroyed by war. There was no place for these people to be resettled. Those who stayed at home were often living in ruins, or were isolated from the outside world by cratered roadways, downed telephone lines, and the disappearance of the postal service.

Rehabilitation of the existing population centers and their inhabitants took top priority, and there were few enough resources on hand for that. So, while AMG had its Refugee Field Section, there was little for it to do. The refugees were pretty much on their own for the duration of the war. It seems that the main effort was toward keeping them out of the way, off the roads, and even away from the towns, since there was a growing problem of thievery and holdups.

And so it was that, in liberated Italy, nearly half a million people milled about aimlessly from mountain to mountain, valley to valley; feared and shunned by the miserable inhabitants of the villages they passed; sometimes attacked, sometimes attacking. They lived in caves and behind rocks. They lived on the ground. They were the flotsam and jetsam of war.

The best that can be said for the food and the refugee situations is that matters did not get completely out of hand. While malnutrition was endemic, and starvation not unknown, widespread famine and raging epidemic diseases were avoided, though just barely. Liberated Italy fared better in such less urgent matters as transportation and power supply. By late 1944, with the fighting front some seventy miles north of Rome, and most of the territory (Naples being the main exception) south of Rome now in the hands of the provisional government, nearly half the electrical power was restored.[14] Coal ships embarked from Philadelphia and Norfolk were stockpiling the basic fuel of the power plants even before many of them were repaired—and more than a few cities got through the war without damage to their main utility systems. At Naples, though, mountains of coal were being built up even as the electrical generators and line equipment from the United States were being installed, to replace machinery thoroughly destroyed by the Germans in early October 1943.

Nearly all the large cities had electricity by this time. Lesser urban centers had to wait, often until the end of the war. The smaller towns were on nobody's list of priorities, and some of the remote mountain villages had never had electricity. Smaller cities, though, even with power systems intact, usually experienced a total cutoff as scarce fuel was hoarded by the cities considered of strategic importance. The situation would not improve noticeably until more than a year after the war was over, mainly because Italy did not have significant coal or oil resources of its own.

Repair of damaged and destroyed roads took precedence over all reconstruction projects after harbor repair and basic big city infrastructure. An asphalt plant was built to expedite work in this area, and rock crushing machines were brought in from the United States.[15]

Small towns and villages were not totally ignored, however. The Allied Military Government always appointed an officer to serve as Allied overseer in each one. Fifth Army assiduously sought out Italian speakers for these interesting assignments. Such men were virtual dictators. Even though they filed all kinds of reports, it was impossible for AMG to keep track of their doings. John Hersey's novel *A Bell for Adano*, perhaps the most famous literary product of the Italian campaign, details the exploits of one of these representatives. Its hero is, authentically enough, an Italian-American. The major concern of the inhabitants of Adano is not food or jobs, but the replacement of a church bell that had been confiscated by the Fascists for melting down into weaponry. A bell is obtained from an American supply ship—named, aptly, for an Italian-American hero of World War I (a war in which Italy and the United States fought on the same side, as they were now doing once again). Some mules are diverted for use in hauling this bell—an event that draws the unwelcome attention of AMG higher-ups, who wonder why the mules aren't carrying ammunition to Allied soldiers fighting up in the mountains (the usual function of army mules, animals which had proved indispensable during combat in Italy). The hero is summarily removed from his post, to the great sorrow of the grateful townspeople.

Remarkably, from the very inception of this lonely assignment (during the Sicilian campaign), it was quickly realized that Allied officers could live in complete safety as overseers among an erstwhile enemy population without aides, bodyguards, or armed garrisons, and possessing no means of self-defense except the pistol each was allowed to carry.

In the British sector, job experience apparently counted more than political coloration, and there were occasions of popular unrest when Fascists were appointed as interim mayors in anticipation of the end of Occupation government. There was a widespread suspicion that this situation could be traced back to Winston Churchill, whose dislike for the Italian politicians of the Provisional Government was well known. His main complaint was that most of them—and their parties—were ready to scuttle the monarchy. Churchill was an ardent monarchist. So, it was thought, seeing these politicians as a greater threat to the monarchy than the Fascists would ever be, Churchill opted for the latter. This was political scuttlebut, but it became an issue when one of FDR's closest advisers, U.S. Secretary Treasurer Henry Morgenthau, accused the British (not Churchill directly) of using Fascists thusly as a shield for the Italian monarchy.[16] In Potenza, one veteran Fascist official was killed by a mob following his reinstatement. Morgenthau's criticism was aired shortly after this incident, during an Allied Council meeting in Washington.[17]

Having a job in liberated Italy was a distinction belonging to only a third of the workforce. In other words, unemployment was twice as high as it had been in the United States in the depths of the Great Depression. The economy of southern Italy was nearly moribund, an indication not only of combat-related dislocations but of the region's dependence on the north, still under German control. The north was not only the source of the country's basic food supply, but also its industrial center—the producer of most of the machinery, equipment, and parts that people in the south needed. The north was also the home of some of the country's major financial institutions—major suppliers of credit and insurance. Finally, it was the prime market for the products (especially agricultural) of the south. Southern Italy could not really function without the north.

Even those lucky enough to have jobs still experienced major hardships. During the twenty-two months that this situation persisted (until the end of the war), the value of Occupation *lire* that workers were paid with was sliced in half. Pay scales, however, lagged behind this inflation by more than 50 percent. If a man had money in the bank when the Occupation *lire* were introduced, his savings were wiped out by an official exchange rate of one new *lire* for a hundred old ones. So even a worker had nothing to fall back on, given prices that meant a month's pay for a pair of shoes, or a week's pay for a trip to the butcher shop (assuming an open butcher shop could be found).[18]

Prices were also subject to unaccountable fluctuations and wide variations from city to city. Rome became noted as the "low price" city—a grim irony to most of its inhabitants, who could not afford much more than a bread and water diet for the duration of the war. But olive oil, a basic cooking necessity in Italy, cost twice as much in Florence as it did in Rome, and so did many other staples.[19]

Economic hardships were made worse by the requisitioning policies of the Allied armed forces. Such policies were far from unique; they seem typical of all wars in all places. Soldiers would requisition vehicles, mules, even household furnishings, and issue pieces of scrip in return. The bits of paper could be redeemed at some ill-defined headquarters at an indeterminate future date for compensation. In practice, the scrip often had to be checked against the very inadequate equipment records of the unit that had done the requisitioning, which entailed endless delay and very often a determination that no payment was due.[20]

Living in a combat zone—as most Italians did for at least a brief while before the occupation settled in—provided some advance preparation for the niceties of requisitioning. This came in the form of looting by the soldiers. German soldiers were well behaved on this score until it was time to evacuate an area. Citizen complaints were dealt with seriously by the German officers. Retreat, though, invariably meant good-bye forever as far as the Germans were concerned. Soldiers coming out of combat were especially callous with regard to citizens' property rights. They wasted little time in the hovels of the poor farmers, however. A Wehrmacht trooper in retreat was invariably drawn to whatever substantial houses and villas stood along his path or anywhere near it. Unless Allied forces were in hot pursuit (a rare event) he would give the place a good working over. Floorboards would be pried loose, walls broken open, and upholstery torn out of chairs in search of the hidden wealth of the inhabitants. Evidence that others had been there first was no deterrent if anything at all was intact within. By the time successive waves of soldiers had completed their passage, such a house would be a complete ruin. Then the first Allied soldiers on the scene would complete any search the Germans had failed to complete. They would be especially watchful for any freshly turned earth—a sign that a resident had made a hurried effort to bury some valuables. Soldiers were ready to dig at the slightest hint. As a result, many a wrecked villa also had "foxholes" around it, to more or less complete the picture of devastation.

Memoirs of life in the combat zones are much more common than memoirs of life under the occupation, or of life under the Provisional Government, after AMG relinquished its control. The best of the combat memoirs from a civilian point of view is Countess Origo's story of the front as it moved northward through Tuscany, following the liberation of Rome. First the partisans became ubiquitous, then German mop-up operations swept through her estate time and time again, always with the threat that she might be arrested for harboring partisan weapons or personnel. Then German officers and a small support unit settled in, remaining for several weeks. One day, seeing ambulances tearing along the roadways, truckloads of soldiers rumbling past, and a Liberator bomber crashing in flames, she asked a German where the front was. His surprised response was that the front was right there where they stood. Indeed, soon there were artillery shells whistling overhead, and the boom of guns came ever closer, lasting through that night and on through the next. Troopers of the 1st Parachute Division, which had heroically re-pelled the February offensive against Monte Cassino, began straggling through. Some of them showed a less heroic side by looting the house. Their general aspect, from Origo's point of view, was that of an army of cynics—soldiers turned hoodlums. It was good to keep out of their way.

And it was good to see the first Americans, even if some behaved wildly. A contrasting story involves the proprietor of a commercial wine cellar in the Alban Hills, just south of Rome, at the time of the Anzio breakout in 1944. The Germans had remained unaware of this subterranean wine store. The happy merchant gave a free glass of wine to the occupants of a Jéep. These were the first Allied soldiers he had ever laid eyes on. They were far from being the last. The merchant had let on that he was guard-ing a commercial cellar, and this information apparently spread like wild-fire, presumably with the aid of a field radio. Every soldier that came by demanded wine for his canteen. Finally, the next day, a truck pulled up. It was carrying a large, empty water tank. The last contents of the wine cellar were requisitioned with the aid of a hose.

Incidents like this were good for the morale of the soldiers, even as they were bad for the morale of the citizenry. For the soldiers, requisi-tioning was a kind of sport; from their point of view, if it was for the good of the unit, it seemed morally justified.

A last, curious episode in the governance of liberated Italy should be related. Before the invasion of Sicily, a Naval Intelligence unit ("F Sec-tion," based at the Federal office center at 90 Church Street in New York) contacted certain Mafia figures. These included Charles (Lucky) Luciano, then in prison; Vito Genovese, a chief of the New York syndi-cate; and a few residents of Licata, Sicily. The latter remain anonymous to this day, but they apparently were persons who had been deported from the United States as undesirable aliens. Contact was also made, via Genovese, with the head of the Sicilian Mafia, Calogero Vizzini.[21]

The exact purposes and results of these contacts have never been re-vealed, but Genovese turned up in Sicily, once the invasion was well underway, wearing a colonel's uniform and designated an unofficial ad-viser to AMG. One can only speculate that the U.S. 3rd Division's easy landing at Licata, where the shore batteries remained silent, even while the invasion force basked in the bright beams of several onshore search-lights (until, one by one, the lights were shot out), was assisted by a Mafia-directed Fifth Column.

It can only be speculated, too, that Governor Dewey's commutation of Luciano's life sentence in 1946 was related somehow to services ren-dered by his associates and underlings. (Luciano, promptly expelled as an undesirable alien, spent the remainder of his life in Italy.) One thing that is certain is that the Allied invasion brought the Sicilian Mafia out from under the thrall of two decades of Fascist rule. The totalitarian Mussolini regime had no tolerance for secret societies of any kind—not even for inoffensive ones that minded their own business. The Mafia was a secret society, but it did not mind its own business. For the Fascists, it was second only to the Communist Party as a subversive force. Moreover, it was a direct rival for money and power at the local level. The end of Fascism could be seen only as the end of a dark age for Italy's Mafiosi and for their Neapolitan counterparts, the *Camorra*.

The tremendous scale of the problem of governing a war-torn country may help explain why an Allied agency would look anywhere for assistance—even to the ranks of organized crime. The project was not administered at the highest levels—Eisenhower and his colleagues were not directly involved, and they may have been unaware of it. But it was not completely contained within the precincts of Naval Intelligence. New York District Attorney Frank Morgan knew about it, and tried to forestall any deal with Vito Genovese in 1943. The latter's arrival in Sicily later that year certainly required the collaboration of other military agencies.

About the same time this deal was hatched, American expatriate poet Ezra Pound was indicted for treason. Long after Churchill and others in the English-speaking world had ceased to admire Mussolini, Pound continued to lionize the Fascist dictator. He and fellow poet T. S. Eliot had learned Italian years before so as to read Dante in the original. Pound finally settled in Italy. When the Allies invaded, they found one of the offerings on Unliberated Radio to be a weekly evening half-hour lecture by Pound.

The program ignored military matters. Unlike Axis Sally and Lord Haw-Haw, Pound never advised his Allied listeners that their only hope for survival was either to go home immediately or surrender. Instead, Pound treated his listeners to news that an international money conspiracy had forced the war on the Axis. There were 110 broadcasts in all, each beginning with an avowal that nothing would be said that was "incompatible with [Pound's] duties as a citizen of the United States of America." In any case, the lectures had not commenced with the Allied invasion, but dated back as far as 1941, when only Americans with short-wave radios could hear them. The broadcasts did not long survive *il Duce*'s overthrow in 1943. Pound himself seems to have lost heart once the Allies reached the mainland, although he did record speeches (never broadcast) in 1943–44 for use on Radio Milan. Pound was arrested at the end of the war and spent most of the remainder of his long life in a mental institution in Washington, D.C. Justice Department lawyers had concluded that the treason charge could be thrown out of court. But it was unthinkable to Washington officials that a noted author could remain on the loose who might continue to extol the virtues of *il Duce* and repeat his radio references to Churchill, Roosevelt, and Stalin as "the three murderers."[22]

Pound may have been crazy, but so too was the politics of chaos as practiced in a society unhinged by war from 1943 to 1945. Yet it is possible to end this discussion on a positive note, with a reference to the Allied concern for Italy's cultural heritage. This concern has already been noted, with reference to the decision—costly, in military terms—to respect Rome's claim to status as an open city. Fifth Army had a Monument, Fine Arts and Archives office in Naples. The State Department in Washington also set up a commission, headed by Supreme Court Justice Owen J. Roberts, whose job was to prepare guides to important cultural sites. These were distributed to U.S. division commanders, as an aid in avoiding unnecessary damage to cultural and historical artifacts. They were used also by AMG in occupied territory, so that buildings containing rare art works could be spared from looting, and to assure that bulldozers and the like would not become careless when operating around important places.

These arrangements were already in place before the great controversy that followed the bombing of Monte Cassino. The railyard bombing at Rome had already highlighted the importance of such safeguards for general morale. The damage done to the historic papal summer residence at Castel Gandolfo, during the Anzio campaign, also underlined the need for careful efforts in this realm. Pius XII himself let it be known that the residence was at the time occupied by refugees—who were also the only casualties of the bombing. Even Cardinal Spelman of New York offered public criticism of this episode.[23]

General Clark, on hearing that the ancient monastery at Capaccio had been heavily damaged by Allied artillery during the Naples campaign, took personal charge of a fund-raising effort to help repair the damage. *Stars and Stripes* advertised for contributions. The abbot expressed his appreciation with a present to Clark.

CHAPTER SIX

LIFE AND DEATH UNDER THE SWASTIKA

Il Duce's dramatic rescue from Gran Sasso was quickly followed by the founding of the Italian Social Republic. The Repubblica held sway across northern Italy, beginning thirty-five miles behind the fighting front. The thirty-five-mile stretch, sometimes inching, sometimes lurching northward, was the bailiwick of the Wehrmacht and the SS. At its outset, *il Duce*'s realm encompassed two-thirds of Italy's population. It also included the nation's industrial centers, and 90 percent of its industry. The Po Valley, not liberated until the fall of Berlin, was the nation's breadbasket—and the heartland of the Repubblica.

But the Repubblica was not Mussolini's creation. It was Hitler's. *Il Duce* was just a front man; to call him a stooge, as Allied propaganda did, was not off the mark. Mussolini could not for a moment forget his total dependence on the Führer, a man he never liked nor trusted.

The Germans constantly worried that the Repubblica would nonetheless get in the way of the war effort, with unpopular moves that might arouse the population (which, as we shall see, was aroused enough already), or possibly even by treacherous negotiations with the Allies. The Repubblica enjoyed neither the trust nor the respect of the Germans. For them, it was a front, a bit of political window dressing, whose purpose was to give their various acts in northern Italy an aura of legitimacy. Considering the joy which had greeted Mussolini's initial downfall in July 1943, there were many who wondered if such window dressing was worth the bother. But the north was the original Fascist stronghold. *Il Duce*'s base was Milan, prior to his appointment as premier in 1922. Bologna had been one of the first cities to fall under the Fascist sway.

Beyond the front, which was Kesselring's area, Germany exerted its influence and control through various agencies. Gen. Rudolf Toussaint, Quartermaster General of the Armed Forces, was transferred to Italy from OKW headquarters in Berlin shortly after Mussolini's overthrow and rescue in 1943. His job was to assure that the Wehrmacht's material needs, ranging from food to ammunition, were met fully and without interruption. This involved the coordination of production in many areas and also the mobilization of the transport system to meet German needs.

The most critical areas of this very broad jurisdiction on the production side were in the armaments industries and agriculture. Gen. Hans Leyers was put in charge of war production. Italy may not have been a major power, but it did have a significant armaments industry. And not only production but even skilled workers were sometimes diverted to the Reich. A report prepared by General Toussaint on 11 May 1944, for instance, details the transfer of nine hundred shipyard workers from Genoa to yards in Rostock and Kiel, plus two thousand metal workers to the Ruhr cities.[1] These were only the latest labor drafts in a program that, since the Quartermaster General set up shop in Italy, had sent a total of seventeen thousand men to work in German industry. (This particular effort was unrelated to the draft of unskilled labor or the deportation to Germany of workers for punitive reasons. The Germans had a separate agency for this.)

The same report details the shipment of a half-million tons of coal (remarkable for a country that imported nearly all of its coal); over seven million tons of bauxite for the manufacture of aluminum; twenty-four thousand pistols; ten thousand rifles; a hundred pieces of medium and light artillery; and eight hundred machine guns—all made in Italy.[2] Other sources indicate that Fiat was turning out an average of fifty motor vehicles a day for the Germans, and also that hundreds of aircraft engines were made or repaired in Italian plants, which also manufactured during the Occupation nearly a hundred complete fighter planes, of German design. Albert Speer, Minister of Armaments in War Production and by now the Führer's closest confidante, had a Colonel Aschoff resident in Milan to help coordinate these efforts on the part of Leyers and Toussaint.

On the food supply front, Baron von Elkart endeavored to superimpose elements of collectivism on the farm country. Quotas were set and fixed prices paid by official middlemen, in the manner of the Stalinist system in Russia, with the official buyers having first priority and free market sales strictly controlled to the point where they became negligible. No effort was made to draw the analogy with Soviet collectivism; the system dovetailed, however, with *il Duce*'s belated rediscovery of Fascism's social mission—specifically, its ideological leanings toward state socialism.

The Germans were not only interested in food for their soldiers. Following their initial conquests in Eastern Europe, they had quickly gotten accustomed to obtaining much of their food supplies from there, even to the point of sharply reducing the ranks of German farmers via diversion to other industries and the military draft. The tide on that front began to turn at the beginning of 1943, and a last, somewhat attenuated harvest was all that could be expected from the east in 1944.

In that year, Italy exported to Germany a quarter of all its rice, fruit, meat and fish production, a sixth of its sugar production (from sugar beets), a tenth of its wine and a tenth of its egg production. Additional amounts of all of these items—a somewhat lesser but indeterminate total—was diverted for use by the Wehrmacht in Italy. Italian wheat was also diverted to feed the soldiers, but none was exported to Germany. In fact, a tenth of the armed forces' wheat supply was actually brought in from other occupied areas.[3]

There was no hunger in the north. The main problem for people living there was inflated food prices, which did result in deprivation for many and which also helped to trigger numerous instances of labor unrest. But since Germany had control over Italy's breadbasket until the very last days of the war, the pursuit of a flexible policy on food supply was always a realistic option. Berlin wanted war production from the Italians. It also wanted to minimize the distractions of the partisan movement. And there was the interest in shoring up Mussolini's republic.

The net effect was that northern Italy was probably the best-fed of all the occupied lands. Italy was, after all, an ally of Germany. The putative reason for the Germans' presence was, in the ultimate interests of Germany's own security, the defense of this ally to the south.

After a year as the man responsible for assuring that all the Wehrmacht's matériel needs were met, General Toussaint was succeeded in August 1944 by Gen. Karl Wolff. The complex logistical system that Toussaint had set in place would not be tampered with for the duration of the war, and the quartermaster general—whose title in Italy was Military Plenipotentiary—went on to still more demanding assignments on both the Eastern and Western fronts.

Wolff was not a supply specialist. He was in the top echelon of the SS hierarchy, and the only man in that security organization who stood above him was Heinrich Himmler. Wolff had been a member—possibly the most influential member—of Himmler's personal staff prior to being sent to Italy as director of security for the entire area outside Allied control. Mussolini himself deferred to Wolff's authority, and it was Wolff who set the rules on telephone access by officials of the Repubblica, and who decided that *il Duce* alone could have unrestricted use of the telephones.

The SS chief did not give up his security job when he replaced Toussaint. It would seem that he was therefore weighted down with excessive responsibilities. The only explanation for this would be that Toussaint had set up a network that was able to run itself, more or less; and that the one pressing need in that supply system was in the area of security, mainly against attacks by partisan bands. Wolff in fact found himself increasingly preoccupied with partisan activities, which evolved from the status of a nuisance in 1943 to a major threat by August 1944. The things that made this possible—more than anything else—were the Germans' ruthless policy of conscripting labor and the Repubblica's program of registering young men for the military draft.

The German labor mobilization operated on two levels. On the one hand, there was the Todt Organization, which rounded up workers for local projects. The biggest single Todt project was construction of the Gothic Line, the Wehrmacht's last defense against the Allied advance. The Gothic Line was more or less complete by August 1944, by which time the Allies were preparing to challenge it.

But this did not mean any serious letting up in the Germans' demand for local labor. As Allied bombing raids grew more intense, there was constant demand to repair roads and clear rubble out of those city streets designated as main military routes. Trains and trucks had to be loaded and unloaded. Repair of the railroad rights-of-way became so pressing a problem that some workers were even brought in from Germany—men considered well-trained in track maintenance and repair.

The other and still larger level of German labor conscription was for workers to be deported, usually for service in German factories but also for clearing bomb damage in German cities and the repair of German roads. Ultimate responsibility for this program rested with Fritz Sauckel, a veteran leader of the Nazi Party. His principal agent *(Sonderbeau-*

ftragter) in Italy was Gen. Otto Zimmermann, who operated out of Turin, close to the giant Fiat plants.

By the end of 1943, there were 280,000 Italians working in Germany.[4] This number included volunteers and special-skilled conscripts from the army divisions that were interned after Italy's surrender in September, and it also includes Italians, numbering about a third of the total, who were working in Germany when the two countries were staunch allies. One year later, Mussolini cited a figure of 786,000 in a speech broadcast over the radio and widely reported in the northern press.[5] In sum, half a million Italian workers were sent to Germany in 1944.

Il Duce's citation, even though widely reported, was not intended to make the people feel proud of his efforts in behalf of the Axis alliance. Rather, it was part of a litany of woe intended to show why the new Repubblica was having such difficulty accomplishing anything. The official records of the regime indicate that Mussolini spent more time pursuing deportee-related issues than anything else. The fate of the interned soldiers was particularly galling to him, but the steady movement northward—under duress—of Italian civilians was also a thorn in the side of the Axis partnership. At the outset of his Republican government, he succeeded in gaining assurances that the *Carabinieri,* Italy's paramilitary national police, would not be deported en masse.[6] This move followed the disbanding, by mutual consent between *il Duce* and German officials (most notably, General Wolff of the SS) of the *Carabinieri* as an institution of doubtful loyalty to the Axis cause. It was also agreed at the commencement of the Repubblica that Italian soldiers in Italy, even if (as most of them were) returned to civilian life, would not then be rounded up for labor service in Germany.[7] In fact, such men ceased to be differentiated from the remainder of the population in very short order, but it was the last concession that *il Duce* would receive for his efforts, which persisted until the last days of the war.

One can imagine that the demands of the Todt Organization for local labor service, the Repubblica's interest in laying the groundwork for a new army with a draft registration program, and finally General Zimmermann's deportation juggernaut, might have come into mutual competition at some points. Actual problems between the Todt Organization and Zimmermann were minimal, for a couple of reasons. First, work under the Todt projects tended to be short-term, with the major exception of the Gothic Line, completed by August 1944. Generally, able-bodied men were rounded up for local needs and many or most of them were turned loose when a local project was completed. The system was very casual, even if Todt administrators did see fit to publish a company paper called *Forced Labor*—something that suggests a stable labor force, until we realize that few except Germans read it.[8] In an extremely casual case, a man might be conscripted to clear bomb rubble out of an avenue for a day, and then sent on his way when darkness fell—although such an assignment might more likely have originated with local military authorities.

In addition, Todt work was recognized as necessary work, and the Todt Organization enjoyed an excellent reputation within the Wehrmacht. That reputation rested not only on such things as tank traps and bunkers, but also on lounges, the conversion of private buildings into mess halls and barracks, and the preparation of headquarters complexes—all the things that made life for the German soldier less Spartan.

The Zimmermann/Sauckel operation, by contrast, played for keeps. Italian shipyard workers and metals craftsmen and others with strategic skills were readily avoided by the Todt Organization in its labor roundups. Hence they were available to the Zimmermann apparatus at all times. Once gone, they would not be seen again for the duration of the war. The same applied to all others caught in the deportation system. All would be "for the duration" withdrawals from the labor pool, and barring a major population drawdown, they would not be missed by Todt.

Also, the Zimmermann office had the special responsibility of invoking deportation as punishment for labor offenses, especially strikes. There was no dearth of these in the north, and the Nazis never had to wait long for the opportunity to stage a punitive roundup for transport to Germany.

The long years of the Mussolini regime, commencing in 1922, had been marked by very few labor stoppages. It was a record of which *il Duce* was proud, for it indicated that a principal mission of Fascism— the elimination of divisive influences in society, most importantly in labor-management relations—was being accomplished. To an opponent of Fascism, of course, that success could be understood in terms of the effectiveness of the secret police and other coercive instruments of the regime.

March 1943 saw the most serious crack in the edifice of Fascist commonalty to appear in twenty-two years. Workers at the Fiat plants in and around Turin went on strike. It was the first real indication of an erosion of support for the Mussolini government—the beginning of the end for *il Duce*. The strike was ended quickly amidst cries of "treason" and "Communist subversion" in the Fascist press, with modest pay increases for the workers. The concessions were widely interpreted as a sign of weakness, although the impending collapse of the North African campaign was sign enough.

The first strike under the German military occupation and the period of the Repubblica came in November 1943, again at Fiat but joined by a sizable number of other industrial concerns, especially around Turin. Considering the vast changes that had overtaken the country in the interim, it is remarkable that the official response to this new outbreak was not unlike the response to the first one—with some novel features. An investigative committee was appointed to look into the workers' grievances. These centered mainly around pay and excessive hours. The committee included German officials because Mussolini had agreed that the Wehrmacht should have direct supervisory powers over all strategic industries (including all the Fiat operations, which remained under Italian management). The workers were told to return to their jobs if they wanted redress of their grievances, and they did. Then, in short order, the committee found that they should receive an immediate 30 percent pay increase, to make up for the erosion that had rapidly developed in the buying power of the *lire* since Italy surrendered. Attached to this generous concession was a rather strong dose of medicine. Men who were accused of being ringleaders, along with a maximum of 10 percent of the rank-and-file workers who had gone out on strike, were going to be sent to work in German factories.[9]

The implementation of the 10-percent segment of the penalty would not necessarily be swift, and indeed it might be reduced, if there were no further instances of labor unrest in the immediate future. Officials let it be known that their definition of labor unrest included slowdowns. In some factories, signs went up urging employees to work diligently, in order to save themselves or co-workers from being sent to Germany. It was also made clear, apropos Germany, that the promises of good pay and pleasant working conditions made in newspaper ads placed by General Zimmermann's office applied only to volunteers—not to men sent away as punishment for disrupting war production.

At this time Dr. Albert Speer, the German Minister of Armaments, decided that he needed resident liaison officers in all the major factories. Part of their mission was to try to head off new labor unrest. Their universal major first impression was that productivity was terribly low. Plant managers and foremen readily agreed that productivity had taken a nose-dive but said that firings and demotions didn't seem to be the answer to this problem. German officials went so far as to hold a conference on the matter in June 1944. It met in Genoa, where a one-day general strike on 9 June (a week before) had totally shut down the city for twenty-four hours. Genoese dockworkers and factory hands had already established a reputation for taking lengthy breaks of up to an hour in the midst of a workday, and neither police nor soldiers had been able to force them back to their tasks, as they lounged around on the premises. Their movements, too, were notably slow.[10] If asked why he could not work faster, a man would reply that he was weak from too long hours and not enough food. In wintertime, he would complain of no heat at home, that he was catching colds and probably had walking pneumonia, and that everybody at home was hacking and wheezing, and it was hard to sleep.

The productivity conference recognized that physical conditions certainly were not conducive to high levels of stamina, but the same held true for soldiers at the front, from whom a great deal was always expected. Morale was the main problem, accompanied by increasingly well-organized Communist agitation. The Genoa strike had obviously been centrally coordinated. At least, this was the conclusion of the local security chief, Colonel Neumann (an officer of the *Sicherheitsdienst*). All present agreed that there was central coordination of the November strike, which lasted for three days in several cities, and which was followed by a one-day general strike in several large cities on 1 December 1943. The latter had been intended apparently to speed the work of the grievance committee, which in fact came up with its 30 percent pay raise recommendation only a few days later.

The raise had not helped productivity. Morale remained very low, and the conference found itself at a loss to find ways to improve worker morale. One possible remedy—the removal of Mussolini—was not discussed for political reasons. Neither was the issue of the German occupation discussed, nor the prospect that, perhaps in a matter of months, the industrial cities would be overrun by the Allies.

It was decided—not by the conference but by General Zimmermann—that the Genoa strike should be severely punished. He ordered that fifteen hundred of the city's workers be immediately rounded up and sent off to Germany.[11] The roundup was widely publicized, along with a warning that another strike would result in the deportation of a much greater number. More than ten months were to pass before Allied forces entered Genoa. During that time long breaks and slow motion continued to be the order of the day for the workers, and there were several more one-day general strikes, culminating in an uprising on May Day (1 May) 1945, the traditional leftist holiday. At that point the Wehrmacht was at last disintegrating, and the last remnants of the German presence were swept out of the city.

Il Duce's concern for the plight of deported workers was tempered by his firm belief (reinforced by German and Italian intelligence reports) that labor troubles were ultimately the work of Communist agitators. He had built his career on Red-baiting. His first venture into anti-Communist activism in 1919 took the form of recruiting, both directly and via his Milan newspaper, strikebreakers to cross "Communist" picket lines and take the jobs of the Bolshevik minions and dupes. He recognized that peer pressure and coercion made many workers leave their workplaces and that such passive pawns in the game of politics were often the ones who went off to an uncertain fate in German labor camps. Mussolini had his hands full working for the release of interned soldiers, who were untainted by any association with a left-wing movement.

The only success he enjoyed in this regard—if it can be considered a success—was to secure volunteers from that large horde sufficient in numbers to fill out four army divisions. The rate of volunteering was extremely low (less than ten percent) considering that the men were promised that their new units would be sent back to Italy. All the soldiers were eager to return home, or at least back to their homeland. But they had been given the distinct impression that these new volunteer units would see front-line duty against the Allies. This impression became a direct promise when *il Duce* was allowed to visit the internment camps, following his meeting with Hitler at Klessheim in late April 1944. He thought they should be proud to defend the Italian Social Republic against the army of Wall Street. Talking among themselves, though, the men conjured up images of being used as human shields or shock troops by the Germans, of serving as decoys to draw enemy fire, and maybe of having to walk mine fields to clear a path for the Wehrmacht.

The organizing and training of these four divisions was the special project of the Repubblica's military chief, Gen. Rodolfo Graziani. It was the one bright spot in a generally sour relationship between the Repubblica and the Reich—a relationship marked even by complaints from *il Duce* that the Wehrmacht had introduced "Mongoli" into his country.[12] This apparently referred to the Turkoman Division which Germany had recruited from POWs of the Russian front. That unit's appearance in the front lines (in the British Eighth Army sector) reflected the Germans' hunger for military manpower—a hunger that was even more urgent than the hunger for labor on the home front. Hitler had actually set a goal of four million foreign workers in Germany by 1945, of whom 1.5 million should come from Italy. Despite the zealous efforts of General Zimmermann and his civilian counterpart in Milan, *Arbeitsführer* Kretschmann, Italy would fall far short of meeting that goal. So too would the volunteer army make only a slight contribution to the war effort.

One aspect of the German occupation that offered no mitigation of outraged feelings was the issue of national boundaries. There were certain areas of what used to be called Unredeemed Italy that Italy had been allowed to annex at the end of World War I, mainly at the expense of Austria. These were in the rugged eastern Alpine region and extended around the northern rim of the Adriatic seacoast to the city of Fiume. These places, like Red-baiting, had also figured into il Duce's rise to power. He had railed in daily editorials against the government's failure to obtain all that rightfully belonged to Italy. It was il Duce himself who finalized Italian control of Fiume, during his first months in power, following a lengthy standoff regarding that city that had greatly embarrassed his predecessors.

Now, in 1943–44, the Führer was making various moves in these places under the rubric of "occupation rights." A further definition of what constituted occupied territory and what constituted the jurisdiction of the Repubblica had added to the thirty-five-miles-behind-the-front definition of occupied territory, the various "entry points" into Italy along the northern border. Mussolini understood this to mean such major railroad stops as Bolzano (where the Wehrmacht had challenged Italian authority in July 1943) and Trento, and such other towns as might be agreed upon at a later date.

The fact that this was a gentlemen's agreement and not something spelled out in a treaty or official memorandum provided the opening for Hitler, who of course was no more a gentleman than his counterpart in this deal. The Germans were in physical control of Fiume only a few days after the king had Mussolini arrested, at the end of July 1943. They also seized the major port city of Trieste at the same time—taking various Italian naval vessels at the same time in both ports, including several submarines.[13] Italy's surrender (which nearly coincided with Mussolini's rescue by Captain Skorzeny) was followed by further German deployments in the Udine, Gorizia, Pola, Belluno, Trento, and Bolzano districts.

When the Italian Social Republic was then set up, nothing was said about its boundary with the Reich. Il Duce just assumed that it was the same as before. But this assumption was not shared by the Führer, although the latter decided that his ally should be kept guessing on the matter.

It was really not much of a guessing game, however. Bolzano, Trento, and Belluno were joined together into an entity known as Alpenvorland. Officials of the Repubblica were debarred from its territory; and the Fascist Party, active in the area since before Mussolini became head of

Hitler (front, left) *greeting Mussolini on his arrival at Nazi headquarters in Poland after escape from Italian prison. A special warfare unit led by Capt. Otto Skorzeny* (not shown) *rescued* il Duce. *Upon returning to Italy from this meeting, Mussolini founded the Italian Social Republic. Courtesy UPI/Bettman Newsphotos*

state in 1922, ceased to operate here. "Bolzano" gave way to "Bolzen" on highway and train station signs, or appeared in parentheses below the German name, which had been the name of the city and district until 1919, when it was transferred from Austria to Italy. A plebiscite there in 1936 showed an Italian majority, although certain parts of the district had a sometimes heavy German majority. After the plebiscite, a number of the Germans resettled in adjacent German territory, or in Austria (annexed by Germany in March 1938). They were motivated by fears of an expanding Italian military draft. German-speaking families with draft-age members preferred the German or Austrian draft, apparently. They were also convinced that any hope of returning this land to either of the German-speaking states was dashed forever by the plebiscite, which had been arranged with Hitler's approval.

Likewise, "Trento" became "Trent." Belluno remained Belluno, however. This reflected the fact that the district was a part of the original modern Italian state, founded as the Kingdom of Italy in 1866. Belluno continued to have an Italian prefect (county manager). Trent (Trento) also retained its Italian prefect, but in Bolzen (Bolzano) a German replaced an Italian. The entire "zone" came under the ultimate sway of the *Gauleiter* of the adjacent German county of Tirol Vorarlberg.

The borderland districts to the east—Udine, Gorizia, Trieste, Pola, and Fiume—did not undergo any major name changes. German-speakers were less common in these areas, being quite insignificant in numbers in Trieste, Pola and Fiume, where the non-Italian constituency consisted mainly of Slovenes, with a significant sprinkling of Croats (much more than a sprinkle in Fiume). Disposition of Trieste and Fiume had proven too much for the peacemakers at Versailles in 1919. Italians tended to be prevalent in the cities, but the surrounding territories were no less overwhelmingly Slovenian in composition. The population pattern was the same in 1943.

Hitler remembered, though, that these lands were a part of Austria when he himself was a young Austrian citizen. So now they became known as Adriatische Kuesterland. Italian prefects were retained just about everywhere, but the Fascist Party was booted out, and no agencies of the Repubblica were admitted. Indeed, since the earliest days of the Occupation (late July 1943) Italians travelling to and from Trieste faced strict travel restrictions—no less stringent than for a trip to Poland or any other occupied country. Ultimate control here was exercised by the *Gauleiter* of the adjacent German district of Kaernten.[14]

Il Duce fulminated against these developments and sent protests via his ambassador in Berlin. This and the issue of the interned Italian soldiers were at the top of his agenda for the Klessheim conference with Hitler in 1944. The Führer listened sympathetically and agreed that these were indeed matters of great moment which needed to be resolved right away. He then proceeded to his own agenda.

Unlike some of his Fascist minions, Mussolini never admired the Führer, nor did he ever come under the spell of the German dictator. He respected and feared Hitler's power, and as that power waned in 1944, his closest associates (who were familiar with his true feelings) wondered how long he could continue in the role of a virtual stooge of the Führer. Would gratitude for his resuscitation from the scrap-heap of history in 1943 see him through these increasingly forbidding times as a German ally? Nobody had ever credited *il Duce* with sentiments of gratitude, beyond the *quid pro quo* instincts of the practical politician.

The leading pro-Nazi fascist, Roberto Farinacci, actually went to the Führer to urge *il Duce*'s replacement. He was shown the door, but, strangely, went unpunished—possibly because the full import of his interview at Hitler's forward headquarters in Poland was never communicated officially by the Germans. Farinacci was an ex-member of the Fascist inner circle, whom *il Duce* had put down as a reckless radical.

He returned to his headquarters in Cremona and resumed his activities as the political chief of Italy's breadbasket, the middle Po Valley.

In February 1945, *il Duce* became suspicious of another of his pro-German associates, Minister of Interior Bufarini-Guidi. That post entailed responsibility for all police functions in the Repubblica. He fired this longtime close comrade. When the SS chief, General Wolff, protested, *il Duce* felt that his suspicions of an impending coup against him were confirmed. Wolff went so far as to engineer the arrest of the chief of the state police, Tamburrini—who was held more or less hostage on behalf of Bufarini-Guidi's reinstatement. But Mussolini held firm.

Wolff himself was the *de facto* commander of the National Republican Guard, which on paper claimed a membership of 150,000. This was a volunteer antipartisan force. Its actual strength may have been closer to fifteen thousand, but the fact that German officers played a prominent role in its activities was bound to give pause to Mussolini loyalists.

Another pocket of pro-German influence was the Navy Commando unit (the *Decima Mas*) commanded by Prince Borghese. Unfazed by the fact that German soldiers shot some of his fellow officers who were held responsible for the escape southward of several navy ships at the time of the surrender, Borghese seemed closer to General Wolff than to *il Duce*.[15] The *Decima Mas*, indeed, enjoyed a high reputation among the Germans.

The army chief, Rodolfo Graziani, was also considered pro-German. By late 1944 he had two of the four volunteer Army units, recruited from the ranks of the internees, on Italian soil. These were the Monte Rosa and the San Marco divisions, comprising the Ligurian army—based in Liguria, the northwestern region that included Genoa and other large cities.

The rump Grand Council of the Fascist Party decreed on 30 October 1943 that members who voted for the Grandi-Ciano Resolution to urge *il Duce*'s resignation, at the fateful July meeting, were herewith condemned to death. Only six of the condemned men actually fell into the clutches of the regime. These were General De Bono, Count Ciano, Carlo Pareschi, Giovanni Marinelli, Luciano Gottardi, and Tullio Cianetti. They were put on trial at Verona, and the death sentence was formalized by a judicial panel in every case but that of Cianetti, who received a prison sentence of thirty years instead. Cianetti had gone to Mussolini the morning after the July meeting to beg his forgiveness (this was before *il Duce*'s meeting with Victor Emmanuel) and then had his "yes" vote changed to "no" in the Council minutes.

The trial was covered in detail in all the newspapers, which capitalized on the human-interest angle: Ciano was married to Mussolini's daughter. They wondered if *il Duce* would show mercy to his son-in-law. When he did not, the outcome was presented as a sort of Greek tragedy. The view they ascribed to *il Duce*, and which he did not refute—that treason within one's family was the worst treason of all—was the stuff of grand opera, at any rate. Galleazzo Ciano, young and handsome, was the glamour boy of the regime and the favorite of the newspaper gossip writers. The acknowledged king of Rome's high society until the war broke out (he was foreign minister at the time), Ciano was probably the most widely known Fascist next to his father-in-law.

The trial lasted from 8 to 10 January 1944. A panel of seven judges (comprising the mayor of Ferrara, a general, a legal scholar, and four experienced jurists, with Judge Aldo Vecchini presiding) heard two days of testimony in the Great Hall of the Castel Vecchio—the same place where the Party Congress had been held only weeks before. The judges wore black shirts throughout the proceedings.

All nineteen of the men who had voted to urge *il Duce*'s resignation at the July 1943 Grand Council meeting were on trial here, but only six were present. Mussolini does not seem to have regarded any of them (least of all Cianetti, who had begged forgiveness and changed his vote the day after the meeting) as ringleaders of the ouster move. The main culprits—Grandi, Bottai, and Federzoni—were out of reach. He personally favored the death penalty only for those three, but felt also that somebody had to be made an example of at Verona.[16]

Cianetti was spared. His co-defendants were all condemned to death—even old General De Bono. None had tried to escape after *il Duce*'s downfall because they still considered themselves good Fascists.[17] On 11 January in the courtyard of the Castel Vecchio each of the five men was set astride a kitchen chair, chest against chair-back and hands tied to a bottom rung. The firing squad marched out in back of them and was quickly given the order to fire. All five were still alive when the roar of rifle fire ended, two sitting upright, the others writhing on the ground, still attached to the chairs. An army captain approached each one with his pistol and administered the *coup de grace*, hesitating slightly over the forty-one-year-old Ciano, who seemed the most lightly wounded of the group.

The Verona trial revealed *il Duce*'s grand capacity for vengeance. What would he have done had he laid hands on Victor Emmanuel himself? When they were still in Rome, the Germans had urged him to establish the capital of the new Repubblica there. Mussolini refused, on the grounds that the Romans' behavior on the day of his firing by the king made them unworthy. Certainly, had he acceded to the request (initially made by General Wolff, the SS chief) Rome's "Open City" status might have come into question. *Il Duce* probably thought of that, and considered it a plus factor for returning. He later expressed regret that a battle was not fought in the city when the Allies arrived and chided Kesselring for leaving the place intact.

An overriding factor in *il Duce's* decision about the placement of his capital was concern for his personal safety. He returned to Italy, on 14 September 1943, riding in one of Hitler's own armor-plated sedans, and nearly bumper-to-bumper with armored cars, front and rear. *Il Duce* got as far as the picturesque western shore of Lake Garda, and then settled in at the Villa Feltrinelli, near the village of Gargagno. This was not deep inside Italy, and there were few towns between this place, the estate of a wealthy banker, and the border. It would be more than a year before Mussolini would make a public appearance—the only one of his republican period—at the Teatro Lirico in Milan.

Il Duce had been wounded by shrapnel during World War I and survived a train wreck in 1920. Learning to fly an airplane in 1935, he was downed by a bolt of lightning (which set the plane's radio afire) but again escaped serious injury. The escape from Gran Sasso had also entailed some flirtation with doom, as the two-seater plane with three large men aboard bounced down a steep mountainside, becoming airborne at the last possible moment before disaster.

This man with a charmed life, who had also dodged assassins' bullets, had obviously lost his nerve. He no longer considered himself a child of destiny and at one point told the German ambassador, Rudolf Rahn, that the people now appeared to him as "a gray mass . . . shaping idols and then destroying them. I am an example of that."[18] *Il Duce,* once something of a workaholic, did not have a busy schedule. The Germans felt that Pavolini, the party chief, was really running the government and was the man to see for hands-on information. Rahn once found Mussolini, in the middle of a working day in his office at the Palazzo, immersed in Plato's *Crito.*[19]

The highlight of *il Duce's* workday was a daily briefing, always at noon, supplied by Colonel Jandl of the German Intelligence branch *(Abwehr)*. Jandl was the Reich's main "eyes and ears" at Feltrinelli, but he was also responsible for Mussolini's personal safety. The only other daily visitors were Captain Dr. Zacharias, formerly aide to Hitler's own personal physician, Dr. Morell, and a German physiotherapist who administered a massage. *Il Duce's* stomach trouble was worse than before, and besides the bland diet of boiled rice, he was now taking pain killing pills pre-scribed by Dr. Zacharias.[20]

Considerable distances separated the president of the Republic from various cabinet-level headquarters. Even the foreign ministry, which Mussolini ran himself, was located in a town at several miles remove—Salò. The interior ministry of Guido Bufarini-Guidi was down the lake-shore in a school building on the outskirts of Maderno. Alessandro Pavolini's Fascist party headquarters was also in the small town. Mar-shal Rodolfo Graziani's defense ministry was located in the more sub-stantial city of Cremona, in the heart of the Po Valley. The Ministry of Economy and Corporations, the center of Mussolini's "socialization" program under Angelo Tarchi, was located in Verona. Agriculture was in Treviso, public works was in Venice, education and the ministry of popular culture were in Padua, and justice was in Brescia. The *Corriere della Sera*, Milan's major newspaper then and now, complained, "In the first place, the government should have not only a political and social address but a postal one as well."[21]

The Repubblica was proclaimed, over the radio, on 23 September 1943. A day later, appointments to all the major Cabinet posts were announced. The Fascist Party changed its name to the Republican Fas-cist Party (Partito Fascista Repubblicana), and held a party convention to adopt new by-laws at Verona on 14 November. The main thrust of changes from the old by-laws (adopted in 1921) were summarized by chairman Pavolini in these terms: "It will, above all, be a workers' party, a proletarian party, creator of a new social cycle."[22]

More than a few people in the world regard Fascism as the pseudo-ideological trappings of an aggressive military-industrial complex, far removed from proletarian sentiments. But then, Mussolini was once a Socialist leader. He invented Fascism because he thought Socialism had become outdated, and liked to describe Fascism as being more advanced than Socialism, not its opposite. Socialism became outdated when it flunked an important test it had set for itself—the test of a workers' strike against the next capitalist war. According to *il Duce*'s formula-tion, International Socialism scored zero on this test in 1914, when World War I broke out. The workers flocked to the colors, and their leaders cringed at the thought of being accused of treason. It was an utter de-bacle for Socialism, in Mussolini's view, and so in 1915 he had parted company with his Socialist comrades. Fascism allegedly dealt with the issue of peace and war in a more realistic (Machiavellian) way. It also absorbed the Hegelian view of war as a medium of revolutionary change—

an idea shared by Lenin and his followers and which may help to explain why a few Communists found their way into the Fascist movement. One, Nicola Bombacci, became *il Duce*'s chief economic advisor as the "socialization" program got underway at the beginning of 1944.

The Repubblica's quest for popular acceptance reached its high point with the promulgation of the "socialization" program. The very name of the new regime, Italian Social Republic, suggested some sort of commitment to a social revolution. The Verona Manifesto and the statements of the party chief, Pavolini, suggested that this was indeed the government of the common man. The papers even carried stories about *"speculazione"*—exposing industrial profiteers and greedy businessmen. These exploiters of the toiling masses were lumped together with the smugglers sneaking food through the lines to the hungry south. Established newspapers such as the *Regima Fascista* (of Cremona), *Resto del Carlino* (of Bologna), and *Gazzetta* (of Venice) suddenly had little good to say about the business community.

The economic situation was not totally unfavorable to social and economic experiments. The food supply was fairly stable, although price swings upset everybody. (Coal, though, was scarcer than ever, and Fascist Man shivered through the last two winters of the war, at work and at home.) Along with the stable food supply was an abundance of jobs. Auto and steel production did not fall below pre-invasion levels, even with Allied bombing raids. Production of machinery and electric fixtures was up, as was the manufacture of paper, wood products, cement, and various other products. Of course, the job situation was strongly influenced by German labor needs. If such were absent there might have been significant unemployment, given the abnormal situation in trade and within the country itself. But in spite of General Zimmermann's rosy advertisements, the general perception was that working for the Germans amounted to enslavement.

On 14 January 1944, workers in "essential" industries were advised that they would soon be given the opportunity to elect, from among themselves, Advisory Councils that would have management powers. The elections were actually held in February and March, after various factories were given an opportunity to nominate candidates. The government reserved the right to disqualify some nominations without giving an explanation (the name would simply not appear on the final list of candidates). But at election time, the workers enjoyed the use of a secret ballot.

Had the aim of this program been to turn over the entire management of the production plants to the workers, this social experiment might have attracted much interest—and in some quarters, of course, considerable alarm. The objective, however, was *"l'equilibre"* (balancing) of the interests of labor and management/ownership. This expressed itself in the assignment of dividends to workers, up to a maximum of 30 percent of total net profit payouts. So, for instance, the Agnelli family still had a paramount interest in the Fiat firm—at least until "socialization" advanced another step.

Elections for "management councils" and "general assemblies" (for some reason, there was no ready consensus on a name) proved a disappointment to the regime. Workers, voting by secret ballot, usually spoiled their ballots. The promise that workers would have an equal voice and would elect managers and shop foremen, had fallen on deaf ears. Corporations Minister Tarchi blamed the outcome on a lack of understanding by the workers of what the new system meant. Ambassador Rahn saw simply a profound *Misstrauen* (mistrust) of the government.[23] Surely one source of the distrust and alleged lack of understanding on the part of the workers was the fact that any attempt to organize a work stoppage would be dealt with as a capital offense. Strike leaders would be sentenced to death.[24]

In sum, the committee movement foundered. But *il Duce* had one more card to play: nationalization. In February and March 1945—just weeks before the end of the war, and a year after the initial elections—Mussolini announced the takeover of Fiat, Montecatini Chemical, and all the other big enterprises. Gen. Hans Leyers, the German liaison for industry, was aghast. *Il Duce* had not tipped his hand to anybody.

At Fiat, another election was now held. This time the workers were not to be offered an ongoing role in management. Instead, they were to elect a management committee, to have hire-and-fire powers over the entire management, from the company president on down. Yet once again the outcome was a fiasco. Only 405 valid ballots were cast by 32,000 workers in various Fiat plants.[25] By this point, everyone knew that the regime's days were numbered. What working man in his right mind would want to be identified as an agent (via committee membership) of the Repubblica? The Allies were getting their new offensive cranked up, and they were already deep inside Germany, almost within striking distance of Berlin. True, the newspapers still carried stories of new secret weapons being prepared in Germany, and accounts of vast destruction in England being caused by V-2 rocket bombs. But few believed that the Axis would see the end of 1945.

The once-stable northern economy had also undergone serious erosion during the time from February 1944 to February 1945. Bombing raids had failed to dislocate industrial production, but they were very effective in causing a widespread slowdown in the transportation system. Damage to railroads and highways was always repaired quickly, but it was just as quickly repeated. Locomotives and railroad cars were difficult to replace, and the toll was felt most strongly in consumer necessities, such as food. Rationing of food finally began in August 1944, for just about everything except bread. The great valley of northern Italy, which seemed in some ways to have been insulated against the worst that the war had to offer, now began to feel the shadow of death creeping over it.[26]

The Repubblica, in its quest for credibility as an actual government, could not bring itself to rely totally on the Reichswehr for the defense of its territory. It was not the Germans who pushed for the four Italian divisions mentioned earlier, but Mussolini and the defense minister, Marshal Graziani. Hitler, though, ever desirous of legitimizing his puppet regime, was fully supportive of the idea. German officers and noncoms were actually in charge of the training, on the premise that Italian units might prove more compatible with German ones if they followed the same procedures and perhaps learned a little German vocabulary on the way.

Only a minority of the enrollees in the new divisions came from among the army internees being held in Germany. At least two-thirds came from the Republican military draft. These were nineteen- and twenty-year-olds, for the most part, who responded to their draft notices after the proclamation of the new Forze Armata on 27 October 1943. The announcement of the new armed forces was accompanied by a statement that the old army had "ceased to exist" ("cessato d'esistere") the day Victor Emmanuel decided to surrender to the Allies. In fact, officers of the old army were offered comparable rank in the new, and Graziani had tried to mobilize those in and near Rome at the time of the German takeover. Four thousand of various rank responded to his order to meet at the Teatro Adriano. They were told that they could either serve the Repubblica (which had not yet proclaimed its Forze Armata) or be interned in Germany for the duration. Anyone who did not wish to serve the Repubblica was asked to stand up. German guards with loaded submachine guns stood at the exits. Nobody stood up, so Graziani then ordered them to march to the train station for transport to a mobilization center. Leaves were promised after they were enrolled in their new units. Two long trains then debarked for a point somewhere in the north— the exact location still not revealed. Once out in the open country, after German guards in several of the cars had been overpowered, men began dropping off the sides of the cars. Relatively few completed the trip.[27]

The following weeks were taken up with an effort to have men born in the years 1922–25 register for military service. The response at first was very poor. Local officials were then ordered to scour the birth records and locate the families of men with a draft obligation. Informers were also invited to provide information for a small reward, full confidentiality guaranteed.

The death penalty was then decreed for non-registrants, such persons now being classified as traitors in wartime. Months later—in August, when food rationing was introduced—families of non-registrants also stood to lose their ration cards.[28] By that time more than a few of the draft-dodgers were enrolled in partisan units. Amnesties had been announced, but the last one expired on 25 May 1944. Some families therefore found themselves deprived of access to food, except for bread (which remained unrationed) and most fresh vegetables, which were freely available as long as there was warm weather.

These coercive measures were accompanied by an option for non-military service, without any need to prove conscientious objector status. This choice was introduced when it was clear that there would be enough men to fill out the ranks of the projected four divisions. Men could join the new Guardia Nazionale (National Guard), described as a successor to the prestigious national police, the *Carabinieri*. (Mussolini had disbanded the *Carabinieri* on the premise that it was too closely identified with the monarchy.) Or, if police work on the home front was still too fraught with the potential for violence, men could fulfill their draft obligation by working full-time for the Todt Organization—fixing bombed roads, building bunkers, refurbishing buildings, and so forth. Yet another option was foreign labor service—in Germany. Four choices in all. It was pointed out that no other government offered such a variety of ways in which to fulfill one's wartime duty. A choice could be made upon receipt of a draft notice.[29]

Draft notices went out in November and December 1943 to 180,000 young men. Local newspapers carried the names of the honorees, and in smaller communities the names also appeared on the walls of post offices and other public buildings. The main purpose of this extensive publicity was to make anyone flouting his draft notice feel unsafe in public, where his neighbors might recognize him as one who had been called.

Marshal Graziani claims that 130,000 answered their notices, of whom 25,000 were dispatched to Germany for training in the new army divisions. A more scholarly source indicates that 87,000 showed up at the designated mobilization centers. Documents show that about 25,000 did enter army service with the four divisions, and that another 25,000 entered the ranks of the Guardia Nazionale.[30] The balance ended up in labor service, working for the Germans. But more than half of the call-ups were prepared to risk execution by not showing up. The prospects of fighting for a losing war effort, and something they did not believe in, were too much for most. The alternatives to military service meant either being slaves of the Germans or, as national policemen, possibly arresting people they considered real patriots, and maybe also being picked off by partisan assassins, who might show up at any time, in any place.

In Florence there were public executions of several draft evaders. A priest referred to them during mass as martyrs, whereupon he was arrested.[31] Subsequent to that, though, captured draft-dodgers were dealt with more discreetly. The new enrollees in the Guardia soon found that a main preoccupation of that force was the tracking down of such traitors, not just in the cities and towns, but also out in the countryside. The *Carabinieri* had rarely encountered situations Guardsmen found commonplace: patrolling through farm country, over terrain that was actually under the control of rebel partisans.[32]

The regime could not in fact rely simply on draftees for that task, even though the Wehrmacht, SS, and Gestapo all had a more than passing interest in controlling partisans. Volunteers were called for, and rank-and-file Fascists joined as officer trainees.

A volunteer adjunct of the Guardia Nazionale was the Muti Legion (La Legione Muti). It was named after the man who had responded to an arrest warrant, following *il Duce*'s overthrow in 1943, with a hand grenade. The Muti group, in league with Pietro Koch's police auxiliary, focused its attention on partisan activity in the big cities. Its leader, a longtime Fascist named Francesco Colombo, was headquartered in Milan. Like the Koch Group, the Muti Legion had an unsavory reputation for torturing suspects and close relatives of suspects.

In addition, there was a group called Decima Mas, consisting of former personnel of the Tenth Torpedo Boat Flotilla of the Italian navy. This unit, led by Prince Junio Valerio Borghese, a naval officer, was considered to be the most effective security force in the Repubblica.[33] Indeed, it attracted significant numbers of volunteers, eventually becoming ten thousand strong. It did not, however, operate at sea. Instead, Borghese challenged partisan strongholds in the Aosta region.[34]

Another loose-cannon organization was the *Banda Carità*, led by Mario Carità. This group enjoyed official status as the Special Services Department (Reparto di Servizi Speciale). It was the closest thing the regime had to a central intelligence-gathering branch. The notorious veteran investigator of the Rome police, Pietro Koch, teamed up with Carità after the Allies reached Rome. Special Services was then based in Florence, at the villa Bolognese, popularly referred to as the "House of Sorrow" (Villa Triste) because suspects were tortured there. It moved north ahead of the Allied advance, always focusing its activities on cities just behind the front. The day after the war ended, in 1945, Carità was shot while resisting arrest by U.S. soldiers. In 1951, 178 of Carità's former agents were tried for torture and murder. Most received lengthy prison terms, and several were given life sentences. (Italy had no death penalty in 1951, nor does it have one today.)

The regime considered it the duty of all Fascists to assist in rooting out all subversive elements. To that end, it sponsored the creation of yet another volunteer group, the Brigate Nere (Black Brigades), as a security arm that all party members were urged to join. Gen. Gaetano Gambara was placed in charge of this somewhat amorphous organization, which attained a membership of about twenty-two thousand.[35] While most of the brigades engaged in little more than passive intelligence—keeping eyes and ears open—a few were more active. Notable in this category was a group headed by Col. Carlo Cesarini, which scrutinized the increasingly fractious factory workers in Milan and Turin. Cesarini was eventually targetted by the partisans and shot down by a hit squad on a Milan street in March 1945.[36]

The Repubblica actually found it difficult to replace the old *Carabinieri* as a national police force. Particularly disturbing was the proliferation of "volunteer police," especially ones that adopted German names, such as the *Sicherheit* group founded by Felice Fiorentini. His assassination by partisans in January 1945 was not regretted by either the regime or the people he "protected." The Guardia Nazionale, intended to function as a national police force, was quickly and totally preoccupied by anti-partisan forays into the lonely valleys. So, in January 1944, the Minister of Interior, Bufarini-Guidi, announced the establishment of the Polizia Repubblicana (PR). Its personnel were recruited from city police forces at first, to form a core cadre. Eventually the PR numbered twenty thousand.

The regime also came up with an Italian version of the SS. Italy had no dearth of German SS men, but apparently they felt the need for some help, especially in high-profile situations that pitted Germans against Italians. The new unit became the enforcement arm of Giovanni Preziosi's Race and Demography office (Razzia e Demografia). It spent the remainder of the war tracking down Jews and others deemed worthy of deportation. It actually outnumbered the fifteen thousand Jews who lived in northern Italy. But in a region overrun with fugitives of so many kinds—partisans, deserters, assorted escapees—Jews found the status of fugitive less forbidding than it was elsewhere. Half of them eluded the racist dragnet. Many took up arms against the regime and the Wehrmacht.[37]

Neither the Repubblica nor the Germans ever entertained any illusions about their popularity in northern Italy. The vote results in the worker-council elections were a stinging reminder of the reality. Much more painful reminders were always at hand, thanks to the partisan bands that roamed the rural valleys and sometimes the city streets.

Initially, the partisan movement consisted almost entirely of fugitive soldiers who had escaped the Wehrmacht dragnet following Italy's surrender in September 1943. For a very brief while, they still considered themselves soldiers. But *il Duce*'s announcement, soon after the founding of the Italian Social Republic, that the king's army had ceased to exist was not countered by any disclaimers from the other side. When captured, such men did not find themselves covered by the Geneva conventions on war prisoners. Instead, they were treated worse than rabid dogs. Before being put to death they were tortured in the hope that they would reveal the location of their comrades.

Still, they carried over from the army the same command structure, including often the same officers, and the army's tradition of political neutrality. This latter characteristic earned them the nickname *Autonomi* (Independents), to distinguish them from the very political bands that sprang up shortly afterward. In truth, their officers were universally suspected of harboring a lingering fondness for the monarchy. This was probably true, although just how true cannot be determined. It certainly had something to do with the fact that the *Autonomi* did not join forces with the CLN or its branch in northern Italy, the CLNAI (Alt' Italia). These groups were dedicated to the end of the monarchy. Even when the Allies recognized the CLN as the provisional government of liberated Italy in June 1944, and in December recognized the Milan-based CLNAI as its agent in German-occupied northern Italy, there was no deal with the *Autonomi*.

These ex-soldiers were not ignored by the Allies, however. The Allies dearly wished that all the partisans were so modest when it came to political labels and outspoken political programs. Churchill was himself pro-monarchist. So the *Autonomi* were not left out when the supply airlift began in late summer 1944, and indeed, they probably received more than their fair share. There is no record, either, of serious clashes between *Autonomi* and civilian partisan bands. The United Front policy pursued by the CLNAI was universally respected by the diverse elements of the anti-German and anti-Fascist resistance. The only serious instance of fighting among partisan bands occurred in the final weeks of the war, when the Communist *Natisone* Brigade quit the CLNAI and joined Tito's partisans near Trieste. This occasioned clashes with the Demo-Christian *Osoppo* Brigade, which feared that Tito had the support of Italian Communists on his claim to territory for Yugoslavia in this border area.

This region happened to be one of the two remaining areas in which *Autonomi* were still a force to be reckoned with. But the *Autonomi* stayed out of this flare-up, even though they had earlier clashed with Slovenian partisans loyal to Tito. The other *Autonomi* stronghold was all the way across the extreme north of Italy, in the Val d'Aosta region near the French border. Here could be found the largest concentration of fugitive soldiers to be found anywhere, numbering more than two thousand. All were veterans of the old IV Army, which had been based in southeastern France when the king surrendered.

Autonomi units could also be found in the Abruzzo region, the rugged mountain country inland from Rome. Men who had been based around Rome at the time of the German takeover could be found in these units, plus some of the military refugees who had crossed the Adriatic Sea from Albania. They were active during the Cassino campaign, and yet at the time were hardly known to the Allies. Mining roads and ambushing convoys well north of the front, even the Germans generally mistook them for Allied commandos who had been parachuted into rear areas. When the Cassino campaign ended in May–June 1944, and the Abruzzo was liberated, they claimed six hundred German casualties. AMG printed up certificates of merit for the men, and then sent them home—if home was south of the front. Others were given an opportunity to apply for the new Italian defense force.[38]

Except for the IV Army elements deployed along the strategic supply route between Italy and France in the Val d'Aosta, *Autonomi* played a minimal role in the resistance after the liberation of Rome. It was at that point, in June 1944, that the partisan movement really began to develop. The leading role was played by the Communist Party, which eventually controlled about 40 percent of all partisan fighters. The larger Communist units were named Garibaldi brigades after the famous nationalist republican firebrand of the 1800s. Combatants sometimes even, like Giuseppe Garibaldi's legendary Redshirts, wore red shirts—or at least red bandannas. This was unusual for plainclothes warriors who relied on surreptitious tactics, especially in an age of accurate rifles and trained sharpshooters. (The Germans had a sniper academy in Berlin, more than a few of whose graduates were sent out to stalk partisan encampments in the mountain fastnesses.) It should be added that not all Communist units engaged in this bravado, and only a few had any sort of required uniform.

The brigades (Communist and otherwise) numbered from four hundred to five hundred men each. They were always divided up into three battalions of about 150 each. Each battalion in turn was split into three detachments, and these could be subdivided into squads.

Unlike other partisan groups, the Communists also had "urban guerrilla units." These were known as the *Gappisti*, for GAP (Gruppi d'Azione Patriottica), which never numbered more than ten each. They performed special, usually very dangerous, missions, such as assassinating Fascist officials or German officers. At harvest time in 1944 they also had the unusual function of somehow laying hands on a portion of the harvest in the Po Valley. They performed this job very well, and kept numerous Garibaldi Brigades well-fed for the remainder of the war.

The British and American authorities were extremely wary of the Red partisans. The situation in Yugoslavia, where the partisan movement was thoroughly dominated by the Communists, seemed somehow more comfortable. What the Allies feared was a repeat performance of what had happened in Greece in 1944. There the Communists were also the largest single partisan entity. They initiated a power play as the Wehrmacht began its retreat in the wake of Soviet advances on the Russian Front, and of course they were well-equipped with weapons supplied by the Allies. In Italy the Communists were very careful to avoid any semblance of such untrustworthiness—even to the point of scandalizing their CLN allies by being noncommittal on the issue of the monarchy. Their leader, Togliatti, did lose patience toward the end of the war, but only briefly. His order for a general uprising in the final days did not exactly accord with Allied wishes, and it seems he was hoping for a revolution from below that the Allies would be hard-pressed to contain. But on the whole, Togliatti followed the Moscow line he had brought back from his long exile in the Soviet Union. This meant conceding Italy to the Western democracies as part of an unspoken spheres-of-influence tradeoff in postwar alignments.

This posture had much to do with CLNAI's success in keeping the peace among the diverse partisan units. Luigi Longo, the second-ranking Communist leader, was co-chairman of CLNAI's military command, along with the head of the Action Party, Ferruccio Parri. That organization, called Commando Generale/Corpo Volontari della Liberta (CG/CVL) was the coordinating arm of all CLN-affiliated partisan groups—meaning the great bulk of the partisan movement. Not the least of its coordinating functions was the fulfillment of objectives spelled out by Allied chiefs. To further this connection with the Allied war effort, Gen. Raffaele Cadorna was sent out from Rome in August 1944 to assume control of day-to-day planning. Cadorna was a non-political entity who had distinguished himself during the Germans' move into Rome in September 1943. He was the only Italian general who had ordered his division to fight the Germans. From September to June, he had been a hunted man within the Eternal City.

Cadorna was officially in control of Communist partisan operations. He could veto proposals made by their leaders, and send them to places they did not want to go. Allied commanders were very attentive to his fate from the moment his plane took off from an airstrip outside Rome. Their initial fear was that he might simply disappear. There were dangers enough from the outset of his new assignment. He had to learn how to parachute out of an airplane, for instance. His pilot was to look for a signal flare outside Milan (where the general would have his secret headquarters). But the Germans were adept at setting off decoy fires and flares, and if they happened to have any burning in the general vicinity of the drop, it would be good-bye to the new CG/CVL commander. Was a reception committee comprised mainly of Communists better than one consisting of Wehrmacht personnel? This was something the British and Americans still wondered about. For the rest, Cadorna would serve them as the monitor of the good behavior of the *Garibaldini*, the *Gappisti*, and the *Sappisti*, and of the politicians in the CG/CVL and the CLNAI. He never had any occasion to raise any serious doubts about the Communists, at least not until the last days of the war.

The second largest force in the partisan movement belonged to the Action Party. About 25 percent of the fighters served in Actionist units.[39] This was a new party with no electoral experience, although some of its founders were veteran politicians from other parties. The party's leader, Ferruccio Parri, would in fact become premier shortly after the war— the first of a very substantial number of postwar premiers in Italy. By 1946, Parri would be in the Republican ranks, a minor political party which also played a very slight role in the partisan movement and did not join the CLN during the war. These facts are mentioned because they contrast so greatly with the important role that the Actionists played in Italy from 1943 to 1945. The party was born of the war and died with the war (a majority of its members ending up, not in the Republican ranks, but in the Socialist Party).

Actionists were essentially left-liberals with a strong commitment to the end of the monarchy. That the monarchy was voted out in 1946 may help to explain the demise of this organization. Their units were called *Giustizia e Liberta* (Justice and Liberty) Brigades, thus causing Actionists to be known generally as *Giellisti*.[40] Like their Communist allies, they were headquartered in the same city that housed the nerve centers of the CLNAI and the CG/CVL—Milan. But whereas Milan and its environs were a major operations area for the Communist *Garibaldini*, a substantial part of the Action forces were to be found in the northwest, mainly in Piemonte. The top field commander there was a Cuneo lawyer, Tancredi "Duccio" Galimberti. Actionist units were also very active in the Genoa area. Their chief there was Luciano Bolis, who survived capture and torture in February 1945; his comrades raided a police station to rescue him.[41]

Communists and Actionists made up together about 65 percent of the partisan ranks, with the *Autonomi* perhaps another 5 percent of the total. The remainder was a mixed bag, with Socialists and Christian Democrats the only organizations worth significant comment. The Socialist Party had been a major force in Italian politics before the Mussolini dictatorship and would become one again immediately after the war. But partisan warfare was not its strong suit, even though a Socialist, Pietro Nenni, served in the cabinet of the CLN provisional government in Rome.

Socialist units were named *Matteotti* Brigades, after a Socialist leader murdered by a Fascist hit squad in 1925. The principal field commander was Antonio "Toni" Giuriolo, who seems to have been more interested in building up for a possible end-of-war showdown with the Communists than anything else. The Socialist underground press, led by the Milan-based newspaper *Avanti*, occasionally questioned Communist motives. The Rome-based Communist paper *Unita* reciprocated by calling the Socialists opportunists and slackers.[42] This war of words—not really a regular feature of either side's newspapers—was the only open sign of dissension within CLN ranks.

Christian Democrat partisans were more active than the Socialists, although they were hardly more numerous. Teresio Olivelli led a unit called *Fiamme Verdi* in the somewhat exposed environs of the Lombard Plain. (Most partisan bands showed a decided preference for remote mountain bases or inner city bailiwicks.) This group also produced a newspaper, *Il Ribelle*. The only other important Christian Democrat force was the aforementioned *Osoppo* Brigade, which clashed with the Communists' renegade *Natisone* Brigade near Trieste. A CD leader, Alcide De Gasperi, sat on the CLN cabinet in Rome. De Gasperi was a veteran politician, but the party—like the Actionists—was new. Unlike the Actionists, however, the CDs would flourish in peacetime. De Gasperi succeeded Parri as premier in December 1945, and would dominate Italian politics for years to come. Decades later, his party was still the largest in Italy.

There was a Trotskyite band, a Republican band, and a pro-monarchist group called the Fronte Militare Clandestino della Resistenza. The last-named specialized in intelligence gathering through a unit called Cento X. Their information was passed directly to the Allies, and the Fronte avoided all contact with the anti-monarchist CLNAI and CLN. On the Eighth Army's front, a partisan company greeted the British soldiers in Tivoli that appeared quite oblivious of CLNAI, as if it had been out of contact with the outside world for some time, only to descend on the city as the Germans made a hasty departure. And there were partisans who appeared at times to be bandits. Rural landowners were sometimes accosted by armed men without any "official" identity, asking for money and jewelry.[43] It was not easy to say no to people wielding rifles and burp guns.

CLNAI was well aware of the potential for trouble of this kind in its own ranks. The great majority of the recruits were draft dodgers and fugitives from various hostage roundups, forced labor levies, and so forth. Interest in fighting the Germans and Fascists was often secondary to a concern for personal safety and regular meals (although food was not a strong feature of the partisan way of life). On the other hand, the great majority of partisans were responsible working people. A third came from the ranks of labor, and another third could be described as middle class. A fifth of the partisans were farmers, and the remainder were students, skilled craftsmen, and ex-soldiers.[44]

All but a few partisan bands maintained a code of conduct. The two-thirds of all partisans who were affiliated with CLNAI adhered to a uniform code of conduct that applied the same standards as the military. But where regular soldiers depended on their own quartermaster and commissary branches for supplies, the partisans relied heavily on the local populace. In some places they even levied regular taxes, payable in cash. Requisitioning was common, and citizens were under great pressure to make donations. Such an irregular system was open to irregularities at every turn. Court martial-like proceedings were part of the control mechanism. CLNAI also maintained an inspectorate at the province level—every province having its own administrative headquarters to coordinate every aspect of the partisan movement within its confines.

Among the Communist *Garibaldini*, stealing from the poor was often treated as a capital offense, although taking from the rich was not easy to distinguish from "requisitioning." The political commissars served as prosecutor, judge, and sometimes jury in cases of stealing. To maintain a Communist spirit in groups that included so many people with only vague political convictions, the party required that at least 15 percent of the membership in all cities should enroll in partisan units.[45]

Fighters convicted of stealing, or disobeying orders, or any other infraction, could not be sent to a brig or stockade. Neither could they be dishonorably discharged. There were no stockades—although some groups actually had barbed-wire pens, mainly for holding enemy prisoners. Punishment had to be immediate and physical. Where, in the normal world, a lengthy prison term might be called for, the remedy in the partisan world was most likely a death sentence.

How many partisans were there? The numbers varied from season to season. A peak was reached in the autumn of 1944, as the Allied armies crashed up against the Gothic Line and an end to the war in Italy seemed imminent. Field Marshal Kesselring states in his memoirs that intelligence estimates placed the figure then at anywhere from two hundred thousand to three hundred thousand. This contrasted sharply with the Repubblica's estimate of eighty thousand in early summer, shortly after the Allies entered Rome. OSS, the American intelligence branch, estimated 99,800 in November 1944.[46]

When the Gothic Line campaign faltered in early December, and a bitter winter descended on the mountain strongholds, the ranks thinned out. Field Marshal Alexander, commander of Allied armies in Italy, ordered a standdown not only at the front but also behind the front, in the partisan war.[47] He indicated that any significant combat for the duration of the winter would have to be at the initiative of the Germans. Otherwise, only minor operations were authorized.

By the time the last Allied offensive got underway in Italy in April 1945, Germany had been invaded, and Allied armies were converging on Berlin. Kesselring's army was cut off from supplies from the Reich, and everybody knew that the end was near. The partisans at this point were given the unfamiliar task of protecting property, rather than destroying it. And after a very rough winter of *Rastrellamenti*—German and Fascist sweeps through the mountain valleys—they found that nobody was looking for them anymore. Indeed, on encountering Germans, the latter were apt to offer their weapons, ammunition, and vehicles in return for safe passage.

There were many people who wished to share in this sudden moment of triumph for the partisans. When bands entered towns and cities, they found it difficult to fend off new volunteers who had never thought to seek them out in the mountain fastnesses. The number of partisans swelled suddenly in those last weeks, but it was an artificial swelling, the stuff of many fake war stories told to children and gullible historians in years to come. So the figures for late 1944 will have to stand as a true measure of the commitment to the partisan movement in northern Italy.

Alexander's standdown order in November 1944 was delivered openly, over the radio. (Millions in the north, although they weren't supposed to do so, listened to BBC broadcasts.) Comando Generale (CG/CVL), the military branch of CLNAI, was no less under his control than the Fifth and Eighth Armies. Indeed, when its co-commander Ferruccio Parri was captured on New Year's Eve in Milan, the Allies made a considerable effort to look after his welfare. Certain warnings were given to Kesselring on the matter of torture, and OSS chief Allen Dulles finally secured his release in Zurich, Switzerland, on 8 March 1945. (Parri was delivered personally by the SS chief, General Wolff, who was feeling out the Allies on a negotiated surrender.)[48]

Relations between CLNAI and the Allies were formalized by the Rome Agreement of 7 December 1944. The Agreement was the product of long, hard negotiations begun at Clark's headquarters in Caserta months before. The inspiration behind it was a feeling among the Resistance leaders that they were simply distrusted by the Allies. CLNAI itself was an Allied product, the brainchild mainly of Harold Macmillan (future prime minister of England), who was the British political delegate to the Allied Control Commission.

Rather than simply serve as the Allies' informal agent in the north, with the aim of reining in any radical tendencies among the partisans, CLNAI wanted clearly defined political powers. These were to come into play as territory was liberated, including enclaves carved out by the partisan bands themselves. What CLNAI got was the right to nominate local officials, subject to review by AMG. Hitherto the situation was somewhat informal and confused, and bad feelings had been generated during the summer by experiences in Tuscany. There, AMG sometimes appointed mayors and other officials without any input from CLNAI; but other times found CLNAI appointees quite acceptable. Partisans tried to move into a town just ahead of Allied forces, in order to have time to appoint a town government. If they got there too late (which seems rarely to have been the case) and didn't have a "liberated government" on hand to greet the soldiers and hold a welcoming ceremony for their commanders, the initiative was lost to AMG. Or so it seemed. Sometimes a stubborn German rearguard action upset things.

CLNAI was also designated to carry out Allied Commission orders.

This was a source of political legitimacy that was expected to win more respect from the military people in AMG, who rarely had much patience with assertive politicians unless they were British or Americans on an official tour.[49]

These concessions to CLNAI were the price of continued cooperation, and the continued success of the partisan movement as an unarguable asset to the Allied cause. Alexander, *et al.*, had been slow to appreciate what the partisans could do for them, and worried constantly about a Communist power play like that of ELAS in Greece. As noted before, the movement didn't amount to much before the liberation of Rome, but its rapid development during the latter half of 1944 commanded respect. The OSS, in one report, noted "a tradition of syndicalist violence in the north" that was bound to give pause. Faced now with the issue of delivering arms and ammunition to the bands, was it enough to have a military professional (Cadorna) in charge? He could easily be ignored in his Milan hideaway, the headquarters of the Comando Generale.

Politics aside, there was also the matter of accountability for the weapons. Who got them? Who needed them? How were they used? The British had some experience in keeping abreast of such matters in Yugoslavia and elsewhere. During the summer Major Temple was parachuted in to serve as Allied liaison for the first big airdrops. He was soon killed during a German *Rastrellamento*, and was replaced by Col. John M. Stevens. In January 1945, Stevens was joined by Maj. Basil Davidson, a veteran of the Yugoslav partisan aid program. It was widely believed, though never admitted, that these officers' most important task was to determine if the Communist *Garibaldini* were stockpiling air-dropped material rather than using it against the enemy.[50]

Britain's Special Forces (SOE) had thirty-three agents among the partisans by the end of 1944, and the American OSS maintained contacts on a more limited scale. (One partisan band in Piemonte was actually led by an escaped British POW, formerly a sailor on a submarine.) And a few partisan units included escaped American and even Russian POWs, the Russians apparently having found their way from Austria. (The only Russian officially in Italy was A. Bogomolov, who had observer status with the Allied Commission.)

Some supplies had been dropped to the partisans as early as January 1944. The prime recipients were the *Autonomi* of the former IV Army, who had made their presence felt in Piemonte as early as autumn 1943. Up to mid-1944, more than half of all supplies were dropped over Piemonte, with the *Giellisti* of the Action Party getting an increasing share. During the summer, the range of the airdrop program increased dramatically, as new units popped up all over the place. Some nine hundred thousand tons were dropped—about half consisting of weapons, a fourth of ammunition, and the remainder "miscellaneous," including mines and radios (which had been a mainstay of the earlier supply drops).

It wasn't until autumn that the United States, though the "arsenal of democracy," surpassed the British in overall tonnage. The Americans might have provided a lot more, but their hearts never seem to have been in this program. That the Yanks (unlike their ally) still held elections in wartime may have had something to do with it. Delivery of guns to the *Garibaldini* in red bandannas was certainly not going to assist FDR in his quest for a fourth term as president. More likely, some scandal might come out of it; and an ELAS-type development might have proved disastrous.

As the airdrop program reached its peak, in autumn 1944, only twenty U.S. transports were assigned to the job. Then, with Field Marshal Alexander's standdown order in November, there was a significant reduction. In February 1945, the supply line became even more restricted.[51] Preparations for the final Allied offensive in April did not result in any significant upgrading. For northern Italy, then, the moment of political truth was at hand: Many wondered if a civil war might not break out in the wake of the German surrender.

The Allies set forth clearly defined procedures for demobilization once the fighting was ended. Most important among them was that all partisans should relinquish their weapons within one month. In the last days, CLNAI "was everywhere in control,"[52] with local governments waiting to greet the soldiers of the Fifth and the Eighth Armies. The Rome Agreement stipulated that CLNAI should dissolve within weeks of the end of hostilities. Would the United Front spirit hold once the Fascists and the Wehrmacht were no more? Had the Allies been confident about this, weapons shipments would have been much more abundant, and the partisan ranks probably would have swelled.

Given these limitations, it is remarkable that the partisans accomplished so much. Next to impeding the Wehrmacht's war effort, a prime goal of the movement was to destabilize and show up the inherent weakness of the Repubblica. To this end partisan brigades endeavored to establish control over territory, and then proclaim the territory "liberated," even though Allied armies might still be some distance to the south. One such territory was the Val d'Aosta, which contained the most important inland highway to France. Here the Fascists of Prince Borghese's *Decima Mas* scored a signal victory in 1944, forcing (with the help of

German and other Italian units) the *Autonomi* of the old Italian IV Army to retire toward the French border. On 2 May 1945, though, the entire province of Aosta was declared a republic, thus taking some of the edge off the humiliation suffered in 1944.

Well before May 1945, however, several other northwestern valleys and the cities and towns within them had been proclaimed "liberated," with results that left the Repubblica and the Wehrmacht humiliated. These included Val Sessera, Val d'Andorno, and Val Chisone, all under the control of Garibaldi brigades. In Val di Lanzo, where a 700-man Garibaldi brigade established itself in June 1944, an attack by 1,500 Fascist Guardsmen and *Decima Mas* troops was fended off with the help of a well-executed ambush. From summer 1944 until the end of the war, no Fascist could enter these places to enforce Fascist laws or collect Fascist taxes. Instead, the people lived according to partisan laws and paid partisan taxes. On 21 September 1944, the town of Monforte d'Alba was declared a free trade center for certain commodities—no price controls, no quotas, no ration cards.[53] This special free trade zone could have been bombed the next day, but instead it flourished under the patronage of brokers from distant cities, who fed supplies into the black market. It is possible that even Fascist Party members and officials might have visited the place, if they determined that the financial opportunities outweighed the risk to their persons.

In the northeast, partisan juntas held sway in large areas of Carnia and Ossola. In Carnia on 26 September 1944, a *tribunale del popolo* declared the end of the death penalty.[54] The province also adopted a mildly progressive tax structure—an unusual move, for even Communist *Garibaldini* tended to soft-pedal reforms in "liberated" areas during the war.

Partisans also established the so-called Repubblica di Torriglio in Liguria and controlled whole counties in the valleys of Emilia between Parma and Modena. In the Veneto, they governed sections of Cansiglio prefecture, and controlled *"una vasta zona"* of Friuli. In all such places, the laws of the Fascist Repubblica were declared null and void.

All of these places were targeted for *Rastrellamenti* by Mussolini and Kesselring but somehow survived as rebel enclaves to the end of the war. Carnia, for instance, was invaded by a force of some thirty thousand men, including *Decima Mas*, *Brigate Nere* (Black Brigade), Militia, and German battalions. The five thousand partisans there, led by Nino "Ninci" Zucchi and Mario "Andrea" Lizzero, had to regroup after a week of fighting, which was heavy during the last week of November. The attack itself was at least in part inspired by Field Marshal Alexander's standdown order, for that told the enemy that the partisans would not be getting large amounts of supplies from the Allies. The partisans had to worry about running out of ammunition. They divided up into squads for the duration of the winter, but continued with some success to govern large areas, even convening an occasional *tribunale del popolo* to resolve civil and criminal matters.

A move against the partisan stronghold in Veneto produced the "second battle of Mount Grappa" (the first having been a World War I engagement between Italian and Austrian armies). The push moved on to the Isonzo River in late September, also the scene of major World War I fighting. Here the town of Faodis, which had survived World War I, was completely destroyed by Fascist and German artillery. But the partisans survived, and reasserted their hold on parts of Veneto when the pressure subsided in the autumn.[55]

Marshal Graziani, chief of staff for the Repubblica's armed forces, concluded not long after the liberation of Rome (in other words, soon into the main period of the partisan movement) that the only place safely under his regime's control was the lowland plain of the Po Valley.[56] Mussolini repeated this sentiment around the end of the year. This was not a negligible area (it includes Milan and several other major cities), but it comprised barely half the territory of the Repubblica as of summer of 1944, when the fighting front extended through Florence and over to the Ortona area on the west coast. Most of the other half was contested territory, with the areas mentioned under the clear domination of the partisans.

Besides liberating territory, the partisans liked to attack as close to the centers of Fascist authority as they dared. The rescue of the Communist leader Giovanni Roveda from a Verona jail cell is one example of this. Verona was the headquarters of several of the Repubblica's ministries and was always crowded with Germans in uniform. This event occurred on 17 July 1944. On the twenty-sixth, a *Gappisti* unit set off a powerful bomb at the Palazzo Giustinian in Venice, where the Guardia had its headquarters for the northeast. The building was heavily damaged and there were numerous casualties. One of the partisans' most daring raids took place in May, when the Ministry of Marine (located at Salò) was overrun by men seeking weapons and ammunition. The ministry proved not to contain a large cache of supplies, but 224 members of the Guardia were disarmed in the process.

Assassinations were also part of the process of striking at the heart of the Repubblica. Mussolini was the big prize, of course, but he remained holed up in his Lake Garda compound for almost the whole of the

Repubblica's existence; mass rallies and arm-waving balcony speeches were a thing of the past. His speech at a Milan theater in December 1944 provided the best opportunity, but the security proved to be too tight.

Members of the cabinet also got through the life of the Repubblica unscathed, until that day in May 1945 when several of them were caught with *il Duce* himself, en route to the Swiss border. The most famous victim of assassination before then was the retired Minister of Education, Giovanni Gentile, who was gunned down on a Florence street on 15 April 1944. Gentile was also an original member of the Grand Council but had resigned in protest against the Lateran Treaty of 1929, which gave the Church the Vatican. This gesture may not have made Gentile popular with devout Catholics, but he stood out among Fascists (in the eyes of most Italians) as a gentleman and also as a philosopher and man of principle. His murder by *Gappisti* produced dissension within CLN, including some caustic anti-Communist editorial comments in the Action Party's clandestine press. GAP did not claim credit. Luigi Longo, chief of the Communist underground, would neither confirm nor deny rumors about this event. Meanwhile, Gentile's sons publicly requested that none of the usual reprisals be carried out, and indeed there were none.[57]

The period of the Verona Congress in November 1943 saw the highwater mark of assassinations in northern Italy. All together, twenty-seven local Fascist leaders were shot or blown up by hand grenades, including the Ras of Ferrara (on 19 November) and the Ras of Milan—Aldo Resega, probably the most important assassination victim of the whole war. Early in 1944, the Ras of Bologna was also killed, but the nine men involved in his murder were all captured and shot. As a result, his was the only murder (except for that of Gentile) not followed by the shooting in reprisal of political prisoners and hostages. The death of the Ferrara chief occasioned seventeen such killings, and two dozen innocent people paid for Resega's murder.[58]

Aside from the capture of Val d'Aosta by *Decima Mas* units, the only signal victory that the regime scored against the partisans was the surprise raid against CLN's Military Command on 1 April 1944. This was before General Cadorna went to Milan to set up his command post for CLNAI (accomplished the following August), so neither he nor the staff of Allied officers who eventually joined him were involved. Instead, the victims were General Perotti; his aide, Captain Balbis (a survivor of El Alamein); the Actionist representative Professor Braccini; a Communist delegate, Mario Giambone; and a Socialist delegate, Bevilacqua.

Seized during a meeting at their basement headquarters in Turin, all were shot on 5 April after four days of torture. Minister of Interior Bufarini-Guidi personally presided at their trial, which received extensive coverage in the newspapers throughout the north.[59]

Actions aimed at the Italian Social Republic were a mere sideshow compared with the partisan war against the Wehrmacht. This was essentially a war for control of supply routes through the mountain valleys. Except for operations around the Ravenna marshes and near Lake Comacchio on the eastern side of the peninsula, most of the fighting, road-mining, and ambushes took place in rugged mountains. In the northern Apennines, partisans often sought to involve themselves in Allied attacks by interfering with German movements well within earshot of the booming guns. The reputed exploits of *Autonomi* in back of Cassino have already been noted. Like those, the brigades that challenged the Wehrmacht generally acted upon their own, not being privy to the secret operational plans of the Fifth and Eighth armies. For these behind-the-lines fighters, it was enough to hear where the guns boomed loudest and to see from mountaintop observation posts—sometimes within a stone's throw of German lookout points—where the Allied troops and tanks were headed.

The Fifth Army became acutely aware of the partisans' presence only after it entered Tuscany in the drive toward Florence, following the liberation of Rome. In town after town, the weary American troops were greeted by carbine-waving men in street clothes—men who had just finished giving the departing Germans a royal sendoff. In some towns, like Pian d'Alberto (more a village than a town), the would-be greeting party was found lying at the base of a wall in a neat row—eighteen men who had taken on a task too big for them to handle.[60] A dozen of their comrades were found in other parts of the village. Some may have been victims of friendly fire, for the Americans shot up the town before they entered it, but all were dead. The ones at the base of the wall had all been wounded and captured by the Germans first.

Months later, Fifth Army troops would have the novel experience of meeting a partisan company led by the escaped English POW-submariner, James F. Wilde. They would also meet the red-bandanna'd 36th Garibaldi Brigade, with its bright red flag on the top of Mt. Battaglia and Mt. La Fine, during a crucial part of the assault on the Gothic Line. The *Garibaldini* supplied detailed maps showing tank traps and enemy bunkers, and diverted fire from some of those mountainside bunkers to assist the Americans' progress. The same unit met the Americans in their winter camp on Mt. Belvedere in December, and helped guard against any raids from the other side. In return, during this standdown period, they were given cases of C-rations.

Front-related partisan actions sometimes achieved the status of pitched battles. The Gramsci Brigade, one week after the Allies entered Rome, launched an attack first at Salto di Cieco, then at Valle Piana. The aim was to slow the German Tenth Army's retreat so the Allies could catch up. A third of the brigade was lost in these actions, but the Gramscis claimed more than twice as many of the enemy—about three hundred men—were also killed or wounded.[61]

On the Eighth Army's front, the Ancona Brigade drove a German battalion out of Osimo in July, and the Maiella Brigade successfully defended its base on Mt. Carotto against a German attack. These actions took place just ahead of the British vanguard, which was moving to consolidate its positions around the port of Ancona.

The Apennine partisans did not always betake themselves to the AMG demobilization centers once the front reached and passed through their accustomed operational areas. They were more inclined to move northward in tandem with the retreating Germans. The mountains ended some twenty miles south of Bologna, though, and the partisans were loath to emerge from their mountain fastnesses, at least not until the Allies burst forth into the Northern Plain themselves. For a brief while, during the autumn of 1944, it looked like this would happen in short order. But the ever-optimistic Kesselring still had a couple of tricks up his sleeve, and the Allies failed to clear the mountains as winter set in.

The net effect of this was that the partisans found themselves heavily concentrated in a rather narrow operational zone, comprising the northernmost peaks of the Apennines. To the south was liberated Italy; to the north, the open-country heartland of the Repubblica. Both places were close at hand.

Three-quarters of the partisans in this area were Communist *Garibaldini*. Greater political variety might have led to jurisdictional disputes, as units that called the northern Apennines home found themselves hemmed in by new arrivals from the south. But there were none. Their ubiquity raised some problems for the Germans, though—and for the inhabitants of the mountain villages. The fact that the front bogged down here for the winter months and on into the spring aggravated the problems. Attacks against German soldiers became an almost daily occurrence. So did German mop-up operations. One day villagers would encounter partisans looking for food, used clothing, blankets, and medical supplies—or just looking for a place to hide. Then the Germans would show up, or perhaps a *Brigatte Nere* unit or a Militia company. If the enemy were simply looking for partisans, things might not go too badly. However, the Germans and the Fascists assumed that, for so many partisans to function in so narrow a space, every village must be implicated in some way. There could be no such thing as innocence or neutrality in such a place. So villagers could not expect to be treated with any consideration, even under the best of circumstances—the best being the absence of any recent partisan actions nearby. If any Germans were killed or wounded near—or, much worse, within—a village, things became especially nasty for the inhabitants.

From the American landing at Gela to the last push toward Rome eleven months later, the Goering Division seemed always to be in the thick of it. Its members had assumed responsibility for the safety of art treasures stored at Monte Cassino, saving a treasure-trove of art works and historical artifacts from destruction. The Goering Division's last official act in Italy, before it was sent away to fight the Russians, was a reprisal for casualties inflicted against some of the its personnel in northern Tuscany. That incident had taken place outside the town of San Martino. A cluster of villages and hamlets lined the ridges and hilltops in the area. Most of the inhabitants fled into the countryside at news of the incident, for they knew what was in prospect. After a few days, when nothing happened and it seemed that the Goering forces might be leaving the area, people began to filter back. The Germans had in fact rounded up more than five hundred hostages, saying that harm would come to these if a colonel taken captive by the partisans was not released immediately. The villagers probably concluded, after a few days of living outdoors away from their homes, that any reprisal would be limited to these hostages, most of whom came from San Martino and Arezzo.

They were wrong. The Hermann Goering Division, under the command of Gen. Wilhelm Schmalz, invaded the area in full force: first, artillery; then tanks; finally, infantrymen armed with flamethrowers, burp guns, grenades, and dynamite charges tore through the communities, leaving more than two thousand dead. This crime, carried out on 27 June, was the Goering Division's farewell to Italy.[62]

Weeks later, and further north, the Allies having narrowed the Apennine front even more, SS Maj. Walter Reder was given the task of commanding several companies of soldiers in reprisal raids for repeated partisan attacks. He commenced his assignment on 12 August at Sant' Anna di Stazzena, where 560 men, women, and children fell before submachine-gun bullets. His itinerary then took him to Valla—still largely abandoned by its inhabitants, but nonetheless able to give up

107 for execution. That was on 19 August. Then it was on to San Terenzio on 24 August, where the *Brigatte Nere* insisted on doing the honors. From there Major Reder and his warriors proceeded to the concentration camp at Mezzano (near Lucca), where the camp commandant was shown an order authorizing a reprisal execution of a hundred of the inmates. The camp housed some draft dodgers, relatives of draft dodgers, "troublemakers" from the factories awaiting deportation, and such. Reder disposed of 108 victims. Then the weary troopers headed for Bergiola, where partisans had ambushed a convoy. On 29 September, they arrived at Marzabotto, at the northern end of the mountains just twenty miles from Bologna. They settled in here, a place reputed to be a longtime bastion of radical sympathies, until 18 October. On 1 October, 147 of the town's inhabitants were shot, including 50 children. Nearby hamlets were visited on succeeding days, but Reder's men had to fan out into the countryside to root out the locals from caves, chicken coops, bushes, and brambles. When this exploit was completed, a total of 1,830 citizens were dead. The total included five priests. The Bologna newspaper, *Resto del Carlino*, felt constrained to deny stories of widespread slaughter in the nearby towns, noting that they sprang from a successful action against a "rebel cell."[63]

Reder was convicted as a war criminal for these acts in an Italian court after the war and sentenced to life in prison. In 1986, he was released due to ill health, and returned to his Austrian home to live out his last days in peace.

From atop the northernmost Apennines peaks, in clear weather, one can make out the dim outlines of the more prominent outcroppings of the Alpine piedmont. The intervening space is the North Italian Plain, bisected by Italy's greatest river, the Po. Those northerly mountains were the other great battlefront of the plainclothes soldiers. There the objective was to disrupt lines of supply and communication between the Reich and Italy. These lines bottlenecked at the Brenner Pass, which lay almost directly ahead as one gazed from the northern face of the Apennines. The one viable alternative route was by way of the Ljubljana Gap, northeast of Trieste, through Istria Province. This was the main line to Austria. Brenner was the main line to Germany itself.

Those partisans not intent on establishing "states" and "republics" in Val d'Aosta and other parts of the northwest tended to concentrate on these two supply routes. The bottleneck was both a challenge and an advantage for both sides. The possibility of a major disruption of transport in the bottleneck was ever-present. Such a disruption could have dire consequences for Wehrmacht forces at the front. This is probably why Kesselring noted these two areas, rather than the northern Apennines rear, as his major trouble spots in the partisan war.[64]

The advantage for both sides lay in being able to concentrate their resources on the task at hand. The Germans had the greater advantage but rankled at the investment in men and material necessary to maintain it. They were acutely aware that their being tied down this way constituted a major victory for the partisans and Allies. Kesselring estimated that on an average day six of his divisions (or the equivalent) were occupied in trying to keep the partisans under control. His Allied counterpart, Field Marshal Alexander, reached the same conclusion from his own sources. The estimate applies to all northern Italy, but half the total (three divisions) can be accounted for by the needs of protecting the main line south from Brenner and the secondary line through Istria.[65]

These lines offered precise targets not only to the partisans but also to Allied bombers. The planes had bombsights that could, from a mile up, assure a direct hit on a length of railroad track or highway. The Brenner Pass area, though, was festooned with antiaircraft guns that limited the Liberator bombers to haphazard drops from very high altitudes. The only occasional successes came from low-level runs by the swift P-38s and other light divebombers. But their ability to cause damage was limited by their small payload capacity. German fighter planes, hardly a factor at the front because of Allied dominance in this area, were a serious factor at the bottlenecks, further limiting the divebombers' effect.

Allied aircraft did a much better job hitting transportation targets in the Po Valley. Such targets were numerous there, and German defenses were accordingly thinned out. To have a telling effect, such raids had to be frequent and massive. The enemy had forced labor platoons out repairing damage almost before the dust was settled on such raids, so the aim was to get ahead of the capacity to repair, and create a growing gap in terms of unusable roadways and bridges and tunnels.

This required not only plenty of planes and crews, but also good flying weather. The Allies had neither. The weather turned very bad at the end of the summer of 1944, and at the same time the Italian front was being bled of men and weapons by the needs of the post–D-Day fighting fronts in France.

All this had the effect of making the partisan effort disproportionately important to the outcome of the campaign. In July and August alone, the partisans destroyed ten railroad bridges. All were located in the mountainous terrain north of the Po Valley—close to the converging bottlenecks, and therefore more important than lowland cross-river

---

bridges. By the end of the year, seven troop trains proceeding from Brenner were derailed and raked with gunfire. In Trieste, partisans even managed to sink an Italian submarine at anchor and to set off a powerful explosive in a movie theater crowded with German soldiers. Monthly reports submitted to Mussolini averaged well over two thousand partisan incidents for all northern Italy, an eighth of these against railroad trains or rights-of-way. Acts of sabotage or shooting incidents on the railroads alone averaged ten per day. Most of these acts occurred in the North Central mountain zone and in Istria.[66]

Kesselring found himself hard-pressed to keep matters from getting out of hand. This is why he requested that authority for dealing with saboteurs and other troublemakers be transferred from the SS to him. He also ordered his troops to execute captured partisans on the spot. Field Marshal Keitel, chief of staff in Berlin, and Heinrich Himmler, the SS chief, had no argument with this. Their premise was that wherever Kesselring's soldiers went, there went also his authority over the partisans. That was the authority to shoot partisans, including those already half-dead.

Torture led to the capture of Ignazio Vian, the *Autonomi* officer who led an ambush of two German officers at Boves in September 1943. That attack was the Wehrmacht's introduction to partisan warfare. The townspeople wisely went into hiding, but then unwisely returned to their homes after three days. The Germans then blasted the place with artillery, killing twenty-four. This was Italy's introduction to reprisal killing. Vian was captured in Turin in July 1944, tortured for information (not forthcoming), and hanged from a tree in a busy square of the city.[67]

The commanders of the *Ortigara* Brigade in Veneto were captured and shot a week before the war ended in Italy. CLNAI field headquarters in Venice, Cuneo, and Genoa were raided, everyone present being shot by firing squads after torture. In Milan, CLNAI set up a command post for the uprising that was to immediately precede the arrival of the Allies. It, too, was raided, and the complete plans for the uprising were taken by the SS.[68]

One may argue that the partisans must have had the initiative, since they controlled so much territory. Their self-proclaimed republics, though, were sleepy mountain valleys. When they had the temerity to raise their flags over large towns, they were quickly driven out, returning only when and if the enemy left. Bold acts, such as the sinking of the submarine at Trieste, suggested that the partisans could strike where they pleased. On New Year's Eve of 1944, for example, men dressed in German uniforms seized the stage of a Milan cabaret-theater filled with

German soldiers. Their leader read a manifesto while his comrades held the audience in check with submachine guns. Then they left by way of the stage door, where a stolen automobile was waiting for them with the motor running. There were no casualties. Yet to think that partisans had the run of Milan would be a mistake. Their public appearances there were usually in front of a firing squad.[69]

Matters of initiative changed drastically in the last two weeks of the war, when the German defenses at the front finally crumbled. The first area of longtime partisan activity to feel the effects of this was Piemonte, in the northwest. The Wehrmacht, which had never maintained a force-in-presence there anyway, was gone before the Fifth Army was even as far north as Genoa. Elsewhere, partisans sometimes found themselves engaged in pitched battles in open combat for the first time. At Belluno, on the frontier, they lost nine hundred men in a single day, probably a record for the whole partisan war.[70] Those last days contributed heavily to the total estimated casualties for the warriors in street shoes from 1943 to 1945: thirty-six thousand dead, plus ten thousand innocent civilians killed in reprisal raids.[71]

CHAPTER SEVEN

LA COMMEDIA È FINITA

Field Marshal Kesselring admitted to but one serious mistake during the course of the Italian Campaign: leaving the Roman bridges across the Tiber River intact when the Wehrmacht made its departure from the Eternal City. He did this because Rome was an open city. The bridges, though sturdy, were historical artifacts.

Still, as Kesselring appreciated later on, it would not have been a violation of the rules of war to render useless a strategic right-of-way, for the purpose of protecting a military retreat. His counterpart on the Allied side, Field Marshal Sir Harold Alexander, decided on a hot pursuit of the Germans, and for that the Tiber bridges were most invaluable. Allied forces did not quite catch up with the Fourteenth Army (whose commander, General Mackensen, was in the process of being sacked for, among other things, allowing the Texas Division to drive unchallenged through a gap in his lines south of Rome). But they unhinged Kesselring's plan to make a determined stand on the north shore of the next big river, the Arno.

The Arno River was the last important natural obstacle before the Gothic Line. The Germans had thus far made the most of natural obstacles, but the Allies' speedy crossing of the Tiber pretty well assured that the Arno would not run red with Allied blood. Things might have gone even worse for the Wehrmacht had not the Allied Fifth and Eighth armies been enmeshed in a massive personnel changeover, with some of their best divisions being despatched to France, their places in the line being taken by green or near-green units, some of which would prove inadequately trained. It is remarkable indeed that, under the circumstances, the pressure was kept on the Germans. Kesselring even found it necessary to abandon Livorno, Italy's third largest seaport, located on the west coast south of the Arno estuary. This became necessary when the U.S. 91st Division (the Powder River Division, shipped in from Oregon during the latter stages of the Anzio campaign) gained a precarious foothold on the south bank of the Arno, several miles inland from Livorno. With its line of retreat thus threatened, the Wehrmacht found it unfeasible to stand and fight when the battle-hardened U.S. 34th Division was sent directly against the city.

The capture of Livorno, on 19 July 1944, afforded the Allies an important depot for seaborne supplies. The fact that the Germans had by now virtually surrendered the skies to the Allies made it even more important, for this harbor, so close to the Gothic Line, was nonetheless rarely attacked by the Luftwaffe. Damage to the port facilities—much less serious than what had been done at Naples—was quickly repaired. During the coming months the only thing that would limit the port's usefulness was that it long remained within German bomber range, and there was always a fear that the Luftwaffe would resurrect itself for a last massive bombing raid. Such a raid, carried out at night or during bad weather, could possibly survive countermeasures by the Allies. But no such raid was ever made.

The focus of Allied efforts at this time was Florence, one of Italy's largest cities. The Arno flows through it before debouching into the sea fifty miles to the west. A major railroad hub, the city had attracted the attention of the Allied air forces as early as 26 September 1943, as the Salerno invasion was just being completed. Railway facilities on the outskirts and just outside the city (especially at Capo di Monte) were the main target. But the main casualty was a children's hospital.[1] A formation of Liberator bombers did not appear over the city again until the following May—the bombs once again aimed at railway targets, especially a locomotive repair facility at Porta al Prato. This raid proved to be more effective, although an unexpected casualty was the historic Teatro Communale, which took a direct hit during a rehearsal of the Mozart opera *Cosi fan tutte*.[2]

This mishap pointed up an important fact about Florence: It was, and had been for some centuries, one of the great repositories of Western culture. The birthplace and principal home of the Italian Renais-

North Italy

sance, the place was still, in 1944, a living museum. Since nobody except Mussolini was totally disillusioned by the status of recently conquered Rome as an open city, the subject of making Florence one as well
was quickly broached by both sides. The pope had played a central role
in achieving this status for Rome, which might easily have been ravaged
without his intercession. Now the two sides took the initiative themselves, and concluded that Florence, in the interests of humanity, should
be considered an open city where no battles or bombings should take
place. This time there was no demurral from *il Duce*, whose own personal fondness for the place rested, in part, on its status as the site of the
founding of the Fascist Party in 1921. It was also the hometown of
Alessandro Pavolini, the party chief and organizer of the *Brigatte Nere*.

Partisan attack on Germans occupying a castle in unidentified town, northern Italy. Courtesy UPI/Bettman

Kesselring declared Florence an open city on 23 June. The new commander of the 14th Army, however, was cautioned to keep at least one division in the city, lest the Allies exploit any opening in the Arno line within the city limits. The new (temporary) commander, Gen. Joachim Lemelsen, selected his best unit for this task, the 1st Parachute Division. It was also necessary to keep an eye out for partisan attacks in the city. Since the first appearance of partisan bands in the area in autumn 1943, the railroad station had been bombed, as had the Excelsior Hotel, at that time occupied mainly by German officers.

The partisans in fact denounced the "open city" declaration as a German ploy to handcuff them—ignoring, in their underground newspapers, full Allied concurrence in this status. Kesselring fully expected an armed uprising during the last days of the Occupation. The 1st Parachute Division, therefore, was given the responsibility for protecting the withdrawal of Fascist officials and their families, along with various SS and Wehrmacht personnel, whenever those last days should arrive.

The assassination of Fiovanni Gentile in February provided a note of urgency and an ingredient of revenge-seeking. The aging president of the Italian Academy was the only Fascist who commanded any respect outside Fascist circles, and we have already noted that even some partisans (specifically, the Actionists) condemned the deed. *Il Duce,* Pavolini, and others would have particularly enjoyed the spectacle of a partisan revolt that might then be bloodily suppressed by the veterans of Cassino.

Florence had also witnessed the public execution of draft dodgers; the imprisonment of a priest who condemned the executions during a Sunday sermon; the arrest of several nuns for hiding Jews; and Archbishop Cardinal della Costa's public assumption of responsibility for the latter deed, for which he voluntarily took the place of the nuns in the city jail. The Germans tried to shore up their image by displaying placards with photographs of alleged Allied atrocities, under banners such as "A Second Katyn" (referring to the now-proven Soviet massacre of Polish military prisoners in 1941), and "Anglo-Russian-American Civilization."[3]

But it was quite clear that disengagement from this large city would be a chancy affair, especially as the railroad station was in the city center. This may explain why the 1st Parachute Division was selected to guard the city during the crisis stage of the Arno campaign.

The New Zealand Corps, which had been repulsed from its attack into Cassino by that same division six months before (the attack which followed the destruction of the Abbey by Allied bombers), reached the southern outskirts of Florence on 4 August. A mile to the north, ranged along the northern bank of the Arno, stood the New Zealanders' old nemesis. The South African Corps, an armored force seeing its first serious combat on this front, moved up close. Further west, the U.S. 91st and 88th divisions, also stood poised for a rush to the river. The line held for a week. Then, on 11 August, Lemelsen ordered an evacuation from the city. At 6 A.M. that morning, the ancient bell of the Palazzo Vecchio began to toll madly. It was the signal for the insurrection.

At this point, dynamite charges that had been placed on five of the seven bridges across the Arno within the city limits were detonated by soldiers of the 1st Parachute Division. Many of the partisans within the city must have been on the south side when this happened, for the neighborhoods north of the river remained relatively safe for the Germans, except for some sniper fire. Certainly, the situation was much less hectic than it had been at Naples, the only other large city to challenge a Wehrmacht withdrawal.

The demolition of the five bridges was the worst instance of cultural damage, or the destruction of historical artifacts, since that of Monte Cassino; it was probably the second worst (again, after the Abbey) of the entire campaign.[4] It is remarkable that these airborne German troopers figured in both incidents—in the first, as the prime targets, and in the second, as the perpetrators. The Bridge of the Graces (Ponte alle Grazie), reduced to a heap of rubble in the riverbed, had been constructed in

1237—the time of Dante and his *Divina Commedia*, and long before the Renaissance that made Florence for a time the cultural center of the West. The Ponte Carraia, noted for its camel-hump shape, contained stanchions and pedestals dating from 1220. That bridge had been partially destroyed by a flood in 1333 and then rebuilt. The Trinity Bridge dated from *circa* 1300. The other two bridges were somewhat newer. Dynamite had been planted under the Ponte della Vittoria also, but (foreshadowing the graver oversight at Remagen, on the Rhine, several months hence) the soldiers simply forgot to set it off.

Kesselring had ordered these bridge blowouts, and was quite incensed by the survival of the Vittoria bridge, which could accommodate heavy vehicles. He did not wish to repeat the error of his decision to leave the Rome bridges intact. Regard for historical artifacts, however, did cause him to order that the seventh Arno bridge, the Ponte Vecchio, be left intact. That span was one of the hallmarks of the city, and, being crowded with shops from end to end, it could not be used by any vehicle larger than a motorcycle or a jeep. Very old buildings stood at either end, however—the dwellings of illustrious Florentines of the past—and the German commander ordered these collapsed into the street, blocking the bridge at both ends.

During the next few days, the German forces guarding the north bank of the river from the west coast to a distance inland, through Pisa and Florence and on to the rugged inland mountains, gradually loosened their grip. The seventy-five thousand men of the 1st and 4th Parachute divisions, and of the 3rd and 29th Panzer Grenadiers, moved northward toward their rendezvous with the Gothic Line and the Wehrmacht's last stand.

Allied commanders had by now spent much time pondering over the issue of how to breach the Gothic Line. Even though their resources were limited, due to the demands of the other fronts, they entertained high hopes that a breakthrough into the Northern Plain could be achieved prior to the onset of severe winter weather—the rainy time when roads turned into sticky mud and life on the mountainsides became very hard.

Clark, always devoted to the element of surprise, favored an attack in what he regarded as the least likely direction. In this war, the least likely direction was the one with the greatest natural obstacles, and also the one at the furthest remove from naval support. So the Fifth Army commander spoke out at meetings in his Caserta headquarters for a thrust into Il Giogo Pass, near the center of the peninsula, and close to the center of the Gothic Line. The Germans had initially been fooled at Anzio (but to no great effect). They had not been fooled at Salerno, when Clark tried to sneak the Texas Division ashore without a preliminary bombardment. They had been victims of naval firepower several times—enough times to expect a main thrust up one of the coasts, probably the west, and possibly involving some sort of amphibious operation.

But the Allies no longer had either the stomach or the landing craft for an amphibious operation—although it is possible that some landing ships could by now have been returned from the English Channel ports. The proposals of the French Expeditionary Corps chief, General Juin, during the Cassino campaign, were cited by Clark as his best authority. The deadlock at Cassino, Juin had said, could be broken by an inland maneuver—through the rugged mountains. And it was such a maneuver, initiated belatedly, that had finally done the trick.

But this difficult endeavor had been executed by Juin's own hardy mountaineers—Berbers, Algerians, and Moroccans who had grown up in the fastnesses of the Atlas Mountains in North Africa. They were gone now, fighting the Germans in France. Nonetheless, Clark's proposal was finally adopted. A highway running from Florence to Bologna, the latest headquarters of the Wehrmacht command, was to be the focal point of the advance. It ran through Il Giogo Pass. Bologna, a major city sixty miles northeast of Florence, was the putative gateway to the Northern Plain. It stood barely twenty miles beyond the northernmost Apennine peaks, on the edge of the great valley of the Po.

The Allied decision was influenced by intelligence received from the partisans, who reported that bunkers, tank traps, and earthworks were less formidable in this sector than in others. In fact, the Todt Organization had assumed, when it commenced the planning and construction of the Gothic Line, that an important route like Highway 65 (the road from Florence to Bologna) would capture the attention of Allied commanders to some degree at least. Todt then made a blunder by expecting that any major attack in this direction would see the Allies short-cutting through nearby Futa Pass. The latter place paralleled Giogo Pass to the west, and was closer to the main body of the Allied advance, which had stuck to the west side of the peninsula even after the liberation of Rome.[5] Unaware of the doggedness of Clark's devotion to the element of surprise, the network of bunkers, minefields, tank traps, etc., was actually more extensive in Futa Pass than in Giogo Pass—a fact duly reported by the partisans via their OSS contacts.

Forward positions of the Gothic Line were barely twenty miles north of Florence. Ranging from coast to coast, its western end followed the Magra River and then cut across the Vernio Pass. Proceeding east, it then cut across the Futa and Il Giogo passes, passed through rugged mountain terrain in the Central Apennines, then descended to the Adriatic Sea along the shores of the Foglia River. The total length of the line was two hundred miles. It was twelve to fourteen miles deep. Included with the bunkers and other obstacles were thirty 88mm gun emplacements in heavy concrete, and a hundred steel shelters—marshalling points for massed infantry attacks.

The front of the line was an obstacle zone in which no troops were deployed. Numerous villages all across the peninsula had been levelled to create this zone, which represented much of the line's overall width— as much as ten of the average twelve miles. The Wehrmacht divisions, with their gun emplacements, stood at the back of the line, ready to pepper the Allies with shrapnel and explosives as (so they hoped) the attack floundered through the minefields and tank traps. Wehrmacht commanders such as Gen. Ernst Guenther Baade and Gen. Fridolin von Senger, veterans of the Cassino campaign from beginning to end, hoped for a repeat of the bloody fiasco at the Rapido. Mark Clark, burned by that episode, was intent on avoiding such a disaster, and trusted that he had learned well.

Fifth Army enjoyed a singular advantage in having the excellent harbor of Livorno. It soon eclipsed Naples as the main supply base and staging area for the western half of the peninsula. Eighth Army had gained a nearly comparable advantage, taking the east coast port of Ancona in July, the same month that Livorno fell to the Americans. These two harbors were within thirty-five miles of the advance emplacements of the Line. Ancona gained in importance when Gen. Sir Oliver Leese, Eighth Army commander, succeeded in having Clark's plan for an attack up the center modified to allow a strong effort up the east coast.

The upcoming offensive, then, enjoyed a logistical advantage unparalleled for the Allies since the beginning of the invasion. The Germans had one important countervailing advantage. This was possession of the only east-west highway of any importance in that part of Italy, Highway 9. It ran along the back of the Gothic Line, and connected such places as Emilia, Modena, Reggio, Parma, Imola and Bologna. All Allied routes were in a north-south direction only. The result was that the Wehrmacht could reinforce pressure points, moving units back and forth along the front, much more easily than the Allies could. The Germans were already noted for a certain managerial adroitness in this regard, especially their ability to move parts of units into and out of other units without generating transport bottlenecks, supply shortages, and other problems.

Aware of the importance of Highway 9, Allied air forces based in Foggia exerted great efforts to minimize the road's usefulness. During the construction of the Line facilities, the Todt Organization found it necessary to keep road repair crews always at the ready to prevent Highway 9 from falling into shambles. In the summer of 1944, Allied bombers passed over this road daily en route to industrial targets in the great cities of the north, and sometimes the lesser cities through which the road passed. Thus the road was occasionally pounded in connection with other operations. It was by no means blameworthy for a B-17 to jettison its bombload, on the occasional aborted mission, over this relatively safe target while en route back to Foggia.

Air raids into northern Italy had been going on steadily since the capture of that major air base, the erstwhile principal home of the Italian Air Force, during the Salerno campaign in 1943. Cities including Milan, Genoa, and Turin had been enduring punishment from the air for a year prior to the commencement of the Gothic Line offensive. The first major raid on Milan, in fact, took place on 12 August 1943, from air fields in Sicily, so eager were the Allies to strike at Italy's industrial base.

The campaign against industrial targets was not a success. At the Fiat plants in Turin, for instance, the main problems were work stoppages and labor requisitions to the Reich, not smashed assembly lines and dead workers. Yet for the U.S. 15th Air Force, commanded by Gen. Ira C. Eaker, these plants were top priority. Even after the escort fighter planes drove the Germans from the air over Italy—a mission all but completed by summer 1944—the threat of ground-level air defense batteries was prohibitive. Theoretically, Fiat should have been attacked every day, until the last wall collapsed. In reality, such an effort would have undermined Allied air strength in Italy.

So it happened, instead, that a place like Tivoli, a middling target that would be liberated by Eighth Army in 1945, was *"devastata"* in a raid on 27 May 1944.[6] And so it happened that a train loaded (the Allies learned later) with POWs headed for Germany crashed into a ravine after bombers knocked out a bridge just ahead, near Chiusi. And so more cultural damage was added to the list compiled by the Monuments, Fine Arts and Archives Commission of AMG: the *Duomo* at Treviso (7 April 1944), and the Tempio Malatestiano at Rimini, a city soon to be liberated by Eighth Army.

By June 1944, 15th Air Force had 1,200 heavy bombers and was dropping bombs over Austria and Bavaria as well as North Italy. Its manpower was in the vicinity of fifty thousand men.[7] It is ironic that Kesselring, a German air marshal and a potential successor to Goering at the Air Ministry in the Reich, was at this point in the war almost entirely dependent on ground-based defenses in the air war, and virtually bereft of offensive capability.

Unlike Livorno, Ancona was subjected to a serious rearguard action by the Germans, using artillery in the nearby mountains. Thus, when Eighth Army would have preferred to be marshalling resources for the impending assault against the Line, it was necessary to pursue the enemy and, if possible, drive him across the Pesaro River to the north. A flanking action was directed toward the little mountain village of Croce (Cross), where the 8th Royal Fusiliers unexpectedly ran across a substantial number of Germans—the 129th Tank Battalion of the 29th Panzer Grenadier Division. The ensuing several hours of close-quarters armored combat on 9 August produced what the British commander, Gen. John Whitfield, later called "the dirtiest battleground I saw during the war."[8] When it was over, nearly five hundred German soldiers (most just in from training camp) and fourteen of their officers lay dead or wounded. The Fusiliers lost twenty-seven of their tanks. Air support had been called in by General Whitfield. It helped to decide the outcome, but at heavy cost: four Spitfires and two Liberator bombers—an amazing figure in an action involving a German battalion aided by no more than one air defense battery.[9]

Eighth Army was scheduled to commence the assault on the Line on 25 August. The attack began with a heavy artillery barrage aimed at German defenses—barbed wire and mined tank traps, strung out along the north bank of the Metauro River. The river had been the scene of a Roman victory over Carthage in 207 B.C. A massed armored attack followed, and the Germans withdrew from the north bank of the river on the second day, 26 August.

This was part of a one-two punch strategy, in which Fifth Army was to administer the second punch via Highway 65 out of Florence toward Giogo Pass. It was hoped that the Wehrmacht would transfer units down Highway 9 toward the Adriatic, in response to the British attack. This the Germans did, leaving themselves less prepared when the Americans launched the main offensive on 30 August 1944. Both the Giogo and Futa passes were the responsibility of the 4th Parachute Division. It faced the U.S. 85th Division (heading toward Giogo Pass) and the 91st Division, launching a "diversion" into the better-defended Futa Pass. The issue, regarding control of both strategic passes, was decided after nearly three weeks of continuous combat. Kesselring found it impossible to send major reinforcements there, because of a fear that there might be even a third punch.

Fifth Army followed up this victory with an assault on Mt. Battaglia, the highest peak between the passes and Imola, a major milestone on the road to Bologna. The capture of this mountain, coming on the heels of the Giogo breakthrough, threatened the defensibility of the entire Line. It also reflected the seriousness of the partisan problem for the Germans, for it was partisans who put the Allies onto the fact that Battaglia was only lightly defended, and partisans who were first to reach the medieval castle on the very top of the mountain. The Wehrmacht's discomfiture was reflected in the fact that a futile attempt was made to recapture this peak. It was a rare example of Germans launching an attack against a well-defended (and easily defended) position.

Giogo Pass had fallen on 17 September, and Mt. Battaglia on the twenty-first. On 22 September, the 91st Division, active now at the eastern end of Fifth Army's operational zone (where it met Eighth Army in central Italy), reached the banks of the Santerno River. The 85th Division, meanwhile, captured the town of Sambuco in a two-day battle, and then moved on to Mt. Canda and Radicata Pass. The intrepid old 34th Division then went into action, yet again, and moved around the eastern flank of the 91st Division, securing control of the Santerno River crossing. On the western side of Fifth Army's front, Pisa was occupied after a lengthy bombardment (which its famous Leaning Tower came through with only minor damage). Lucca and Pistoia were also liberated in September.

On Eighth Army's front, the Germans fought a stubborn defense on Coriano Ridge, not far from the star-crossed village of Croce. They next made a stand at the Marecchia River, which the Canadian Corps succeeded in crossing on 21 September. The following day, Canadian units entered the Republic of San Marino, population 14,000 (plus 120,000 refugees). San Marino, which Germany recognized as an independent state but then occupied in 1944, was in the midst of a serious typhoid epidemic.

The main action at this time, however, was several miles to the east, near the Adriatic coast. There the Royal Bays and the 9th Lancers of the British were moving against Rimini. On 19 September, a massed tank assault over two miles of open ground resulted in the destruction of twenty-four of the twenty-seven tanks involved.[10] The commander of the defending forces, the 90th Panzer Grenadier Division, was General Ernst Guenther Baade, who had figured in the bloodletting on the Rapido back in January. Also taking part in the defense of Rimini, an eastern anchor of the Gothic Line, were the 356 Infantry and the 20th Luftwaffe Field Division. All three of these units were newly arrived on the Adriatic Coast, the latter two fresh from training camps in Germany. Rimini fell to the British after two more days of desperate fighting, on 21 September.

At this point the advance on the Gothic Line was barely four weeks old. It appeared that the work of the Todt Organization, which had been going on all through 1944, was virtually for nought. Kesselring's now-legendary talent for bottling up the Allies also seemed to have lapsed. The American drive from Florence to Bologna had already covered forty-five of the sixty miles' distance. At that rate, Fifth Army might emerge into the Northern Plain by the end of the month.

The last ten days of September, however, were marked by heavy rains. Roads that had sent up choking clouds of white dust now became sticky quagmires that could suck the boots off a soldier or cause a tank to slide sideways until it toppled into a roadside ditch or ravine. The business of replacing men and matériel lost in the combat of those four weeks was greatly impeded by the weather. The Americans alone had sustained ten thousand casualties.[11] Eight army infantry divisions were cut from four to three battalions until further notice, due to manpower losses averaging eight hundred per day during the offensive. The British had also lost 71 of 150 tanks used in the first ten days (25 August–5 September), and at the end of September they counted 250 tanks lost in combat, plus 230 disabled as a result of non-combat causes, mainly in road mishaps during the rainy last days of the month.[12] (Many of the latter were, however, back in action when the offensive resumed.) The 56th Division, veteran of many battles in Italy, was disbanded except for its Headquarters unit; disbanded, too, was the 1st Armored Division.

On 5 October, Fifth Army launched another drive, along a seven-mile front centered on the road to Bologna, Route 65. Intermittent rainfall was still a problem, and supply lines stretching back to Livorno now had to contend with serious flooding on all the rivers. The 91st Division headed up the highway, flanked by the 34th, the 85th and the recently arrived "Blue Devils" of the 88th Division. The towns of Loiano and Livergnano were captured, but after ten days of furious activity the advance had covered barely three miles. Eighth Army meanwhile secured the north bank of the Marecchia River, in the vicinity of a bridge built in the time of Emperor Tiberius (1st century A.D.). The Marecchia, in dry weather only two feet deep, was now running strong at a twelve-foot depth due to the rain. Further progress proved very difficult, and Eighth Army's entire front became static. On 25 October, Fifth Army made a lunge toward Highway 9, the east-west roadway that served the Wehrmacht so well. The 88th and 91st divisions fought their way to the peak of Mt. Grande, which afforded them a good view of a considerable stretch of Highway 9. Now the Americans could fire on specific targets moving along the highway, provided such targets were available in daylight. The Germans lost part of their freedom of use of this highway.

The three-day battle of Mt. Grande took place in continuous heavy rain. It was the rainiest October in living memory. Both armies were awash in mud and flooded rivers. The weather, plus the heavy losses of the September fighting, had a telling effect on the Allies' hopes of breaking out of the mountains before winter. The momentum and the initiative now seemed lost. They *were* lost. An added factor, which became apparent late in the month, was the steady drying up of the supply line. By the end of October the Allies had lost 465 tanks,[13] destroyed or damaged beyond repair. They were not able to make good half of the loss. By early November, Fifth Army found itself with but fifteen shells for each piece of artillery—a level of armament that could have spelled disaster in coming battles.[14]

These shortages were due to the intense activity on the other fronts. Late September, for instance, saw the temporary derailment of the Allied advance through the Low Countries (stopped at Arnhem, 26 September). In the Pacific, General MacArthur was in the midst of his largest campaign, the liberation of the Philippines. Had the Germans not also seen the first serious cutback in their own resupply situation, things might have become critical indeed for the Allies.

The problems that began to crop up here prevented Kesselring from gloating over his October successes. Indeed, while the Americans launched their attack on Mt. Grande on 25 October, Kesselring was injured in a collision and had to be hospitalized. Responsibility for Highway 9 fell suddenly into the hands of Gen. Heinrich Gottfried von Vietinghoff, Tenth Army commander on the Adriatic front. Kesselring, with an arm and leg in a cast, was permitted by his doctors to follow the action only through brief oral reports delivered to him by his chief assistant, Gen. Siegfried Westphal. His injuries kept him out of action until February, and any impulses to second-guess Vietinghoff were repressed during that long recovery in the interests of morale and efficiency in the Wehrmacht command. As it happened, this was virtually the effective end of Kesselring's role in Italy. He returned to duty, but only a few weeks later, in March 1945, he was summoned to take charge of the defense of Berlin. Vietinghoff then resumed, on a permanent basis (as permanent as anything could be for the Wehrmacht then), command of German forces in Italy.

On the last day of October, Eighth Army fought its way across the Ronco River. Ten days later the city of Forli was liberated, and the British were tantalizingly close to the end of the great mountain chain. It was widely assumed that the Germans would not be a match for the Allies once the fighting reached the Northern Plain. Visions of Germans fleeing across open, treeless fields, raked by Spitfires and P-38s, were fondly held by every Allied soldier.

The Germans in fact did not intend to stand and fight battles in the Plain, although some talked of turning Milan into a German Stalingrad. Stalingrad had proven, with its stone buildings and narrow streets, to be a natural fortress for the Russians. If the Allies repeated in Milan the mistake the Germans had made at Stalingrad—going in after the defenders with tanks and infantry—some Wehrmacht officers believed that the Germans could win. But Milan was inhabited by Germany's enemies, not by its citizens. It was the headquarters of the Underground. And the element of an overlong supply line, of the type that had failed the Germans in Russia, was absent—unless the weather remained very foul. But even though, by November, it seemed that the rain would never end, everybody knew that it would eventually, and a strong defense in the Plain would be challenging fate at best.

The Germans instead planned to fall back quickly to the Alpine foothills in the northeast, where an impressive network of World War I tunnels, bunkers, and the like, built by the Austrians and Italians, was still intact. Rommel had suggested that the Alpine region comprise the only defense line after the fall of Sicily. He was then talking of a line that stretched all the way across northern Italy to France. But Rommel thought such a line could be held for the duration of the war. So, too, from the vantage point of late 1944, could a shorter line stretching from the Brenner Pass to the Ljubliana Gap—a line that would block off the entry points to Central Europe.

Kesselring had broached the idea to the Führer before his accident, in September, while the Allies were apparently making mincemeat of the Gothic Line. It was more a talking point than a solid proposal, but Hitler had quashed the idea immediately, telling the field marshal to hold the Apennine barrier for as long as possible—to head for the Alps only when there was no longer any alternative.

Shortages in November on both sides made the front exceptionally quiet. For the first time, at least after the capture of Forlì, all was quiet on the Italian front. Soldiers devoted their time not to preparing for or engaging in attacks, but in planting barbed wire and digging more foxholes and dugouts.[15] It continued to rain frequently enough to keep the roads and rivers impassable, and cold weather set in early, so that on the higher mountainsides rain turned into windblown sleet. On 13 November, Field Marshal Alexander delivered his standdown order to the partisans—over the radio, to the great enlightenment of the Wehrmacht.

The Allies, however, still entertained hopes of driving the Germans out of their mountain stronghold, and marshalled their thin resources for one last attempt before the worst winter weather set in. The drive was tentatively set for mid-December, with Bologna its main objective. U.S. and British forces would converge on the city—the Americans continuing up Highway 65, the British rounding the northeast corner of the Apennines. The distance to be covered for the Americans was little more than ten miles in places, and not much more than twenty miles for the nearest Eighth Army units.

But the Germans reinforced Imola, on the American front, with the 29th Panzer Grenadier Division. They also sent reinforcements to Faenza, in front of Eighth Army, and also to Ravenna. There would be no easy victories here.

Eighth Army made its move against Ravenna at the beginning of December, hoping to improve its chances of converging on Bologna in tandem with the Americans. The city fell on 5 December. On the sixteenth, Eighth Army secured Faenza after a fierce battle with the 90th Panzer Grenadiers.

The drive on Bologna was then put on temporary hold when the OSS reported that the German Fourteenth Army, in concert with the new Ligurian Army of Mussolini's republic, was plotting a daring move to attack down the west coast and seize the harbor at Livorno. Such a move seemed highly implausible, since it involved an attack down thirty miles of coastline. The Wehrmacht's only previous counteroffensive—the one at Anzio—had involved only a few miles of territory, from the Alban Hills to the Allied landing site. It was also well-known what naval guns could do to an army fighting near the shore. Both the Germans and the Italians had learned a hard lesson on that score. Then there was the likelihood of Fifth Army cutting in behind the advance, out of its fortified mountain bases that paralleled the entire length of this putative attack.

This brief scare finally dissipated, and preliminary action for the offensive against Bologna got underway just before Christmas. By this time hard winter weather had already settled in. But the prospect of spending two or three more months amidst snow drifts at the higher altitudes, sitting under sleet storms at the middle altitudes, and walking through icy quagmires in the valleys, was enough to impel at least one more effort to bid farewell to the Apennines, before it was time to sing "Auld Lang Syne" to the hellish year 1944.

The German Fourteenth Army, however, managed to catch everybody by surprise after all. The rumored west-coast offensive turned out to be more than a rumor. On 26 December, the 51st Mountain Corps, assisted by two Italian divisions of the Ligurian Army, came roaring into the Serchio Valley. This westernmost sector of the Allied front was the responsibility of the U.S. 92nd Division. The troopers of the 92nd found themselves heavily outnumbered—a quite unique experience for an American combat unit in Italy. No less unusual was taking the brunt of a German offensive. The nearest parallel was the Fourteenth Army attack at Anzio in January, but even there it was the British who took the first blows. The British forces, moreover, were seasoned units with veteran commanders.

The 92nd had some combat veterans, but it had reached operational strength for the first time only weeks before. The German-Italian attack covered three miles in little more than a day, and then paused to allow ammunition and supplies to catch up. Fifth Army hastily gathered reinforcements. The 8th Indian Division (on temporary assignment with Fifth Army) was first on the scene. Units of the U.S. 85th Infantry and 1st Armored gathered around Lucca, a short distance to the south. Navy ships also steamed up the coast from Livorno, and the Fourteenth Air Force was called on for repeated bombing and strafing runs. The Indians led an attack on 28 December that recovered much of the lost territory almost as rapidly as it was lost. The Germans and their Italian allies withdrew from the Serchio Valley on the 29 December.

The planned move against Bologna was cancelled for the time being. A post mortem on the Serchio Valley attack indicated that the Allied front had to be fortified in greater depth, to prevent another attempt at a breakthrough in some quiet sector. This meant a reduction of offensive capability in the interests of defense. Mark Clark, who had succeeded Alexander as commander of operations in Italy (Fifth and Eighth armies) two weeks earlier, reluctantly concluded that the Bologna campaign would have to be scrubbed for the duration of the winter. His successor as Fifth Army chief, Gen. Lucian Truscott (who had to leave his 3rd Division in Southern France for this unexpected assignment back to Italy) had argued against overreaction to the Serchio Valley offensive. He characterized it as more a "reconnaissance in force" than a true attempt to capture and hold major targets.[16] The new Fifth Army commander was sorely disappointed at the prospect of sitting the winter out. He was impatient to lead this army the way he had led his old division.

Truscott also argued that the problem was not with general deployments, but with the unfortunate 92nd Division itself. It was the largest black combat unit in the American army, and the men's conduct under fire became a topic of discussion, even attracting the attention of General

Marshall in Washington, who had last visited the front on the eve of the Gothic Line offensive in August. Truscott himself had some biting comments, saying that the Serchio defenses on 26 December "melted away— a term which was to be frequently used in describing action of colored troops."[17]

A German commander has been quoted to the same effect[18] and the belief was definitely shared by Clark and Marshall. Clark noted in his memoirs that the 92nd had a "less favorable" record than any other unit in Fifth Army,[19] and concluded that the division's performance on 26 December was its low point. He went on to blame segregation for this, considering it a negative morale factor. But then he went on to say that the Army was not ready for desegregation. Truscott shared this view.

All of the 92nd's officers above the rank of lieutenant colonel were white, while all the troops were black. The commander was Gen. Edward M. Almond, who would lead a desegregated force into the jaws of the Chinese military behemoth exactly five years later, in North Korea, provoking the longest retreat of an American army in U.S. history.

Two British historians have offered a novel view of the 92nd's problems. Claiming it to be the U.S. equivalent of the familiar British colonial forces (such as the 8th Indian Division that saved the day in the Serchio Valley), they noted that unlike the spirited colonials, the men of the 92nd lacked a distinctive traditional uniform—in itself a sign that they lacked a clear identity and the pride that goes with it.[20] These writers also note, however, that the front here was woefully thin and that Axis forces enjoyed the advantage of "complete surprise."[21] Add to this the fact that the 92nd was, as a functioning combat unit, only a few weeks old, and one wonders just how blameworthy the troopers were.

The story was covered in the American newspapers with little reference to the battlefield realities. An official War Department investigation led by Truman Gibson, a respected black American, was similarly two-dimensional. Gibson found himself, afterward, under attack in the black press. The episode was the one thing that put Italy on the front pages during those winter months.

The 92nd was reorganized in the aftermath, at one point being pared down to a regiment of black troops and a regiment of white troops that ate and slept separately. In subsequent operations, especially in the final offensive of April and May that brought the 92nd up to the vicinity of Genoa, the division sustained hundreds of casualties. In March the ranks were filled out with the addition of the Japanese-American 442nd Regiment, transferred in from southern France. The 442nd enjoyed an excellent reputation; it, too, had always been a segregated unit. The 92nd ended the war, then, being segregated three ways, with a black regiment, a yellow regiment, and a white regiment. Dying together was sometimes unavoidable, but the bodies went to segregated cemeteries.

At midnight, New Year's Eve, whole sections of the front across Italy were lit up with tracer bullets. In some of the villages within earshot of soldiers shivering on the mountainsides, church bells pealed. The bells were often rung by fellow soldiers, because some of the villages were virtually abandoned. But in some churches there were midnight masses, as there had been on Christmas Eve, and the churches were lit up despite the dictum that any light in nighttime would draw artillery fire. But the guns were silent, and only the tracer bullets resounded.

Three more months passed with the scale of operations limited to attacks on adjacent enemy-held mountain peaks. For these activities the newly arrived U.S. 10th Mountain Division—trained in the Rocky Mountains, and whose standard equipment included skis and snowshoes—proved invaluable. It was said that the enlisted ranks of this unit were better educated than the officer corps of some other divisions. This late arrival was destined to compile a lengthy and distinguished combat record before the war was over in just a few months.

April saw the resumption of full-scale hostilities. It was time at long last to complete the journey down Highway 65. Eighth Army set forth from its base in Ravenna for its first taste of open-country fighting, in the area around Lake Comacchio. Here the Tommies met the Turcoman Division, which surrendered hastily in the face of a massed tank attack, and secured by 4 April access to the rolling hill country east of the city of Bologna.

The Polish Corps followed up by fighting its way across the Senio River on 10 April. The British then captured Porto Garibaldi, and crossed the Santerno River on the twelfth.

The long-delayed drive into Bologna began on 14 April. The city had lived under the Allied guns for more than six months, expecting to be engulfed in a great battle at any moment. The sense of impending doom was constantly reinforced by the daily booming of artillery and tanks somewhere along the front, and by occasional bombing raids. The latter, though, were remarkably perfunctory, the worst being an October raid on the government center at Piazza Maggiore (formerly Piazza Vittorio Emmanuele II). Partisan activity added to the general unease. The men who harassed the Wehrmacht supply lines in the so-called triangle of death considered the city their base of operations. And they had been active there since at least January 1944, when the Fascist chief, Eugenio Facchini, was gunned down by bicycle-riding *Gappisti.*

Anti-German feeling had expressed itself at the time of Italy's surrender to the Allies, in September 1943, when a *"comitato"* was hastily
formed and demanded that weapons of the local Italian Army contin-
gents be turned over to it. (The area commander, Gen. Alberto Terziani,
turned them down.) In November 1943 four German soldiers were shot
while dining at the Fagiano Restaurant. No group claimed credit for
this, possibly because it occasioned the first roundup of hostages. No
more such incidents occurred in Bologna until June 1944, when a soldier was shot by a sniper. Ten hostages were then executed near the scene
of the assassination, on Via del Pratello.

Partisans captured in the immediate countryside were sometimes executed in the Piazza Nettuno, site of one of the city's landmarks, a statue
of Neptune by Arbizzani. Such executions were especially common in October, when everybody thought that the Allied soldiers would be in the
streets almost at any hour. On 18 October, partisans bombed the Hotel
Baglione, then home to many German officers. Two days later, students
at the university (site of one of Europe's oldest medical schools) rioted
when police staged a raid looking for the source of the new underground
newspaper, *Rivoluzione Socialista.* One of the most effective partisan
attacks of the whole war also occurred in Bologna, on 10 August, when
the 83rd Garibaldi Brigade invaded an aircraft engine plant that was a
major supplier to the Luftwaffe in Germany.

Yet, in spite of the months of foreboding, Bolognese enjoyed the highest standard of living in all Italy, at least in terms of food supplies. The
surrounding countryside was one of the country's most productive farming areas—a reason why Bologna has always been famous for its cuisine.
Disruptions in transportation caused by bombing raids therefore did
not affect the city very much. Neither was it a major haven for refugees,
most of whom avoided cities not in liberated areas. Shortages did not
appear until March, and these were the result of exceptional diversions
to meet emergencies elsewhere in the North, and in Germany. That month
saw disturbances over food shortages, including an invasion of city hall
during a demonstration that got out of hand.

The Allied offensive was marked by a diversionary strike by British
forces up the Adriatic coast. Then units of the Polish Corps (most of the
3rd Carpathian Division) headed around Lake Comacchio and made
straight for the city from the southeast. Meanwhile, to the west, the U.S.
10th Mountain Division secured control of the three thousand-foot
heights of Riva Ridge (using ropes to scale a sheer cliff at one point) and
then broke across the east-west highway, Route 9.

On 21 April, units of the U.S. 88th Division fought their way into the city on the southwest side. The same day, Polish forces entered the city from the east. Of even greater concern to the Germans was the maneuvering of Allied divisions outside the city. Fifth Army was pouring men and armor across Highway 9 to the west, heading north against limited opposition. It was expected at Vietinghoff's headquarters that these would cut eastward, within the next few days, in order to envelop the defenders of Bologna. Eighth Army was conducting a similar maneuver around the north end of Lake Comacchio, which the Germans thought might even be related to an amphibious landing up the coast.

On 24 April, Vietinghoff ordered the Fourteenth Army to begin a complete disengagement. This violated an order direct from the Führer, who had expressed a desire that the Allies be held out of the Northern Plain for as long as possible. The implication of this order, issued when Berlin was already in flames, was that the Wehrmacht should make its last stand not in the foothills of the Alps but at the northern end of the Apennines, and that it should expend its last resources there.

Amazingly, had Vietinghoff ordered his troops back to Germany, at this juncture, they would not have been able to fight their way back into their homeland. Virtually the entire Reich had already been overrun by the Allies. Eleven days earlier, Vienna had fallen to the Russians, who then quickly advanced to the foothills of the Austrian Alps, within striking distance of the Italian border. Parts of General Patton's Seventh Army were close to the northern outlet of the Brenner Pass. The climactic Battle of Berlin—the city's defense in the hands of Kesselring—was already well underway.

Beyond the streets and battered houses of Berlin, an inferno of noise and smoke, the last surviving dominion of Fascism was to be found in the expanses of the Italian north. The situation was not to last for very long. Bologna proved to be the last stand of the Wehrmacht in Italy. The SS chief in Italy, General Wolff, was already negotiating the details of a German surrender with OSS head Allen Dulles. General Vietinghoff was apprised of these negotiations and, as he ordered the retreat from Bologna, without referring to Wolff's dealings, asked Berlin for guidance as to the proper timing for any capitulation.

The answer came back, from the eternal optimist Kesselring (who could not have been overly optimistic at this juncture), that surrender was not to be considered. A spirited fighting retreat across the Northern Plain was the least that Berlin expected of Vietinghoff. At the very moment that this message was sent, Allied artillery shells were landing in the immediate vicinity of Kesselring's command center, sending reverberations through the subterranean structure and creating a pall of dust in some of its rooms.

Even though Vietinghoff was expected to make a stand south of the Po, German units began crossing that river as early as 23 April. With the order to disengage from Bologna the following day, units sometimes fought for road space in a frantic effort to get across this great natural obstacle. All of the bridges had long since been destroyed by Allied bombers. Engineers laid out pontoon bridges which promptly attracted the attention of the British and American pilots. Daytime activity proved to be extremely hazardous. The terrible carnage produced by strafing runs against columns on the north-south roads on 24 April and twenty-fifth in daylight impressed the Germans with the fact that the day belonged totally to the Allies. Henceforth, movement—including the construction of pontoon bridges was reserved for the night.

But Fifth and Eighth Army forces were rushing ahead. Some British units crossed the Po at about the same time the Germans did. A major part of the famous 1st Parachute Division, and most of the 4th Parachute Division, were cut off before they reached the river. Other divisions scrambled across, leaving behind large numbers of dead and wounded, and virtually all of their artillery, tanks, trucks, and supplies.

The Wehrmacht was finally broken. Allied units sped along toward their northerly objectives with little or no opposition, sometimes passing hapless German soldiers waving white flags and standing clear of the roads. The U.S. 91st Division reached the banks of the Adige River—the Germans' putative last line of defense in the Northeast—on 27 April. On the twenty-ninth, the British 56th Division was in Venice. On 2 May, the New Zealand Corps entered Trieste—just ahead of Tito's forces, who were not supposed to be there.[22]

Even Milan, the industrial metropolis of the North and Italy's largest city, fell without a battle. German forces were ordered out on the 26 April, barely forty-eight hours after the evacuation from Bologna. The fact that Milan is fifty miles north of Bologna, and separated from it by the mighty Po River, suggests how speedy was the Wehrmacht's collapse. The great city, though, had not been completely spared from the ravages of war. It was a prime target of the Fifteenth Air Force, and had sustained heavy damage as early as 12 August 1943, when the Allies were still struggling for a foothold in Sicily.[23] By a month later, it was estimated, an eighth of Milan's buildings had been destroyed or heavily damaged. At such a rate, the city might have been levelled, like Munich and Dresden, by the war's end. But the raids became less frequent after Italy's official surrender in September 1943, although the surrender probably had nothing to do with this. For the duration of the war, nonetheless, up to half a million of Milan's citizens boarded trains in the evening to spend the night in the homes of people living in nearby towns and villages. And many of the city's children were boarded in country towns for the duration.

That late summer night, in 1943, when Italy's surrender had been announced on the radio, great crowds paraded through the streets, some waving Italian flags, others waving red flags and singing the "Internationale." German soldiers were in the streets the next day. Now, a year and a half later, they were going away, just as suddenly and unexpectedly as they had arrived. In the interim, Milan had become the headquarters of the Resistance. The Resistance, however, kept a relatively low profile there during the Occupation. A German division, assisted by up to forty thousand Fascist militiamen, Black Brigade men, *Decima Mas* men, and others, secured at least a semblance of control. The worst disruption of Occupation authority occurred in November 1944, during the wave of strikes that swept across the north, and which was orchestrated by the Resistance leaders in their damp cellars and hidden rooms.

The most prominent public figure through it all was Cardinal Alfredo Aldefonse Schuster, Archbishop of Milan since 1928 and, next to the pope, the leading clergyman in Italy. Schuster sometimes complained to Mussolini about conditions, such as the presence of seven different police authorities (SS, Wehrmacht military police, Fascist police, Guardsmen, Pietro Koch "investigators," and so forth). He also sermonized on Sundays about "a new kind of *vendetta*," in which citizens denounced each other to one or another of these police forces, in order to settle old or sometimes new scores.[24]

Schuster has been characterized as "once an ardent admirer of Fascism,"[25] who, by 1943, was somewhat disillusioned with the regime. On 25 April, the day before the Germans left, he received a phone call asking if he would host a meeting between *il Duce* and Resistance leaders at his official residence. The cardinal promptly agreed, and the rather unlikely confabulation convened that afternoon. That very day, these same Resistance leaders had proclaimed a general insurrection in the city, and armed partisans were taking over the streets.

SS chief General Karl Wolff was supposed to be at the meeting. *Il Duce* was surprised to learn that Wolff was busy working out details of a German capitulation. He was still more taken aback when General Cadorna, military commandant of the Resistance, refused to discuss safe conducts to Switzerland or any other schemes for saving Fascist hides. He demanded simply that Mussolini surrender himself unconditionally, and announce to all the Fascists that they should do likewise—that very day.

Il Duce was allowed two hours to think things over, and left the meeting promising to reply promptly, after conferring with his closest advisers and family members. It was not unrealistic to expect, with the North quickly falling under the control of the partisans or the Allied armies, that Mussolini would return within the hour (he said he would only need an hour) and allow Cadorna to place him under arrest.

But all his life Mussolini had been a political gambler, and now he would make one last gamble. His car headed straight out of the city. Aides notified members of his family and whatever top government leaders they could find. The town hall in Como (on Lake Como) was selected as a rendezvous point. Requests also went out for a German military escort, to help *il Duce* make his way to the Swiss border and possible political asylum in that neutral country.

Mussolini and a coterie of his followers spent the night in Como, and the following day set out up the lake shore. On the evening of 26 April, they joined up with a German column, consisting of an armored car and thirty trucks, with three hundred soldiers. The Germans were also headed for Switzerland, where they hoped to be briefly interned and then repatriated. The caravan moved along through the night, but was stopped by a partisan roadblock at 8 A.M. on the morning of 27 April. There were only a dozen partisans, but the Germans knew that fighting partisans was no longer the thing to do. The word had quickly spread that the partisans controlled all the roads, and that to fight past one roadblock would mean running a deadly gauntlet the rest of the way, with the partisans probably taking no prisoners. On the other hand, it was known that partisans might let Germans through, after assuring themselves that there were no Fascist fugitives in disguise among them.

The inspection of the three hundred Germans' papers took a few hours. Meanwhile, Italian militiamen in service of the Italian Social Republic were separated out and told they would be detained. Most of these men were armed, but they surrendered their weapons willingly. Mussolini, at this point, was sitting in one of the trucks among the Germans, dressed up in a German uniform, replete with helmet and overcoat. One of the partisans recognized him.

Il Duce was conducted to an army barracks in Dongo, a town located close by, and spent the night there. The partisans, members of a Communist Garibaldi unit (the 52nd Garibaldi Brigade) notified their commandant, "Pedro" (Count Pier Luigi Bellini delle Stelle), and in short order the Communist chiefs in Milan were notified. The Insurrection Commit-

Fascist leaders executed by Italian patriots and hung for public display in center of Milan. The two on the left are Claretta Petacci, Mussolini's mistress, and Mussolini. The Allies wanted il duce *alive but did not condemn this act of revenge against the brutal dictatorship.* Courtesy UPI/Bettman

tee, a CLNAI unit whose job was to co-ordinate partisan activities during the Insurrection that had been proclaimed on 24 April (not only in Milan, but all over the north) was then notified. Luigi Longo, head of the Communist brigades, was the leading figure on this committee by virtue of the fact that a substantial majority of partisans were enrolled in Garibaldi units. The committee had announced, on 25 April, that all captured Fascist officials were subject to summary execution. Longo and his associates, Sereni, Pertini and Valiani, lost no time in deciding that this policy applied to *il Duce* himself—even though the final armistice agreement between the Allies and Italy required that Mussolini be turned over to the Allies if he ever fell into the hands of Italian authorities. The Insurrection Committee and the *Garibaldini* were all adjuncts of CLNAI, itself an agent of the provisional government in Rome.

General Cadorna, who happened to be the provisional government's highest-ranking official in Milan, was notified of the decision. He made no objection, but communicated the news to the Bonomi government in Rome. The Insurrection Committee, meanwhile, dispatched an execution team, headed by one Walter Audisio. By the time Audisio and his aide reached Dongo by car, *il Duce* had been joined by his longtime paramour, Clara Petacci.

Clara Petacci was a widely recognized figure in Italy, having even been featured in newsreels at the movie theatres. Every Italian knew that *il Duce*, a married man with a family, whiled away his leisure hours with Clara. She had moved to Lake Garda when the Italian Social Republic was set up, and in recent months had occupied the chateau of the late Fascist poet Gabriele d'Annunzio.[26] It was widely believed that she exerted influence over political appointments and general access to *il Duce*. For this, she was somewhat controversial in Fascist circles. Edda Ciano, the widow of Count Ciano and Mussolini's daughter, claimed that Clara was the *de facto* head of state in the Italian Social Republic, making decisions on behalf of the often depressed and passive *Duce*.[27]

In 1943, after Mussolini's firing, she had been arrested on a charge of possessing stolen property (Persian carpets) and sent to jail to await trial. Then the Germans freed her, shortly after their rescue of *il Duce*. This time nobody was looking for her, but when Walter Audisio showed up in Dongo, there she was, insisting that wherever *il Duce* went she would go.

She therefore joined Mussolini in Audisio's car, when *il Duce* was advised that he was being returned to Milan for processing. After a few miles, on the outskirts of Giuliano di Mezzagra, the car stopped, and Audisio ordered his two prisoners to stand side by side against a wall by the roadside. He then pulled from his pocket a paper, prepared by the Insurrection Committee, indicating that *il Duce* was condemned to death for his crimes and that the sentence was to be carried out forthwith. Audisio then produced a firearm, raised it, and shot *il Duce* and Clara.

The bodies were then returned to the car, and brought to Milan. It was the will of the Insurrection Committee that they be exhibited in the Piazzale Loreto, where hostages had been massacred in summer 1944, as a reprisal for partisan deeds. Two other high-ranking Fascists, Achille Starace (party chairman throughout much of the Mussolini era) and Roberto Farinacci (the strongly pro-Hitler veteran of the Fascist Council) were also placed on exhibit, although they had been captured and killed elsewhere. That gruesome exhibit, captured in newsreel footage, is one of the most famous scenes of the war. It marked the one instance in which the partisans took matters into their own hands and stopped obeying the Allies. There was no demur. This was a purely Italian affair, and the visitors from abroad, though they had spilled their own blood abundantly in this war, simply stood by quietly and watched.

CONCLUSION

It is rare indeed for both contestants in a military endeavor to come away with their minimum objectives achieved. Usually there is a winner and a loser. In a case where there is no winner, neither side is apt to feel satisfied unless there was a case of one surviving against heavy odds, in which case the other side has suffered a moral defeat.

In Italy, the armed forces of both sides succeeded in their respective missions. The Germans elected to go into Italy for the purpose of staging a delaying action, to keep the Allies at some remove from the boundaries of the Reich. They succeeded fully and may have been surprised at how successful they were.

Their success was due in no small part to the vagueness of the Allied objectives. The Allies hoped Italy would fall like a ripe plum. But barring that, they looked at Naples and the Foggia airfields as a minimum objective. Then they looked at Rome. And then they looked at the Alpine frontier. The official U.S. histories of the campaign reveal another objective: to tie down scarce German manpower and exploit the Allied manpower advantage by maintaining an "extra" fighting front. But then, even this aim was not present at the time the campaign got underway. It materialized only after the Germans made their commitment.

The Allies did capture Naples, Rome, etc., and they did tie down a dozen Wehrmacht divisions, so they won too. It cannot be said that the campaign was a failure for either side. We can even add a shopping list of additional benefits that accrued to each side.

For the Germans, there were the matters of rescuing Mussolini, resuscitating Italian fascism, and "rectifying" the frontier with Italy. There was the slightly encouraging prospect of the Allied advance in Italy being slower than elsewhere and stopped altogether for extended periods. But most important, there was the matter of exploiting Italy's resources. We have already described what Germany took from North Italy. The Allies were satisfied in tying down a dozen German divisions, but those divisions secured large quantities of vital war materials. On the whole, the Wehrmacht made an excellent investment in Italy.

A shopping list of added benefits for the Allies would include the overthrow of *il Duce*. True, he was revived by Hitler but only as a stooge. He ceased to be a true head of government before the Sicilian operations were over. If the Allies had not invaded Italy, what would have been Mussolini's status at the end of the war? By then, he might have tried changing sides. In any case, there would be the problem of knowing how to deal with him. And also in any case, it would have been unseemly for Italy, an Axis land, to get through the war without being invaded.

The Allies—particularly the Americans—also enjoyed one of the triumphal moments of the war, the liberation of Rome. The image of Pius XII, raising his arms in thanksgiving from the Vatican balcony, is a highlight of our collective memory of the war.

There was also the issue of having something to do while preparing for the cross-Channel invasion. This was a realistic concern, especially as fighting raged on the Russian front. It was an issue of morale and hope.

Further, there was the matter of the lesser Allies. Quite a large number of countries declared war on Germany. Virtually none but the "major allies" saw action on the eastern front or in the west after D-Day. In Italy, however, were to be found Poles, New Zealanders, Indians, Brazilians, Moroccans, etc. It was a veritable United Nations army—and referred to as such, late in the war, even before the signing of the UN charter. General Clark complained of the problems of language, customs, and command structures that confronted him in managing multinational forces. Such problems were not to be welcomed on the major fronts, but Italy, as a Sideshow War, could afford to cope with them and give the lesser Allies a chance for action.

Neither side lost in Italy. But that only highlights the real tragedy of the Italian campaign. Nobody lost because, from a military standpoint, it wasn't all that important. It really didn't have to happen.

NOTES

CHAPTER ONE

1. Clay Blair, *Ridgway's Paratroopers: The American Airborne in World War II* (New York: The Dial Press, 1985), p. 90.
2. *Records of the Italian Army* (Washington, D.C.: National Archives Microfilm, 1967), roll T 21, frames 725–26, 736–37, 751, 757, 774, 846, 858, 949.
3. Office of Strategic Services (OSS), "Survey of Italy." Washington, D.C.:National Archives Microfilm. Roll 17, frame 39.
4. Blair, *Ridgway's Paratroopers*, p. 84.
5. Ibid., pp. 92–93.
6. Albert N. Garland, and Howard McGraw Smyth. *Sicily and the Surrender of Italy* (Washington, D.C.: USGPO, Office of the Chief of Military History, 1965), pp. 171–72. Also, J. Lee Ready, *Forgotten Allies: The Military Contribution of the Colonies, Exiled Governments, and Lesser Powers to the Allied Victory in World War II* Vol. I. *The European Theatre.* (Jefferson, N.C.: McFarland, Inc., 1985), p. 195; and Blair, *Ridgway's Paratroopers*, p. 99.
7. Garland, *Sicily*, p. 170.
8. Ibid., p. 182.
9. Blair, *Ridway's Paratroopers*, p. 103n.
10. *The Papers of Dwight David Eisenhower: The War Years*, ed. Albert D. Chandler, Jr. (Baltimore: Johns Hopkins Press, 1970), p. 1303.
11. *The New York Times*, 15 July 1943, p. 1.
12. Garland, *Sicily*, p. 17.
13. *Records of the Italian Army*, Roll 30, frames 428, 431; Roll 21, frame 34. For the German reaction, see F. W. Deakin, *The Brutal Friendship: Mussolini, Hitler and the Fall of Italian Fascism* (Garden City, N.Y.: Doubleday, 1966), p. 373.

14. *Records,* Roll 21, frames 18, 88 (21/18, 88) for Axis troop deployments prior to Montgomery's move.
15. *Times,* 18 July 1943, p. 1.
16. Cf. Blair, *Ridgway's Paratroopers,* p. 110. Ridgway called it "more like a maneuver than a shooting war." The author also cites the official history of the campaign, (Garland, *Sicily*), which referred to the western swing as "little more than a road march."
17. *Times,* 30 July 1943, p. 4.
18. *Records,* 21/168.
19. *Times,* 7 August 1943, p. 1.
20. Dwight D. Eisenhower, *Crusade in Europe* (New York: Dolphin Books, 1961), p. 190.
21. Blair, *Ridway's Paratroopers,* p. 104.
22. *Records,* 21/212.
23. OSS, "Survey of Italy," 17/38.
24. *Records,* 21/14.
25. *Records,* 21/230, 233.
26. *Times,* 16 August 1943, p. 2.
27. *Records,* 21/18, 24.
28. *Times,* 3 August 1943, p. 1.
29. Trumbull Higgins, *Soft Underbelly: The Anglo-American Controversy Over the Italian Campaign, 1939–1945* (New York: Macmillan, 1968), p. 98.
30. Cf. W. G. F. Jackson, *The Battle for Italy* (New York: Harper & Row, 1967), p. 77.
31. *Records,* 21/239, 241 (Daily Reports).
32. David W. Ellwood, *Italy, 1943–1945* (New York: Holmes & Meier, 1985), pp. 9, 10.
33. Martin Blumenson, *The Mediterranean Theatre of Operations: Salerno to Cassino* (U.S. Army in World War II. Washington, D.C.: USGPO, Office of the Chief of Military History), p. 217.
34. Hugh Pond, *Salerno* (Boston: Little, Brown, 1962), p. 24.
35. Martin Gilbert, *Winston S. Churchill.* Vol. VII: *Road to Victory, 1940–1945* (Boston: Houghton Mifflin, 1986), p. 403.
36. Josef Stalin, *Correspondence,* pp. 136–37.
37. Ibid., p. 138.
38. Gilbert, *Churchill,* p. 430.
39. Ibid., pp. 445, 449.
40. Ibid., p. 475.
41. Harry L. Coles, and Albert K. Weinberg, *Civil Affairs: Soldiers Become Governors* (Washington, D.C.: Office of the Chief of Military History, Department of the Army, 1964), p. 223.
42. G. A. Sheppard, *The Italian Campaign, 1943–1945* (New York: Frederick A. Praeger, 1968), p. 69. Also, *Times,* 17 August 1943, p. 1.
43. *Records,* 21/18, and *Times,* 21 July 1943, p. 5.
44. *Records,* 21/168 (map).
45. Garland, *Sicily,* p. 240.
46. *Times,* 30 July 1943, p. 4. Gen. Giuseppi Molineri escorted General Keyes into Palermo.
47. *Records,* 21/600, 757.
48. Jackson, *Battle for Italy,* p. 40.

49. Chandler, *Papers of Dwight David Eisenhower*, p. 1347.
50. *Records*, 21/190 "Operazioni in Sicilia." Cf. also Garland, *Sicily*, p. 240.

CHAPTER TWO

1. Benito Mussolini, *The Fall of Mussolini*, ed. Max Ascoli (New York: Farrar, Strauss, 1948), p. 138.
2. Cf. Denis Mack Smith, *Mussolini: A Biography* (New York: Vintage, 1982), p. 383. An order to "act with utmost prudence" in the event of any rescue attempt had just be received that day.
3. M. de Wyss, *Rome Under the Terror* (London: Robert Hale, 1945), p. 39, notes that the Roman newspapers passed the event off as "unimportant."
4. *Records*, 21/198. For example, the 171st battalion of the Aosta Division was decimated by desertions. General Roatta, in a report to the *Comando Supremo*, stated that unit *"era constituto da elementi Siciliani."*
5. OSS. "Sicilian Separatism With Particular Reference to the Report of Lord Rennell." R & A No. 1521. Washington, D.C.: National Archives Micro film. Report dated 19 November 1943, p. 5. Separatists were most active in 1945, when L'independenza della Sicilia (the main separatist group) organized the Ecercito Volontario, the nucleus of a hoped-for volunteer "army of independence." The movement all but expired in 1946, the year Italy produced a new constitution.
6. Cf. Deakin, *Brutal Friendship*, pp. 439–40.
7. Wyss, *Rome Under the Terror*, p. 57. Grandi related this later to the Swiss ambassador.
8. Mussolini, *Fall of Mussolini*, p. 71.
9. Wyss, *Rome Under the Terror*, p. 48.
10. Deakin, *Brutal Friendship*, p. 541.
11. Wyss, *Rome Under the Terror*, p. 91. Muti was suspected of leading a cabal of old Fascists in a scheme to overthrow the king and set up General Cavallero as a military dictator.
12. Deakin, *Brutal Friendship*, p. 502.
13. Wyss, *Rome Under the Terror*, p. 101. The writer adds that generals Roatta and Rossi refused to attend the meeting.
14. Ibid.
15. Ibid., p. 114.
16. Friedrich-Karl Plehue, *The End of an Alliance: Rome's Defection from the Axis in 1943*, trans. Erich Mosbacher (London: Oxford University Press, 1971), pp. 66–67; Garland, *Sicily*, p. 290.
17. Garland, *Sicily*, p. 293.
18. *Records*, 21/500
19. *Records*, 21/495.
20. *Records*, 21/506.
21. *Records*.
22. *Records*, 21/544.
23. *Records*, 21/519.
24. *Records*, 21/520, 571.
25. Silvio Bertoldi, *I Tedesci in Italia* (Milan: Rizzoli, 1964), pp. 103–104.

26. Rudolf Rahn, *Ruheloses Leben: Aufzeichnungen und Erinnerungen* (Duesseldorf: Diederichs Verlag, 1949), p. 275.

27. Bertoldi, *I Tedesci*, 93. Cf. also OSS R & A No. 2268, "The German De Facto Annexation of the Italian Northeastern Provinces," (Survey of Italy), Roll 17, p. 4.

28. Deakin, *Brutal Friendship*, p. 615.

29. *Records*, 21/505.

30. Cf. Enzo Collotti, *L'amministrazione tedesca dell' Italia occupata, 1943–1945: Studio e documenti* (Milan: Lerici Editori, 1963), p. 81; Iris Origo, *War in Val D'Orcia: An Italian War Diary, 1943–1944* (Boston: David R. Godine, 1984), p. 70; *Times*, 27 July 1943, p. 4; Jackson, *Battle for Italy*, p. 25.

31. Deakin, *Brutal Friendship*, p. 597.

32. Roberto Battaglia, and Giuseppe Garritano, *Breve Storia della Resistenza italiana* (Turin: Giulio Einaudi, 1955), pp. 58–59.

33. Ibid., p. 62.

34. Origo, *War in Val D'Orcia*, p. 151.

35. Battaglia and Garritano, *Breve Storia*, p. 58.

36. Sheppard, *Italian Campaign*, p. 27; Charles G. Delzell, *Mussolini's Enemies: The Italian Anti-Fascist Resistance* (Princeton, N.J.: Princeton University Press, 1961), p. 32.

37. Ready, *Forgotten Allies*, p. 203. The destroyer *Ardito* was sunk by a bomb; the destroyer *Avisto Sella* sunk by a German E-boat; the destroyer *Ugolino Vivaldi* scuttled after being disabled by a bomb; the destroyer *Antonio Da Noli* sunk by a mine.

38. *Records*, 21/636, 642.

39. Cf. Blair, *Ridgway's Paratroopers*, p. 147. The Italian fleet based there was already en route to surrender at Malta, and sighted the British invasion force heading toward the city. There was one costly mishap at Taranto: The cruiser *Abdiel* struck a German mine in the harbor; 55 sailors and 101 paratroopers were lost.

40. Kesselring saw the attack as a virtual assassination attempt, and believed that some Italian officer had delivered plans of the compound to the Allies. Another momentous event occurred at the same place a day later: Count Ugo Cavallero, the pro-German former chief of staff (replaced in January by Ambrosio) allegedly shot himself following a meeting with Kesselring. The two occurrences have not been tied together, but there was widespread belief among Italians that he had been murdered by the Germans. Rumor had it that the bullet entered the back of his head.

41. Meyer, *Stars and Stripes*, p. 127.

42. Blair, *Ridgway's Paratroopers*, p. 142.

43. Pond, *Salerno*, p. 12. On 1 August, the Germans complained that nobody was on duty during an Allied fly-over the night before. An investigation ordered by *Commando Supremo* found this accusation to be "*parimente falsa*." 21/652.

44. Chandler, *Papers of Dwight David Eisenhower*, p. 1321 (Eisenhower cable to Combined Chiefs of Staff).

45. Wolfgang Werthen, *Geschichte der 16. Panzer-Division, 1939–1945* (Friedberg: Podzun-Pallas Verlag, 1958), p. 145.

46. Eric Morris, *Salerno: A Military Fiasco* (New York: Stein & Day, 1983), p. 89. There was a fifteen-minute preliminary bombardment on the British beach. Cf. Blumenson, *Mediterranean*, p. 74.

47. Sheppard, *Italian Campaign*, p. 12. The ammunition and supplies, on the other hand, did land in the right place—thus making matters even worse, as many of the soldiers found themselves under fire without ammunition.

48. Dominick Graham, and Shelford Bidwell, *Tug of War: The Battle for Italy, 1943–1945* (New York: St. Martin's Press, 1986), p. 54. General McCreery, commander on the British front, shared this view.

49. Blumenson, *Mediterranean*, p. 97.

50. Albert Kesselring, *The Memoirs of Field-Marshal Kesselring* (London: William Kimber, 1953), p. 205, notes that General Clark (in his memoir, *Calculated Risk*) criticized the Germans for not massing their tanks during attacks. Kesselring credits accurate naval gunfire for preventing such massing and compelling the Germans instead to disperse their tank forces in small attacks.

51. Kesselring, *Memoirs*, p. 184, places the blame for this decision on Rommel.

52. Graham, *Tug of War*, pp. 93–94.

53. Morris, *Salerno*, p. 242. All 38 planes missed the drop zone, some by as much as 25 miles. Two planes were still "unaccounted for" a month later, according to Blumenson, *Mediterranean*, p. 132.

54. Mark Clark, *Calculated Risk* (New York: Harper & Brothers, 1950), p. 200.

55. Col. (later General) James Gavin of the 82nd Airborne was especially critical of Clark, and placed most of the blame on him. Cf. Blair, *Ridgway's Paratroopers*, p. 157. Eisenhower, on the other hand, cites Dawley's "lack of skill" in *Crusade in Europe*, p. 199, and made similar remarks in his report to General Marshall. Morris, *Salerno*, p. 243, cites Dawley's "unauthorized" move to the beach on the first day as the prime cause of his alleged loss of control. Meanwhile Graham, elsewhere quite generous to Clark, holds him primarily responsible for the shortcomings of the campaign (p. 199). Graham also criticizes General Walker, 36th Division commander, for not having trained his men well enough. Other assessments of blame can be found on pp. 144 and 283 of Morris's book, and also in Pond, *Salerno*, p. 125.

56. Maj. Gen. Lucian K. Truscott, *Command Missions: A Personal Story* (New York: E. P. Dutton, 1954), p. 262. Cf. also Blair, *Ridgway's Paratroopers*, p. 159, for General Walker's observations.

57. Graham, *Tug of War*, p. 91; and Pond, *Salerno*, p. 195.

58. Blumenson, *Mediterranean*, p. 102.

59. Delzell, *Mussolini's Enemies*, p. 283.

60. Cf. OSS, Roll 17 ("Political Dilemma in Italy," p. 7); and Giorgio Bocca, *Storia Dell' Italia Partigiana: Septembre 1943–Maggio 1945* (Bari: Editori Laterza, 1966), p. 75.

61. Blumenson, *Mediterranean*, p. 166, writes that the city was "utterly destroyed." A similar characterization can be found in *Stars and Stripes*, 4 October 1943, p. 1.

62. Coles and Weinberg, *Civil Affairs*, p. 322.

63. Ibid., p. 241.

64. Ibid., p. 322; Blumenson, *Mediterranean*, p. 169; Chandler, *Papers of Dwight David Eisenhower*, p. 524.

CHAPTER THREE

1. Graham, *Tug of War*, p. 118.
2. The film, *The Battle of San Pietro*, was directed by John Huston. It is available at several film libraries.
3. *New York Times*, 23 January 1944, p. 1.
4. Robert L. Wagner, *The Texas Army: A History of the 36th Division in the Italian Campaign* (Austin, Tex.: Robert L. Wagner, 1972), p. 115n, referred to it as a "great aid to the enemy."
5. *Times*, 5 February 1944, p. 2.
6. Maj. Jack S. Berry, who was in charge of the engineers, felt that Fifth Army headquarters had failed to address the problems of effecting a crossing of the Rapido. (Blumenson, *Mediterranean*, p. 350.)
7. Graham, *Tug of War*, p. 118.
8. Blumenson, *Mediterranean*, p. 348 (quotation from Walker's diary).
9. Blumenson, *Mediterranean*, p. 350.
10. Col. William H. Martin, who won a Silver Star at the Rapido, was the leading critic of the operation. He told the Congressmen that men were sacrificed as "cannon fodder," and that his 143rd Regiment was "destroyed" for no reason. (Wagner, *The Texas Army*, p. 115n.) Truscott called the attack "overly optimistic." (*Command Decisions*, p. 289.) A summary of the Germans' assessment can be found in Blumenson, *Mediterranean*, pp. 121, 350. Clark, in his memoir *Calculated Risk*, says the operation was "not impossible," and states that such a rate of casualties was not unknown. He cited the losses of the 34th Division (a newcomer to the campaign) during the push to Cassino as an example of this, noting that there were no complaints from that quarter (pp. 279–80).
11. Blumenson, *Mediterranean*, p. 134.
12. Westphal, *Memoirs*, p. 419.
13. *Times*, 25 January 1944, p. 3.
14. *Times*
15. Gilbert, *Churchill*, p. 662. The message was addressed to the prime minister.
16. *Times*, 24 January 1944, p. 1.
17. Vaughan, *Anzio*, p. 58.
18. Martin Blumenson, *Mark Clark: The Last of the Great World War II Commanders* (New York: Congdon & Weed, 1984), p. 171. For Churchill's role, cf. Gilbert, *Churchill*, pp. 621–22; and for Clark's statement, cf. Graham, *Tug of War*, p. 110.
19. Sheppard, *Italian Campaign*, p. 209, and Blumenson, *Mark Clark*, p. 165.
20. Blumenson, *Mark Clark*, p. 165. The worst previous air raid was on 8 February.
21. Sheppard, *Italian Campaign*, p. 217.
22. Churchill to Lord Moran: "Anzio was my worst moment in the war." Cf. Anthony Cave Brown, *Bodyguard of Lies* (New York: Harper & Row, 1975), p. 420. This book describes how the Allies tracked the Germans via access to their coded messages provided by the Enigma decoding device. Every German move was anticipated by the Allies, in stark contrast to the grossly incompetent intelligence about the invasion supplied by Admiral Canaris to Marshal Kesselring.
23. Brown, *Bodyguard*, p. 414.

24. Wilson, *Report*, p. 24.
25. Wilson, *Report*, p. 31, contains the erroneous information that the Abbey was "occupied and fortified," an assertion that oversteps even the claims of General Tuker. An equally spurious account appeared in the *Times of London* just days before the decision to bomb was made. (Cf. David Hapgood, and David Richardson, *Monte Cassino* (New York: Congdon & Meed, 1984), p. 162.) Eaker's inspection flight is noted on p. 185.
26. Graham, *Tug of War*, p. 192. The sanitary zone was supposed to be 330 yards wide.
27. Clark nonetheless concludes that the bombing was a "mistake." (*Calculated Risk*, p. 246.)
28. Sir Harold Alexander, *The Alexander Memoirs*, ed. John North (London: Hutchinson, 1962), p. 245. He asked, "How could a structure which dominated the fighting field be allowed to stand?"
29. This was, according to Blumenson in *Mark Clark*, p. 186, the first time heavy bombers were used against a combat target. Such planes normally were used against transportation and industrial targets, usually in urban areas far removed from combat zones.

CHAPTER FOUR

1. *New York Times*, 21 July 1943, p. 1.
2. Wyss, *Rome under the Terror*, p. 44.
3. Ibid., pp. 41–42.
4. Ibid., p. 135.
5. Eugen Dollmann, *Roma Nazista* (Milan: Langanesi, 1949), pp. 256, 276–77.
6. Reported in *Giornale d'Italia*, 23 February 1944, p. 3.
7. Wyss, *Rome under the Terror*, p. 137.
8. Ibid., p. 139. Battaglia and Garritano, *Breve Storia*, p. 107, states that 2,091 Jews were arrested.
9. David W. Ellwood, *Italy, 1943–1945* (New York: Holmes & Meier, 1985), p. 130.
10. Wyss, *Rome under the Terror*, p. 140.
11. Origo, *War in Val D'Orcia*, pp. 106–109.
12. Wyss, *Rome under the Terror*, p. 140.
13. Named for Fritz Todt, its founder, this unit constructed major defensive works in occupied territories.
14. *War Crimes*, XIV, p. 292. Testimony of Ambassador Weizsaecker.
15. Wyss, *Rome under the Terror*, p. 111.
16. Dan Kurzman, *The Race for Rome* (New York: Doubleday, 1975), p. 325, notes that there was a lively fear of a Naples-like last-minute insurrection.
17. Wyss, *Rome under the Terror*, p. 151.
18. Hapgood and Richardson, *Monte Cassino*, p. 227; also Bruce Quarrie, *Fallschirmpanzerdivision Hermann Goering* (Warren, Mich.: Squadron/Signal Publications, 1978), p. 18; and *War Crimes*, IX, p. 552.
19. Dollmann, *Nazista*, pp. 241, 244, 255. Cf. also Kurzman, *Race for Rome*, p. 174.
20. Battaglia and Garritano, *Breve Storia*, pp. 126–27.
21. Ibid., p. 126.
22. Plehue, *End of an Alliance*, p. 25.
23. Blumenson, *Anzio*, p. 257.
24. Sheppard, *Italy*, p. 252.

25. Blumenson, *Anzio*, p. 257.
26. Christopher Hibbert, *Anzio: The Bid for Rome* (New York: Ballantine, 1970) p. 150.
27. Martin Blumenson, *Mark Clark: The Last of the Great World War II Commanders* (New York: Congdon & Weed, 1984), p. 210. Alexander virtually assigned (at an earlier date) the city to Clark's Fifth Army. Cf. Nicholson, Alexander p. 248. Cf. also Jackson, *Battle for Italy*, p. 241, for more insight into this issue.
28. Gen. Friso von Senger und Etterlin, "Probleme." Article in Andreas Hillgruber (Ed.), *Probleme des Zweiten Waltkrieges* (Cologne and Berlin: Kiepenheuer & Witsch, 1965), p. 286. (Article pp. 277–91.)

CHAPTER FIVE

1. Cf. Kurzman, *Race for Rome*, p. 385.
2. E. Piscitelli, *Storia della Resistenza Romana* (Bari: Laterza, 1965), p. 413, describes American and British attitudes.
3. Coles and Weinberg, *Civil Affairs*, 327; Ellwood, *Italy*, p. 79.
4. OSS. R & A No. 1211 (11/15/43). "Basic Political and Social Information on Central Italy," p. 19.
5. *New York Times*, 30 Jan 1944, p. 7.
6. Cf. Ellwood, *Italy*, pp. 81, 88.
7. Delzell, *Mussolini's Enemies*, p. 398. The Provisional Government's denazification program was guided by the provisions of the Sforza Decree. Before the capture of Rome, the Badoglio administration included a Committee on De-Fascistization (appointed in April). Its chairman was Prof. Adolfo Amodio, one of the leaders of the anti-monarchist Action Party.
8. OSS. "Occupied Terr." Reel 17. "Food Distribution in Italy," p. 14.
9. Ibid.
10. *Records of the Italian Army*. Reel 474. "Ernährungslage in Süditalien." (Anlage zu Amt VI—München). Nr. 914 (23 Nov. 1944), p. 34.
11. Ellwood, *Italy*, p. 169.
12. Ibid., p. 116. The decision to step up food shipments came after the latest Roosevelt-Churchill summit meeting. The matter was given a certain amount of fanfare, and even carried a special designation, the "Hyde Park Declaration."
13. Coles and Weinberg, *Civil Affairs*, p. 307.
14. *Records.* Reel 474. OKW/Feldwirtschaftsamt. "*Italian wiederaufbau probleme in feindbesetsten Italian,*" p. 10.
15. *Records.* The Americans also built a new brickyard and a windowglass plant near Naples.
16. Ellwood, *Italy*, p. 171.
17. Coles and Weinberg, *Civil Affairs*, p. 385.
18. Cf. Battaglia and Garritano, *Breve Storia*, p. 112.
19. *Records*, Reel 474. "*VAA heim Uberbefehls Südwest (3 Nov. 1944)*", p. 21.
20. Coles and Weinberg, *Civil Affairs*, pp. 377–78.
21. Rodney Campbell, *The Luciano Project: The Secret Wartime Collaboration of the Mafia and the United States Navy* (New York: McGraw-Hill, 1977), p. 174.
22. *Ezra Pound Speaks: Radio Speeches of World War II*, ed. Leonard Doob (Westport, Conn.: Greenwood Press, 1978), p. 368.
23. *New York Times*, 23 Feb. 1944, p. 4. Spelman's remarks were made at a Knights of Columbus mass commemorating Washington's Birthday. He noted

that the Vatican was a neutral state, and that the victims were "homeless and helpless people."

CHAPTER SIX

1. Enzo Collotti, *L'amministrazione tedesca dell' Italia occupata, 1943–1945: Studio e documenti* (Milan: Lerici Editori, 1963), p. 208.
2. Ibid., p. 370. The Germans also "looted" 16,000 tons of steel rails.
3. Ibid., p. 176. Cf. also Paul L. Schultz, *The 85th Infantry Division in World War II* (Washington, D.C.: Infantry Journal Press, 1949), p. 201.
4. OSS, "Population Movements in Italy," Reel 17, p. 8.
5. Deakin, *The Brutal Friendship*, p. 743. The speech originated in the Lyric Theatre in Milan before a large audience. It was *il Duce's* sole public appearance from the time he was rescued to his capture and execution by Communist partisans.
6. Deakin, *Brutal Friendship*, p. 396.
7. Ibid., p. 398.
8. *Lavori forzati* was published at San Pietri in Casale, and was obviously intended for an Italian readership.
9. OSS, R & A No. 2161, "German Administrative Control in Northern Italy," (7/24/44) p. 11. The policy of punitive labor requisitions was combined with the threat of plant closings and removal of machinery to Germany in an order promulgated by Industry chief General Leyers on 26 March 1944. (Cf. Collotti, *L'amministrazione*, p. 204.)
10. Collotti, *L'amministrazione*, pp. 190, 205.
11. Ibid., p. 205.
12. Bertoldi, *I Tedesci*, p. 108. The Udine newspaper *Gazzetta* was closed temporarily for printing Mussolini's complaint.
13. *New York Times*, 31 July 1943, p. 1.
14. OSS, R & A No. 2200, "The German De Facto Annexation of the Northeast Italian Provinces," pp. iv, 20, 27. A new Fascist newspaper was allowed in Adriatische Kuesterland in May 1944, shortly after the Klessheim conference. It was titled *Italia Repubblicana*. Also, while Fiume district was still administered by an Italian, the city itself came under a German-appointed Croatian mayor.
15. Cf. Garland, *Sicily*, p. 533.
16. Roman Dombrowski, *Mussolini: Twilight and Fall*, trans. H. C. Stevens (London: William Heinemann, 1956), p. 92. Farinacci and Pavolini shared this view.
17. Giovanni Marinelli, one of the condemned, was reputedly the mastermind of the assassination of opposition leader Matteotti in 1925—an event that aroused so much popular unrest it nearly derailed the Fascist juggernaut. (Dombrowski, p. 152.)
18. Rahn, *Ruheloses Leben*, p. 251.
19. Ibid., p. 244.
20. Deakin, *Brutal Friendship*, p. 609.
21. *Corriere della sera*, 23 Dec. 1943, p. 23.
22. OSS, R & H #1740, "The Italian Social Republic," Reel 18, p. 17.
23. Rahn, *Ruheloses Leben*, p. 280. Details of the reorganization plan can be found

in Colotti, Enzo, *L'amministrazione tedesca dell' Italia occupata, 1943–1945: Studio e documenti* (Milan: Lerici Editori, 1963), pp. 157, 325; and in Deakin, p. 671.

24. Colotti, *L'amministrazione*, p. 204.
25. Delzell, *Mussolini's Enemies*, p. 474.
26. Massobrio and Guglielmotti, *Storia*, p. 319, provides details of the rationing program. Monthly limits per person included 2 kilos pasta, 1 rice, 5 potatoes; 150 grams red meat (available Saturdays only), 100 grams pork.
27. Origo, *War in Val D'Orcia*, p. 101.
28. Ibid., p. 118.
29. Bertoldi, *Salò*, p. 68.
30. Deakin, p. 660.
31. Origo, *War in Val D'Orcia*, p. 181.
32. Rodolfo Graziani, *Ho Difesa La Patria* (Milano: Garzanti, 1948), p. 427. Cf. also Delzell, *Mussolini's Enemies*, p. 266; and Deakin, *Brutal Friendship*, p. 750.
33. Cf. Delzell, *Mussolini's Enemies*, p. 266.
34. Susan Zuccotti, *The Italians and the Holocaust: Persecution, Rescue and Survival* (New York: Basic Books, 1987), p. 284.
35. Graziani, pp. 427, 436; Zuccotti, *Italians and the Holocaust*, p. 153.
36. Giovanni Pesce, *Soldati senza uniforme: Diario di un Gappista* (Rome: Edizioni di Culture Sociale, 1950), p. 259.
37. Of Italy's 30,000 Jews, 6,885 died in 1943–45. Assembly camps for transfer to Germany were located at Verona, Bolzano and Fossoli. Cf. Bertoldi, *Salò*, p. 341.
38. According to Bocca, *Storia*, p. 104, there were 10,000 *Autonomi*. Cf. also Delzell, *Mussolini's Enemies*, p. 322. Civilian partisan groups active in the Abruzzi region included the Bosco Martese, the Armando Ammazzalonga and the Rocca brigades.
39. Delzell, *Mussolini's Enemies*, p. 291; p. 290 for the Communists as 40 percent of the total. Cf. also *Historical Dictionary of Fascist Italy*, ed. Philip V. Canistraro (Westport, Conn.: Greenwood Press, 1982), p. 454.
40. Their most important groups were the Rosselli and the Italia Libera brigades.
41. See Luciano Bolis' war memoir, *Il mio granello di sabbia*, (Canoa, 1947).
42. *Rinascità*, June 1944, p. 50.
43. Origo, *War in Val D'Orcia*, pp. 157, 160.
44. Delzell, *Mussolini's Enemies*, pp. 295–96.
45. Ibid., p. 288.
46. Ibid., p. 283, estimates 100,000 in 1945. OSS, "The Contribution of the partisans to the Allied War Effort," R & A #2992, 3/31/45, p. i, estimated a three-fold increase in numbers between January and November 1944, at which time a figure of 99,800 is given. Kesselring's *Memoirs* present a figure of 200,000–300,000 (p. 225). Haestrup, p. 346, estimates 250,000.
47. Luigi Longo, the number-two man in the Communist hierarchy and head of the Communist Resistance, calls it an *"instruzzione."* Cf. Longo, *Continuita della Resistenza* (Turin: Giulio Einaudi, 1977), p. 56.
48. Parri initially met Dulles in November 1943. Cf. Haestrup, p. 345.
49. Battaglia and Garritano, *Breve Storia*, p. 286.
50. Delzell, *Mussolini's Enemies*, p. 469.
51. Coles and Weinberg, *Civil Affairs*, p. 545.
52. Ibid., p. 551.
53. Battaglia and Garritano, *Breve Storia*, p. 225.

54. Ibid., p. 229.
55. Twenty thousand Fascist Guardia, *Decima Mas*, and other troops composed the principal manpower in this attack. Battaglia and Garritano, *Breve Storia*, p. 245.
56. Deakin, *Brutal Friendship*, p. 704. Graziani made his estimate in June 1944.
57. Massabrio, *Storia*, *II*, p. 829. The Action paper *Libertà* deplored *("deploriamo")* the assassination, and directly blamed the Communist *Gappisti*. (*Libertà*, 4/30/44, p. 1.)
58. Deakin, *Brutal Friendship*, p. 631.
59. Battaglia and Garritano, *Breve Storia*, p. 141.
60. Ibid., p. 189.
61. Ibid., p. 86.
62. *Trials of the Major War Criminals*, Vol. 35, p. 2.
63. Elements of the 6th Panzer Division assisted SS troops in this operation. The elusive Red Star Brigade, commanded by "Major Lopo" (Mario Musolesi) had lately attacked a German convoy. Cf. Longo, *Continuita*, p. 60, and Battaglia and Garritano, *Breve Storia*, pp. 252, 260.
64. Kesselring, *Memoirs*, p. 225.
65. This figure is corroborated in OSS, "Contribution," p. 1, Delzell, *Mussolini's Enemies*, p. 379, Ellwood, p. 157. Battaglia and Garritano, *Breve Storia*, pp. 307–308, says as many as 14 of the 26 German divisions were thus tied down in 1945.
66. OSS, "Contribution," pp. 8–9.
67. Delzell, *Mussolini's Enemies*, pp. 298–99. Cf. also Erich Kuby, *Verrat auf deutsch: Wie das Dritte Reich Italien ruinierte* (Hamburg: Hoffmann und Campe, 1982), p. 480.
68. Battaglia and Garritano, *Breve Storia*, pp. 324–26.
69. Elizabeth Wiskemann, *The Rome-Berlin Axis: A Study of the Relationship Between Hitler and Mussolini* (London: Collins, 1966), p. 394.
70. Battaglia and Garritano, *Breve Storia*, p. 336.
71. Canistraro, *Historical Dictionary*, p. 455, has the latest and probably most realistic figures. *War Crimes*, Vol. 1, p. 46, puts the figure on civilian reprisal deaths at 7,500.

CHAPTER SEVEN

1. Origo, *War in Val D'Orica*, p. 83.
2. Ibid., p. 180.
3. Ibid., p. 125.
4. Other notable instances of cultural damage: The ruins of Pompeii were peppered with flak falling from the sky, as German ground batteries fired at Allied aircraft. The main damage to Castel Gandolfo (already mentioned) consisted of a bomb hole through the west wall. At Velletri, which Fifth Army should have taken before pushing into Rome to block the German retreat from Cassino, the old cathedral was destroyed by aerial bombing, along with murals and paintings within dating from the Renaissance. Cf. Monuments, Fine Arts and Archives Commission report in *New York Times*, 18 July 1944, p. 3.
5. Cf. Jackson, *Battle for Italy*, p. 276.
6. *Il Giornale d'Italia*, 28 May 1944, p. 2.
7. Sheppard, *Italian Campaign*, p. 156.

8. Douglas Orgill, *The Gothic Line: The Italian Campaign, Autumn, 1944* (New York: W. W. Norton, 1967), p. 11.

9. Harry Hoppe, *Die 278, Infanterie-Division in Italien, 1944/1945* (Bad Nauheim: Verlag Hans-Henning Podzun, 1953), p. 39.

10. Orgill, *Gothic Line*, p. 156.

11. Blumenson, *Mark Clark*, p. 230.

12. Orgill, *Gothic Line*, p. 93.

13. Sheppard, *Italian Campaign*, p. 157.

14. Clark, *Calculated Risk*, p. 406. Clark viewed the problem as "critical."

15. Cf. Maj. Robert A. Robbins, *The 91st Division in World War II* (Washington, D.C.: Infantry Journal Press, 1947), p. 186.

16. Truscott, *Command*, p. 455.

17. Ibid.

18. Ulysses Lee, *The Employment of Negro Troops* (U.S. Army in World War II: Special Studies. Washington, D.C.: Office of the Chief of Military History, 1966), p. 557.

19. Clark, *Calculated*, p. 414.

20. Graham, *Tug of War*, p. 383.

21. Ibid.

22. Gilbert, *Churchill*, p. 1326. Tito had promised to stand clear, in the interests of Allied amity.

23. Melton Davis, *Who Defends Rome? The Forty-Five Days, July 25–September 8, 1943* (New York: The Dial Press, 1972), p. 239.

24. Wyss, *Rome under the Terror*, p. 148; Deakin, *Brutal Friendship*, p. 742.

25. Delzell, *Mussolini's Enemies*, p. 495.

26. Dollmann, *Interpreter*, p. 329.

27. Dombrowski, *Mussolini*, p. 100.

BIBLIOGRAPHY

UNPUBLISHED DOCUMENTS

International Military Tribunal. *Trials of the Major War Criminals, Nuremberg, Germany, 14 November 1945–1 October 1946*. Washington, D.C.: USGPO, 1946.

Italy, Comando Supremo. "Records of the Italian Army." Washington, D.C.: National Archives Microfilm, 1967.

Office of Strategic Services (OSS), United States.

"Sicilian Separatism With Particular Reference to the Report of Lord Rennell." R. & A No. 1521. 19 November 1943.

"Political Dilemma in Italy." R. & A No. 1539. 15 October 1943.

"Basic Political and Social Information on Central Italy." R & A No. 1211. 15 November 1943.

"Food Distribution in Italy." R & A No. 1568. 1 January 1944.

"Population Movements in Italy." R & A No. 1189: 30 June 1943.

"German Administrative Control in Northern Italy." R & A No. 2161. 24 July 1944.

"The German De Facto Annexation of the Northeast Italian Provinces." R & A No. 2200, 1 February 1944.

"The Contribution of the Partisans to the Allied War Effort." R & A No. 2992, 31 March 1945.

"The Italian Social Republic." R & A No. 1711. 15 March 1944. Series: *Germany and Its Occupied Territories During World War II*. Microfilm. Reels XVII, XVIII. Washington, D.C.: University Publications of America, 1977.

BOOKS

Adelman, Robert H., and Col. George Walton. *Rome Fell Today*. Boston: Little, Brown, 1968.

Alexander, Sir Harold. *Report by the Supreme Allied Commander Mediterranean, Field-*

Marshal The Earl Alexander of Tunis, to the Combined Chiefs of Staff. London: HMSO, 1951.

————. *The Alexander Memoirs.* Edited by John North. London: Hutchinson, 1962.

Amendola, Giorgio. *Lettere a Milano: Ricordi e documenti.* Rome: Editori Riuniti, 1974.

Anfuso, Alberto. *Da Palazzo Venezia al Lago di Garda.* Bologna: Cappelli, 1957.

Arbizzani, Luigi. *Guerra, Nazifascismo: Lotta di Liberazione nel Bolognese.* Bologna: Amministrazione Provinciale di Bologna, 1976.

Badoglio, Pietro. *L'Italia nella seconda guerra mondiale (memorie e documenti).* Milan: Mondadori, 1946.

Bailey, D. C. *Engineers in the Italian Campaign: 1943–1945.* London: Printing and Stationery Services, C.M.F. 1945.

Battaglia, Roberto. *Un Uomo, un Partigiano.* Torino: Giulio Einaudi, 1965.

————, and Giuseppe Garritano. *Breve Storia della Resistenza italiana.* Torino: Giulio Einaudi, 1955.

Bergwitz, Hubertus. *Die Partisanenrepublik Ossola.* Frankfurt: Verlag fur Literatur und Zeitgesehen, 1972.

Bertoldi, Silvio. *I Tedeschi in Italia.* Milan: Rizzoli, 1964.

————. *Vittorio Emmanuelle III.* Torino: Unione Tipografico Editrice Torinese, 1970.

————. *Salò: Vita e Morte della Repubblica Sociale Italiana.* Milan: Rizzoli, 1976.

Bishop, Leo V., Frank L. Glasgow, and George A. Fisher. *The Fighting Forty-Fifth: The Combat Report of an Infantry Division.* Baton Rouge: Army & Navy Publishing Company, 1946.

Blair, Clay. *Ridgway's Paratroopers: The American Airborne in World War II.* New York: The Dial Press, 1985.

Blumenson, Martin. *The Mediterranean Theatre of Operations: Salerno to Cassino.* (United States Army in World War II.) Washington, D.C.: GPO, 1962.

————. *Anzio: The Gamble that Failed.* Boston: J. B. Lippincott, 1963.

————. *Bloody River: The Real Tragedy of the Rapido.* Boston: Houghton Mifflin, 1970.

————. *Mark Clark: The Last of the Great World War II Commanders.* New York: Congdon & Weed, Inc., 1984.

Bocca, Giorgio. *Storia Dell Italia Partigiana: Septembre 1943–Maggio 1945.* Bari: Editori Laterza, 1966.

————. *La Repubblica di Mussolini.* Roma: Editori Laterza, 1977.

Bonomi, Ivanoe. *Diario di un Anno: 2 giugno 1943–10 giugno 1944.* Rome: Garzanti, 1949.

Bravo, Anna. *La repubblica partigiana del' Alto Monferrato.* Torino: G. Giappichelli Editori, 1965.

Brown, Anthony Cave. *Bodyguard of Lies.* New York: Harper & Row, 1975.

Brown, John Sloan. *Draftee Division: The 88th Infantry Division in World War II.* Lexington: University of Kentucky Press, 1986.

Buckley, Christopher. *The Road to Rome.* London: Hodder & Stoughton, 1945.

Campbell, Rodney. *The Luciano Project: The Secret Wartime Collaboration of the Mafia and the U. S. Navy.* New York: McGraw-Hill, 1977.

Catalano, Franco. *Storia del CLNAI.* Bari: Laterza, 1956.

Cavallero, Ugo. *Comando Supremo Diario, 1940–1943.* Bologna: Cappelli, 1948.

Clark, Mark. *Calculated Risk.* New York: Harper & Brothers, 1950.

Coles, Harry L., and Albert K. Weinberg. *Civil Affairs: Soldiers Become Governors.* Washington, D.C.: Office of the Chief of Military History, Department of the Army, 1964.

Collotti, Enzo. *L'amministrazione tedesca dell' Italia occupata, 1943–1945: Studio e documenti*. Milano: Lerici Editori, 1963.

Craveti, Raimondo. *La Campagne D'Italia E I Servizi Segreti: La Storia Dell' ORI (1943–1945)*. Milano: La Pietra, 1980.

Davis, Melton. *Who Defends Rome? The Forty-Five Days, July 25–September 8, 1943*. New York: The Dial Press, 1972.

Deakin, F. W. *The Brutal Friendship: Mussolini, Hitler, and the Fall of Italian Fascism*. Garden City, N.Y.: Doubleday, 1966.

Delaney, John P. *The Blue Devils in Italy: A History of the 88th Infantry Division in World War II*. Washington, D.C.: Infantry Journal Press, 1947.

Delzell, Charles G. *Mussolini's Enemies: The Italian Anti-Fascist Resistance*. Princeton, N.J.: Princeton University Press, 1961.

Dollmann, Eugen. *Roma Nazista*. Milano: Langanesi & Co., 1949.

———. *The Interpreter*. London: Hutchinson & Co., 1967.

Dombrowski, Roman. *Mussolini: Twilight and Fall*. Translated by H. C. Stevens. London: William Heinemann, Ltd., 1956.

Eisenhower, Dwight D. *Crusade in Europe*. New York: Dolphin Books, 1961.

———. *The Papers of Dwight David Eisenhower: The War Years*. Edited by Alfred D. Chandler, Jr. Baltimore: Johns Hopkins Press, 1970.

Ellis, John. *Cassino: The Hollow Victory*. London: Andre Deutsch, Ltd., 1984.

Ellwood, David W. *Italy, 1943–1945*. New York: Holmes & Meier, 1985.

"Ezra Pound Speaking": Radio Speeches of World War II. Edited by Leonard W. Doob. Westport, Conn.: Greenwood Press, 1978.

Fisher, Ernest F. *Cassino to the Alps*. Washington, D.C.: Center for Military History, U.S. Army, 1977.

Forty, George. *Fifth Army at War*. London: Ian Allan, 1980.

Garland, Albert N., and Howard McGraw Smyth. *Sicily and the Surrender of Italy*. Washington, D.C.: USGPO, Office of the Chief of Military History, 1965.

Gasparri, Tamara. *La Resistenza in Italia*. Firenze: Guaraldi Editori, 1977.

Gilbert, Martin. *Winston S. Churchill*. Vol. VII: *Road to Victory, 1940–1945*. Boston: Houghton Mifflin, 1986.

Graham, Dominick, and Shelford Bidwell. *Tug of War: The Battle for Italy, 1943–1945*. New York: St. Martin's Press, 1986.

Graziani, Rodolfo. *Ho Difesa La Patria*. Milano: Garzanti, 1948.

Haestrup, Jorgen. *European Resistance Movements, 1939–1945: A Complete History*. Westport, Conn.: Meckler Publishing, 1981.

Hapgood, David, and David Richardson. *Monte Cassino*. New York: Congdon & Weed, 1984.

Harvey, J. M. Lee. *D-Day Dodger*. London: William Kinber, 1979.

Hibbert, Christopher. *Anzio: The Bid for Rome*. New York: Ballantine, 1970.

Higgins, Trumbull. *Soft Underbelly: The Anglo-American Controversy over the Italian Campaign, 1939–1945*. New York: Macmillan, 1968.

Historical Dictionary of Fascist Italy. Edited by Philip V. Cannistraro. Westport, Conn.: Greenwood Press, 1982.

Hoppe, Harry, *Die 278. Infanterie-Division in Italien, 1944/1945*. Bad Nauheim: Verlag Hans-Henning Podzun, 1953.

Istituto Storico della Resistenza in Piemonte. *Studi e Documenti, No. 7*. Parma: Guarda Editore Parma, 1972.

Istituto Storico della Resistenza in Toscana. *Atti e Studi, Nos. 6–10*. Firenze: La Nuova Italia Editrice, 1966–70.

Jackson, W. G. F. *The Battle for Italy.* New York: Harper & Row, 1967.
Katz, Robert. *Death in Rome.* New York: Macmillan, 1967.
Kesselring, Albert. *Soldat bis zum letzten Tag.* Bonn: Athenaeum, 1953.
———. *Memoirs of Field-Marshal Kesselring.* London: William Kimber, 1953.
Kuby, Erich. *Verrat auf deutsch: Wie das Dritte Reich Italien ruinierte.* Hamburg: Hoffmann und Campe, 1982.
Kurzman, Dan. *The Race for Rome.* New York: Doubleday, 1975.
Lee, Ulysses. *The Employment of Negro Troops.* (U.S. Army in World War II: Special Studies.) Washington, D.C.: Office of the Chief of Military History, U.S. Army, 1966.
Lewin, Ronald. *Ultra Goes to War: The Secret Story.* London: Book Club Associates, 1978.
Linklater, Eric. *The Campaign in Italy.* London: HMSO, 1951. .
Longo, Luigi. *Continuita della Resistenza.* Torino: Giulia Einaudi, 1977.
———. *I centri divegenti del PCI nella Resistenza.* Roma: Editori Riuniti, 1973.
Massobrio, Franco, and Umberto Guglielmotti. *Storia della Repubblica Sociale Italiana.* 2 Vols. Roma: Centro Editoriche Nazionale, 1967.
Mellini, Alberto. *Guerra diplomatica a Salò.* Bologna: Cappelli, 1950.
Monelli, Paolo. *Roma 1943.* Rome: Migliaresi, 1946.
Morison, Samuel Eliot. *Sicily—Salerno—Anzio.* (Vol. IX, History of U.S. Naval Operations in World War II.) Boston: Little, Brown, 1958.
Morris, Eric. *Salerno: A Military Fiasco.* New York: Stein and Day, 1983.
Mussolini, Benito. *The Fall of Mussolini.* Edited by Max Ascoli. New York: Farrar, Strauss, 1948.
Nelson, Guy. *Thunderbird: A History of the 45th Infantry Division.* Oklahoma City: Oklahoma Publishing Company, 1969.
Orgill, Douglas. *The Gothic Line: The Italian Campaign, Autumn, 1944.* New York: W. W. Norton, 1967.
Origo, Iris. *War in Val d'Orcia: An Italian War Diary, 1943–1944.* Boston: David R. Godine, 1984.
Pack, S. W. C. *Operation "Husky": The Allied Invasion of Sicily.* Vancouver: David & Charles, 1977.
Parri, Ferruccio. *Due mesi con i Nazisti.* Roma: Edizioni Carecas, 1973.
Pausa, Gianpaolo. *Guerra partigiana tra Genova e il Po.* Bari: Editori Laterza, 1967.
Pesce, Giovanni. *Soldati senza uniforme: Diario di un Gappista.* Rome: Edizioni di Culture Sociale, 1950.
Piscitelli, E. *Storia della Resistenza Romana.* Bari: Laterza, 1965.
Plehue, Friedrich Karl. *The End of an Alliance: Rome's Defection from the Axis in 1943.* Translated by Eric Mosbacher. London: Oxford University Press, 1971.
Pond, Hugh. *Salerno.* Boston: Little, Brown, 1962.
Puntoni, P. *Parla Vittoria Emmanuele III.* Milan: Palazzi, Editore, 1958.
Quarrie, Bruce. *Fallschirmpanzerdivision Hermann Göring.* Warren, Mich.: Squadron/ Signal Publications, 1978.
Rahn, Rudolf. *Ruheloses Leben: Aufzeichnungen und Erinnerungen.* Düsseldorf: Diederichs Verlag, 1949.
Ready, J. Lee. *Forgotten Allies: The Military Contribution of the Colonies, Exiled Governments, and Lesser Powers to the Allied Victory in World War II.* Vol. I., *The European Theater.* Jefferson, N.C.: McFarland & Co., Inc., 1985.
Robbins, Maj. Robert A. *The 91st Infantry Division in World War II.* Washington, D.C.: Infantry Journal Press, 1947.
Salvadori, Massimo. *La Resistenza nell' Anconetano e nel Piceno.* Roma: Opere Nuove, 1962.

Schultz, Paul L. *The 85th Infantry Division in World War II.* Washington, D.C.: Infantry Journal Press, 1949.

Scorza, Carlo. *La notte del Gran Consiglio.* Milan: Palazzi, 1968.

Senger und Etterlin, Gen. Frido von. *Neither Fear nor Hope.* New York: E. P. Dutton, 1963.

Sheppard, G. A. *The Italian Campaign, 1943–1945.* New York: Frederick A. Praeger, 1968.

Skorzeny, Otto. *Skorzeny's Secret Missions: War Memoirs of the Most Dangerous Man in Europe.* Translated from French by Jacques LeClerq. New York: E. P. Durton, 1950.

Smith, Denis Mack. *Mussolini: A Biography.* New York: Vintage Press, 1982.

Sogno, Edgardo. *La seconda repubblica.* Firenze: Sansoni, 1974.

Starr, Chester G. *From Salerno to the Alps: A History of the Fifth Army, 1943–1945.* Washington, D.C.: Infantry Journal Press, 1948.

Steinhoff, Johannes. *The Straits of Messina: Diary of a Fighter Commander.* London: Andre Deutsch, 1971.

Tamaro, Attilio. *Due Anni di Storia, 1943–1945.* Rome: Tosi, 1948.

Togliatti, Palmiro. *La Politica di Salerno: Aprile–Decembre 1944.* Roma: Editori Riuniti, 1969.

Truscott, Maj. Gen. Lucian K. *Command Missions: A Personal Story.* New York: E. P. Dutton, 1954.

Wagner, Robert L. *The Texas Army: A History of the 36th Division in the Italian Campaign.* Austin, Tex.: Robert L. Wagner, 1972.

Warren, C. E. T., and James Benson. *The Broken Column: The Story of James Frederick Wilde's Adventures with the Italian Partisans.* London: George G. Harrop, 1966.

Werthen, Wolfgang. *Geschichte der 16. Panzer–Division., 1939–1945.* Friedberg: Podzun Pallas Verlag, 1958.

Wilson, Henry Maitland. *Report of the Supreme Commander Mediterranean to the Combined Chiefs of Staff on the Italian Campaign, 8 January 1944 to 10 May 1944.* London: HMSO, 1946.

Wiskemann, Elizabeth. *The Rome-Berlin Axis: A Study of the Relationship Between Hitler and Mussolini.* London: Collins, 1966.

Wyss, M. de. *Rome Under the Terror.* London: Robert Hale, Ltd., 1945.

Zangrandi, Ruggero. *1943: 21 Iuglio–8 Settembre.* Milano: Feltrinelli Editore, 1964.

Zingali, Gaetano. *L'invasione della Sicilia (1943).* Catania, 1962.

Zuccotti, Susan. *The Italians and the Holocaust: Persecution, Rescue and Survival.* New York: Basic Books, 1987.

INDEX

Note: Pages with illustrations or maps are indicated by italics.

183–84. *See also* Eighth Army, U.K.;
Fifth Army, U.S.
Allied Military Government (AMG): and
anti-Fascist actions, 113; and attitude
to partisans, 112, 115, 152; and attitude to political parties, 109; and civilian hardships, 118–21; Mafia advisors
to, 125–26; rural representatives of,
122; and support for Autonomi, 150–
51; and support for monarchy, 111
Almond, Gen. Edward M., 186
Altavilla, 59
Alt' Italia. *See* CLNAI (Committee of Na-
tional Liberation for Upper Italy)
Ambrosio, Gen. Vittorio, 5, 29, 38, 43, 47–
48
Amendola, Giorgio, 91
Americans, 21–26, 116. *See also* Fifth
Army, U.S.; Seventh Army, U.S.
amphibious operations: Allied lack of re-
sources for, 176; at Anzio, 72, 74–77; at
Salerno, 52–53; in Sicily, 6–7, 17–19
Ancona, 177, 179
Ancona Brigade, 164
antiaircraft artillery, 19–20, 76, 86, 167,
178
anti-Semitism, 92
Anzio, Battle of, 72–78, *78*, 80, 102–106
Aosta Division, at Messina, 16–17, 20
Apennine mountain range, 164, 177
Ardeatine Massacre, 98–101
Ariete Division, 88
armaments industries, 129
arming of partisans, 115–16, 158–59
Arno River campaign, 170–75
Artemisio, Mt., 105
artillery: and Alban Hills threat, 105; at
Anzio, 74; at Cassino, 68–70; at
Salerno, 52–53; at San Pietro, 67; in
Sicily, 9, 21
art works, preservation campaigns, 95–97,
127. *See also* cultural heritage
assassinations, 161–62

Assieta Division, 20
atrocities: and Ardeatine Massacre, 97–
101; as Fascist Italian, 148–50; and
forced labor conditions, 94; and German reprisals, 62, 165–66, 168, 174,
188
Audisio, Walter, 194
Augusta, 11–13, 27
Autonomi, 114, 150–51, 158
Avellino, 57, 59
Axis forces: and anti-partisan raids, 162–
63; and Augusta loss, 12; communication problems of, 29; internal conflicts
of, 7–8, 27–28, 137–39; and reconstitution of Italian army, 136, 146–47; in
Sicily, 16–21, 25. *See also* German
forces; Italian forces

Badoglio, Field Marshal Pietro, 38–41, 108
Balkans, 6, 29–30, 47
Banda Carità, 148–49
Bari, 79
Bari Conference, 109–11
Basilica of St. John in Lateran, *86*
Battaglia, Mt., 179–80
Battipaglia, 59
battle fatigue, at Cassino, 70, 82
Bencivenga, General, 91
Benevento, 60
Bergolo, Gen. Calvi di, 88, 93
Black Brigades, Fascist, 101–102, 149,
166
black market, 92, 160
Bolis, Luciano, 154
Bologna, 184, 187–88
Bombacci, Nicola, 144
Bonomi, Ivanoe, 109, 112–13
border issues, 137–39
Borghese, Prince Junio Valerio, 140, 148
Bozen Regiment, German, 97–98
Brenner Pass, 42–43, 166–67
bridges, strategic value of, 170, 174–75
Brigatte Nere, 101–102, 149, 166

Apennines, 183; doubts about Italian military, 28; and Gustav Line, 80; and Mussolini, 45, 137, 139; and terrorist acts, 99; and pessimism on ability to repel Allies, 56; and support for defense of Italy, 46

Hopkinson, Maj. Gen. G. F., 11, 59

Hube, Gen. Hans Valentin, 16

il Duce. See Mussolini, Benito

Il Giogo Pass, 175–80

industrial production, 123, 146, 178, 196

inflation problems, 113, 123, 130

infrastructure, 121–22

Insurrection Committee, 192–94

intelligence operations: and Allied surveillance of partisans, 116, 158; and American communications advantage, 19; and German lack of information at Anzio, 72–73; and German west-coast offensive report, 184; and partisan role, 148–49, 155, 176, 180; and predicting Allied landing sites, 4–6, 50–51

Italian campaign: debate on wisdom of, 21–24; and defensive debate, 44–45; and strategy debate, 24–25; and success of both sides, 195–96

Italian Communist Movement, 110

Italian forces: and CLN participation, 101; debate on loyalties of, 48–49; and disposition of navy, 50; foreign deployments of, 4, 29–30, 47; and German occupiers, 49; and internment of soldiers in Germany, 132; and lack of fighting spirit, 28–29, 52; and lack of resources, 47–48; and loyalty to king, 38; and mistrust of Germany, 35, 43–44; and post-armistice status, 41; pro-German elements in, 140; reconstitution of, 136, 146–47; and Rome's occupation, 88; at Salerno, 51–52; in Sicily, 7–9, 11–18, 20, 25; and soldiers as partisans, 91, 114, 150–51, 158; and

soldiers as refugees, 120; and west-coast offensive of 1944, 184–85. *See also specific units*

Italian Social Republic: and anti-partisan activities, 159–61; as Fascist refuge, 114; as government organization, 143; and lack of popular support, 150; political position of, 128–29; refugees from, 120

Italy, 5, *172;* British hatred of, 21–22, 116; Cold War position of, 108–109; and fear of German reaction to armistice, 39–40; German attitudes of, 19, 27–28, 44–46; and humanitarian aid problems, 116–17, 119, 126; surrender of, 34–41, 43, 51

Japanese-American unit, 186–87

Jewish people in Italy, 91–92, 99, 149–50

judicial system, 113

Juin, Gen. Alphonse, 68

Kappler, Col. Herbert, 99–100

Kesselring, Field Marshal Albert, *8,* 167, 168; at Catania, 18; and criticism of Clark, 71; and ground-based air defense, 178–79; and desire for fighting retreat, 189–90; injury of, 182; on Italy's defense, 45; optimism of, 26–27, 33, 75; in Rome, 88, 107–108; and Salerno, 54; and Sicily defense, 7–8; and treatment of Florence, 173, 175

Keyes, Gen. Geoffrey, 15–16, 81

Koch, Pietro, 149

labor conscription, German: civilian attitude to, 144; Naples attempt, 62; in Rome, 92–94; and skilled workers, 129; system of, 46–47, 131–33

labor-management relations, 134

labor movement, 110, 130, 133, 144–45

La Malfa, Ugo, 109

Leese, Lt. Gen. Oliver, *14,* 177

left-wing politics: Action Party role in, 110, 153–54; Fascist Party use of, 130, 143–44; northern strength of, 114; and Socialist Party, 109, 111, 153–54. *See also* Communist Party

legal system, 113, 155–56

Lemelsen, Gen. Joachim, 173

Leonardi, Rear Adm. Priamo, 12

Leyers, Gen. Hans, 129, 145

Liberal Party, 109

Liebenstein, Capt. Baron Gustav, 19

Ligurian Army, 184–85

Livorno, 171, 177, 184

Livorno Division, 8–9, 17, 20

Lizzero, Mario, 160

Ljubljana Gap, 166–67

logistics, 71, 76, 89, 103, 129, 181. *See also* supply lines

Longo, Luigi, 152, 193

looting by soldiers, 94, 124–25. *See also* requisitioning practices

Lucas, Gen. John, 75, 77–78

Luciano, Charles, 125–26

Luftwaffe in Italy, 8–10, 79, 104, 171

Lungo, Mt., 67

McCreery, Gen. Richard L., 57

Mackensen, Gen. Eberhard, 73, 75, 99–100, 105, 170

MacMillan, Harold, 22, 157

Maelzer, Gen., Ardeatine massacre, 98–100

Mafia support for Allies, 113, 117, 125–26

Maiella Brigade, 164

Manfredi, Adm. Giuseppe, 15

manpower problems, German, 136

Marecchia River, 180–81

Marshall, Gen. George C., 23, 66–67, 186

Matteotti Brigades, 154

Messina, Battle of, 7, 14–15, 19–21

Mezzano concentration camp, 166

Milan, 129, 154, 183, 190–91

military, Italian. *See* Italian forces

military draft, in northern Italy, 146–48

mine fields, at Cassino, 69–70

Misurata, Volpi di, 92

Molinaro, Gen. Giuseppe, 15–16

monarchy, Italian: Churchill's support for, 109, 111, 122; and erosion of position, 111–12; military support for, 114, 150; republican challenge to, 107–10, 115; supporters of, 93, 101; weaknesses of, 40–41

Monte Cassino, Abbey of, 78–83, 89, 95–97

Montgomery, Gen. Bernard, 13, 15, 26

morale, 70, 82, 125, 134–35, 196. *See also* civilians

Morgan, Frank, 126

Morganthau, Henry, 122–23

Moroccan Brigade, 68

Mussolini, Benito, *36, 138, 193;* Churchill's admiration for, 22; and criticism of military, 33; and distrust of Hitler, 139; and distrust of Italian military, 12, 28; and escape from Milan, 191–92; and fall from power, 33–38; and fear of coup, 140; and Florence, 172; and forced labor issue, 94, 132; and German need to reinstate, 45–46; and handling of military, 48–49; and hatred of Communists, 135–36; and hatred of Rome, 87, 107; as Hitler's puppet, 128–29, 131; paranoia of, 142; prison rescue of, 31–32; and restoration of Papal State, 90; security measures of, 161–62; and Sicily, 24

Muti, Carlo, 38

Muti Legion, 148

mutiny, 57, 82

Naples, 25, 61–65, 112, 114, 117

Napoli Division, 11–13, 18, 20

nationalization program, in Italian Social Republic, 145

National Republican Guard, 140

naval operations: and American ships' collision, 15; at Anzio, 72–74, 76, 103; at

Bari, 79; Italian, disposition of, 50; and Italian threat to British, 21; at Livorno, 185; at Rapido River, 70–72; at Salerno, 55, 59–60; in Sicily, 11–12, 19–20; and superiority of Allies, 3, 9, 13, 18; technological advances of, 21–22

Nazi regime, Italian fascist sympathizers, 139–40. *See also* German forces; German High Command (OKW)

Nenni, Pietro, 109, 154

Nettuno, 72–75

New Zealand Corps: at Cassino, 80–81, 83; at Florence, 174; at Serchio Valley, 185; at Trieste, 190

Nicosia, 17

night bombing, 19–20

90th Panzer-Grenadier Division, 79, 180, 184

91st Division, U.S., 171, 174, 179–82, 190

94th Division, German, 70

92nd Infantry Division, U.S., 185–86

93rd Panzer-Grenadier Division, 88

9th Infantry Division, U.S., 17–19

9th Lancers, 180

North African campaign, 4, 29

Nuti, Col. Enrico, 91

Office of Strategic Services (OSS), 33, 158. *See also* intelligence operations

Olivelli, Teresio, 154

111th Engineer Battalion, 71

143rd Regiment, 36th U.S. Div, 71

Operation Mincemeat, 4

Origo, Countess, 124–25

Ortigara Brigade, 168

Ortona, 79

Osoppo Brigade, 151, 154

OSS (Organization for Strategic Services), 33, 158. *See also* intelligence operations

Palermo, 15–16

Pantilleria, 28

paratroops. *See* airborne operations

Parri, Ferruccio, 152–53, 157

partisan movement, *173;* Allied attitude toward, 115–16; and Axis aids against, 162–63, 165–66; in Bologna, 187–88; draft-dodgers in, 147; and Florentine open city policy, 173–74; and hatred of monarchy, 107–108; independent actions of, 192–94; in Milan, 183, 191; missions of, 149, 159–69; and Mussolini, 192–94; in northern Italy, 114–16; organizations of, 150–55; political powers of, 156–58; population fluctuations in, 155–56; supply issues, 158–59; tactical intelligence role in, 180; and threat to German logistics, 131. *See also* CLNAI (Committee of National Liberation for Upper Italy)

Patton, Gen. George S., 13–16, 55

Pavolini, Alessandro, 142–44, *172*

peace negotiations, 38–39, 87–88, 189

Penney, Gen. W. R. C., 74

Petacci, Claretta, *193*, 194

Piemonte, 154

Pisa, 180

Pius XII, Pope, 85–86, *86*, 87–90, 94, 97, 127

Pizzono, Alfredo, 114

Podolski Lancers, 83

Polish Corps, 83, 187–88

politics, 119; and Italian parties, 102, 107, 109–15, 153–55, 158–59

Polizia Repubblicana (PR), 149

Ponte alle Grazie, 174

Ponte Becchio, 175

Ponte Carraia, 174

Ponte Olivo airfield, 10–11

Pontine Marshes, 73–74, 83

Ponza Island, 37

Porto Empedocle, 15

Pound, Ezra, 126–27

Po Valley, 117, 128

Preziosi, Giovanni, 149

Primasole Bridge, 18

prisoners of war, 18, 25, 49–50, 77

productivity problems, 134–35
propaganda war, 66–67, 96–97, 118, 174
Provisional Corps, Patton's, Sicily actions, 14–16
public relations activities, 94–97

Quebec Conference, 24–25, 39

Race and Demography Office, 149–50
racism, 185–87
radar, and safety of British navy in Mediterranean, 21
railroad system, 89, 167–68, 171
Randazzo, 18
Rangers, U.S., 9, 52, 56, 75, 76–77
Rapido-Garigliano Allied Offensive, 68–84
Rastrellamenti, 156, 160. *See also* reprisal executions, German
Ravenna, 184
reconnaissance activities, 80–81, 163
Reder, Maj. Walter, 165–66
refugee situation, in southern Italy, 120–21
Regina Coeli Prison, 92
reprisal executions, German, 164–65, 168, 174, 188
republicanism, 108–13
Republican Party, 110, 153
requisitioning practices, 123–25, 155–56
resistance, Italian. *See* partisan movement
Rhodes, Island of, battle at, 49
Ribbentrop, Joachim von, 48
Ridgway, Gen. Matthew, 6, 15
Riva Ridge, 188
Roatta, Gen. Mario, 12, 32, 114
Roberts, Owen J., 127
Rodt, Gen. Eberhard, 70
Rome: fall of, 107; German occupation of, 44, 49, 91–101; German preservation of bridges in, 170; liberation of, 103–106; Mussolini's hatred of, 141–42; and partisan activities, 90–91, 95, 97–98, 101–102; and Vatican preservation attempt, 85–90
Rome Agreement of 1944, 157

Rome Protocols, 115
Rommel, Gen. Erwin, 19, 44–45
Roosevelt, Franklin Delano, 23, 119
Roveda, Giovanni, 161
Royal Bays, 180
Ruini, Meuccio, 109
Russia. *See* Soviet Union

sabotage operations, 62–64. *See also* partisan movement
St. Paul's Basilica, 90–91
Salerno: Battle of, 46, 50–62; lack of food sources, 117–18
Salonika, Greece, 4–5
Sambuco, 180
San Lorenzo Railway Yard, 86
San Marco Battalion, 91
San Marino, Republic of, 180
San Martino, 165
San Pietro, Battle of, 66–68
San Stefano, 16–17
Sant' Anna de Stazzena, 165
Santerno River, 180, 187
Sardinia, 4–6
Sauckel, Fritz, 94, 131–32
Schlegel, Lt. Col. Julius, 95–97
Schmalz, Col. Wilhelm, 11–12
Schmalz Group, 11–13, 18
Schuster, Cardinal Alfredo Aldefonse, 191
Schutz-Staffel (SS), 97–101, 131
Scoccimaro, Mauro, 109
Scorza, Carlo, 38
2nd Armored Division, U.S., 15–16
security, 131, 135, 148
segregation, in U.S. army, 185–87
Sele River, 55–56
Serchio Valley, 184–85
715th Infantry Division, Axis, 77
Seventh Army, U.S., 15–17, 53
Sicily, 32; Allied objectives in, 4, 7; Allied progress in, 8–21; amphibious operations at, 6–8, 11–12; consequences of, 21–30; food shortages in, 117–18; and intelligence battle, 3–6

Sieckenius, Gen. Rudolf, 54
Sikh fighters, 80–81, 83
sit-down strike, of British non-coms, 57, 82
16th Panzer Division, 15, 51–52, 54–55
skilled workers, transfer to Germany, 129
Skorzeny, Capt. Otto, 31–32
Slovenians, in northern Italy, 139
slowdowns, labor, 134–35
smoke screens, 69–71, 76
Socialist Party, 109, 111, 153–54
socialization program of Italian Social Republic, 143–45
sonar, 21
Sorrento Peninsula, 52, 56
South Africa Corps, 174
Soviet Union: British fear of, 22–23; and incarceration of Poles, 83; and Italian campaign, 23–24; and partition of Europe, 108–109; Russian POWs in partisan movement in, 158
Special Forces (SOE), British, 158
Special Service Department of Italian Social Republic, 148–49
Speer, Albert, 46, 129
Spellman, Cardinal Francis, 127
SS (Schutz-Staffel), 97–101, 131
Stalin, Joseph, 23–24
Starace, Achille, *193*, 194
starvation. *See* food supplies
Stelle, Count Pier Luigi Bellini delle, 192–93
Stevens, John M., 116
Stimson, Henry L., 24
strikes, labor, 133–35, 145, 191
submarine warfare, 20–22, 50–51, 168
supply lines: Allied problems with, 76, 182; Axis problems with, 18; and important bases, 64–65, 171, 177; partisan disruption of, 163, 166–67; partisan sources of, 158–59; and shortages for both sides, 183. *See also* logistics
Syracuse, 11–12

tank operations: and Allied losses, 67, 104, 181–82; and British losses, 179–80; and Italian losses, 9; in Mt. Artemisio operation, 106; at Salerno, 55
Tarchi, Angelo, 143
Taylor, Gen. Maxwell, 39
Teatro Communale, 171
Tenth Army, German, 83–84, 164. *See also* German forces
10th Mountain Division, U.S., 187–88
terrain. *See* topography
Texas Division. *See* 36th Infantry Division, U.S.
3rd Carpathian Division, Polish, 188
3rd Infantry Division, U.S., 15, 74–75, 82, 104
3rd Panzer-Grenadier Division, 76
34th Infantry Division, U.S., 82, 171, 180–81
36th Infantry Division, U.S., 51–53, 55–56, 70–72, 105–106
356th Infantry Division, German, 180
362nd Infantry Division, German, 104
334th Infantry Division, German, 79
Todt Organization, and draft labor, 46–47, 94, 131–33, 147
Togliatti, Palmiro, 102, 108, 152
topography, Italian: and defensive advantages, 27, 45, 59, 66–69, 176–77; and Normandy *vs.* Italy debate, 23; and partisan operations, 163
totalitarianism, 113
Toussaint, Gen. Rudolf, 129–31
transportation system, 121–22, 129, 146, 177
Trieste, 44, 137
Trinity Bridge, 174
Trocchio, Mt., 68, 70
Troina, 17
Truscott, Gen. Lucian, 15, 59, 71, 77–78, 185–86
Tuker, Gen. Francis, 80–81
Turkoman Division, 136, 187
20th Luftwaffe Field Division, 180